HOW TO BE THE
WORLD'S
SMARTEST
TRAVELER
(and Save Time, Money, and Hassle)

HOW TO BE THE
WORLD'S
SMARTEST
TRAVELER

(and Save Time, Money, and Hassle)

CHRISTOPHER ELLIOTT

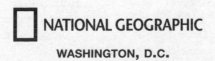 NATIONAL GEOGRAPHIC

WASHINGTON, D.C.

CONTENTS >>>>>>>>>>>>>>>>>>>>>>>>>>>>

Introduction

Let's get one thing out of the way: I'm *not* the world's smartest traveler.

As *National Geographic Traveler* magazine's reader advocate, I've been helping solve your vacation problems for more than a decade. I'm an inveterate traveler, having spent the last four years crisscrossing the United States with my family, and many years before that exploring the world on my own.

But simply traipsing from point A to point B didn't turn me into a travel genius. Neither did the thousands of cases that crossed my desk as a magazine ombudsman. Instead, with each refund I secured and every botched reservation I helped repair, I learned what *not* to do when I'm on the road.

I have you, my readers, to thank for that education. I'm beyond grateful. Now it's time for a little payback.

In this book, I'll show you . . .

→ HOW TO SAVE TIME. Whether you're planning a honeymoon or a business trip to close a deal, time is a finite and precious commodity. The travel industry likes to waste yours by making you stand in line, wait on hold, or read pointless form letters. I'll show you my favorite shortcuts.

→ HOW TO SAVE MONEY. Let's face it, no one likes to overspend. I'll tell you when you don't need to shell out more—and when you should. I'll also give you a heads-up on where the bargains can be found and I'll disclose which ones are too good to be true.

→ HOW TO PREVENT HASSLES. From onerous contracts to come-ons by opportunistic timeshare salesmen, the last thing you want when you're traveling is to be harassed. I can show you how to avoid these annoying roadblocks.

I've spent my career covering an industry that's perfected the art of separating you from your money. *How to Be the World's Smartest Traveler* is the antidote to a business that has lost its way, too often relying on customer-hostile policies and junk fees to eke out an undeserved profit. I'll explain precisely how the travel industry takes your hardearned vacation dollars and time from you and then coughs up a substandard product.

You deserve better. I'll help you get it.

Use this book to plan and enjoy your next trip. If you do, you'll vacation like the world's smartest traveler.

How to Use This Book

Think of *How to Be the World's Smartest Traveler* as a survival manual for your next trip. Everything that can possibly go wrong, from misspelling the name on your ticket to falling for a scammy timeshare pitch—it's all here. The wisdom I'll offer in these pages is focused on keeping you out of trouble and surviving your trip with your health, dignity, and bank account intact.

You can read *How to Be the World's Smartest Traveler* in two ways. Either review it from cover to cover, and learn about common mistakes and solutions at each step. Or turn to this book when you're in trouble, find your travel problem, and fix it.

• Most chapters start with a **decision matrix** to help you figure out if the chapter applies to you. If it doesn't, just skip it.
• Look for the **Smart** and **Not Smart** boxes throughout the chapters. These are quick tips that you can use right now to improve your trip.
• Throughout the book, be on the lookout for the **Problem Solved** headers. They're real travel problems I've helped mediate.

If you're reading this as an ebook, I recommend downloading it on your reader, tablet, or phone before your next trip. When you're in trouble, type the keyword or phrase that describes the problem to find a fast and authoritative answer. I've also included an appendix

with the contact information for most of the large travel companies mentioned in this book. For some truly subversive bonus information, including the names and email addresses of managers at these companies, check out my website at *elliott.org/contacts*.

If you're a seasoned traveler, I'm sure you'll find most of the information in *How to Be the World's Smartest Traveler* incredibly useful. But some of the material, particularly in the first few chapters, may also seem to be laughably commonsense advice. I'll be honest; I'm laughing with you because I wish it wasn't necessary to share these strategies. I wish everyone *knew*. But my years of advocating for customers—and making so many of these mistakes myself—tells me otherwise.

Also, some of the tips, especially when it comes to problem-solving advice, overlap with advice in other chapters. That's because some of you will read the sections separately when trouble rears its ugly head. I want all the information to be *right there* when you need it.

By the way, if this book makes you want to stay home, I don't blame you. While most trips are incident-free, some are not. I'm a realist. I'm not going to apologize to a travel industry that too often tries to put a positive spin on everything for telling you the truth about what could happen. If you don't go on your next trip with your eyes wide open, then what kind of consumer advocate would I be?

1

Find the Most Reliable Travel Advice

The truth about online reviews, guidebooks, and what your friends won't tell you about their travel advice.

Where should I go? Stay? Eat? If you're having trouble sorting it all out, take a number. Thanks to the proliferation of blogs, social media, and user-generated review sites, we're drowning in information. And while it's hard to know what's authoritative, that shouldn't stop you from trying. I'll help you make sense of it.

A little knowledge can be a dangerous thing

Many of the dominant online review sites, such as TripAdvisor and Yelp, position themselves as definitive guides to everything from accommodations to shopping. Other sources, such as blogs and guidebooks, would have you believe they're one-stop resources for travelers who need to know the "best" hotel, restaurant, or destination, and would just as soon skip the comparison shopping.

But make no mistake: Consulting just one site can be a serious error. Any single source—and that's especially true of user-generated sites where travelers write the reviews—is prone to manipulation by innkeepers, restaurant owners, and reputation-management operatives. (For more on how reputation management works, check out my last book, *Scammed: How to Save Money and Find Better Service in a World of Schemes, Swindles, and Shady Deals*.) On top of that you'll need to factor in the inevitable instances of plain old bad judgment on the part of some reviewers. When it comes to travel, you simply can't place all your trust in a single source. Instead, you have to use multiple resources to triangulate the truth. Don't worry, I'll explain.

What's out there?

• **Guidebooks,** such as Fodor's, Lonely Planet, and, ahem, National Geographic, are printed-on-paper books written and researched by professional travel writers. Some of the information in these guides may also be available online or as ebooks. These have traditionally been the go-to source for travelers. Also, articles in mainstream media publications such as *National Geographic Traveler* can be excellent resources, although they often focus on just one aspect of a destination or experience.

👍SMART TRIANGULATE A TRAVEL RECOMMENDATION.

Facts have to be verified by at least three independent sources when you're a journalist. The same rule applies to travel recommendations. Don't put all your money on one review from a single source, or even on many reviews from one source. Ideally, you'll want to make sure three sources that are independent of one another confirm the review.

• **User-generated review sites,** such as TripAdvisor and Yelp, are free crowdsourced guides that you can find online. They are relatively new, in comparison to guidebooks, and are still developing and evolving as credible sources.

• **Social media sites,** such as Facebook and Twitter, connect you to your friends and colleagues, but they can also put you in touch with a broader community of travelers, who might offer reliable and customized advice.

• **Word-of-mouth recommendations,** often the source of the best advice you can find.

GUIDEBOOKS

Printed guidebooks have seen better days. (A little ironic that I should be writing this in, of all places, a travel book.) But guidebooks can still be an excellent resource for your next trip. Spend a little time on *Amazon.com, BN.com,* or at your local bookstore browsing through the guidebooks still being published. Look for the following qualities:

➔ **UPDATES.** When was the last time the book was updated? Always check the copyright date. Did the publisher simply slap a new date on the cover or did it revise the entire manuscript? Updating only the cover is a time-honored guidebook trick that serves to line the pockets of the publisher. The best way to tell is to look at the previous version and, perhaps, to read some of the reviews of an individual guidebook or a guidebook series on a book retail site like *Amazon.com*.

➔ **FOCUS.** Does the guide cover the aspects of a destination that interest you most? For example, if you're retired, you probably won't want a *Let's Go* guidebook on your next trip to Europe; that series is written for students. If money is no object, you might prefer a Luxe guide to a Rick Steves tome.

➔ **CREDIBILITY.** Look for guidebooks that at least give a nod to ethics. For

NOT SMART BRANDISHING YOUR GUIDEBOOK WHEN YOU'RE ABROAD.

Not only does the guidebook peg you as a tourist—making you an easy mark for any number of crimes—but it can also distract from the enjoyment of a destination. Visitors who obsessively consult their guidebooks risk missing the best part of their vacation: the spontaneous experiences no book can anticipate.

(Of course, that doesn't apply to *this* book.) Most guidebooks are available as ebooks, which you can download to your tablet or smartphone before leaving home. Still, don't forget that electronic devices are tempting targets for thieves the world over, so hold on tight to that iPad.

example, writers for the Moon series "don't accept free goods or services in exchange for positive coverage"; nor does money buy inclusion in the guides. Too often, guidebooks rely on an army of underpaid—or unpaid—contributors who write only about hotels and attractions that offer them free stays, services, or products. It offers them a powerful incentive to write about those businesses in flattering terms and to ignore other deserving places that refuse to play the game.

→ **A CAUTIONARY NOTE ABOUT MAIN-STREAM TRAVEL PUBLICATIONS.** A magazine or newspaper travel section is a smart place to consult for vacation ideas, since many publications don't accept articles based on sponsored trips. However, don't make the mistake of booking a trip based solely on the word of a professional journalist, no matter how prestigious the publication. Good travel reporters pride themselves on providing useful, objective content, but like anyone else, they have their own perspectives that may or may not match your tastes.

What about "star" ratings?

The best known of the American ratings are the American Automobile Association (AAA) Diamond Ratings. These reflect a combination of overall quality, range of facilities, physical attributes, and level of services offered.

These can be useful in identifying first-rate hotels and restaurants—so-called "five diamond" establishments. For the rest of us, the "AAA Approved" sign out front signals a minimum standard of cleanliness and service.

Outside the United States, star ratings are sometimes regulated by the government or an industry group, and they have a more specific meaning. Any ratings system based on a clear, consistent, and easy to find methodology is more credible than something cobbled together willy-nilly online. More on that in a moment.

USER-GENERATED REVIEW SITES

"Should I trust user-generated reviews?" is a question I hear a lot. The short answer is: not entirely. For the purpose of exploring how they can be used to make more informed booking decisions, I'm dividing user-generated reviews into two general categories: forums, or sites that don't use any discernible methodology to review and rate a travel product; and review sites, which use a numeric or star rating.

Should I turn to a forum for help or advice?

Forums such as Lonely Planet's Thorn Tree *(lonelyplanet.com/thorntree)* or FlyerTalk *(flyertalk.com)* are unstructured: In general, they aren't organized around a particular cruise ship, individual hotel property, or restaurant. Instead, they're loosely grouped by topic or destination and follow a discussion thread based on the poster's personal interest.

These sites predate the blogging revolution, and were, originally, helpful places to post questions and get a fast answer from one of your peers. To some extent, they still are helpful, but because of the way these sites are structured, they also have some inherent weaknesses.

→ THEY'RE SOMEWHAT RANDOM. If you're looking for information about a particular product, you have to sift through a lot of posts to determine what's relevant to you.

→ THE TROLLS OFTEN RULE. Perhaps the most disappointing aspect of forums is that the discussions often devolve into name-calling and negativity. Contributors who actually want to help and have meaningful information to share are too often drowned out by angry know-it-alls.

→ THE INFORMATION IS SOMETIMES INACCURATE. Finally, there's the problem of fact. Most of the information is highly subjective—one person's opinion versus another person's. It's like a guidebook, minus the research.

No effort is made to verify any of the content on these forums, so you can never be entirely sure about accuracy. For this reason, I would advise extreme caution in using or believing anything you find in a forum. The information may be fact, but then again, it may be fiction.

How about review sites? Aren't they believable?

Sort of. Yes, these sites are organized around some sort of quantifying system, awarding stars or number ratings in ascending order based on quality. But no, the reviewers are not verified and they often remain anonymous. Even though sites such as TripAdvisor and Yelp do their best to convince us that they comb through their reviews looking for fakes, they often miss the bogus write-ups and delete the real ones. The sites operate on the assumption that because they have so many reviews, and the ratings look legitimate, their credibility can't be challenged. That's wrong.

How about the star ratings used by some online travel agencies?

Some online travel agencies where you can book travel products, notably Hotwire and Priceline, use aggregate "star" ratings based on their own reader feedback and user-generated reviews to classify hotels. This is particularly important for sites like Hotwire because when you book through them, you're buying an anonymous star rated hotel. The sites don't generally reveal the name of the hotel —only its star rating and location—before you make a nonrefundable reservation.

Although the sites claim to use a methodology in compiling their ratings, the classifications are too often called into question by travelers. These are, by far, the least credible of the user-generated reviews, and while the travel sites that publish them almost always stand behind them, in the sense that the nonrefundable purchase you made based on the rating really *is* nonrefundable, the online agencies can't always tell you how they came up with a particular rating.

If someone posts a favorable review about a restaurant or hotel you're considering, check the person's previous posts.

Should I just ignore the reviews?

No. The reviews, like the blog and forum posts, are just single data points. Individually, the recommendations are not reliable, but put them together and they may guide you to a reliable recommendation. Here are some methods used by smart travelers to distinguish the true from the false.

→ DISREGARD THE TOP AND BOTTOM 5 PERCENT OF THE REVIEWS. Assume that the top reviews are written by employees or relatives of employees and that the bottom 5 percent are penned by competitors. The rest are probably submitted by real travelers.

→ WEED OUT THE ONES YOU'RE LIKELY TO DISAGREE WITH If someone posts a favorable review about a restaurant or hotel you're considering, check the person's previous posts. If that same person has reviewed another establishment you've been to, and you disagree with what they've written, odds are good that you'll also have a problem with the current assessment.

→ LOOK FOR SUSPICIOUS FLAGS THE "ALGORITHM" MISSED. The review sites' vaunted fraud-detection algorithms—programs designed to identify fake reviews—are deeply flawed and often unreliable. If you see an obviously suspicious account (for example, someone who only posts once with something very positive or very negative), then ignore the advice—it might be bogus.

→ **WATCH FOR A REACTION FROM THE BUSINESS.** If a hotel or restaurant responds to negative reviews in a responsible and non-dismissive way, it's hard evidence the owners care what customers think and will try to do better. That's a good sign.

→ **USE COMMON SENSE.** If something looks too good to be true, it probably is too good to be true. (Brace yourself: I'm gonna say that a few times in this book.) Sure, it's well-worn advice, but you would be surprised at how often common sense and reason go out the window when you're researching your dream vacation.

SOCIAL MEDIA SITES

Social networks are only as helpful as the people who are on them. So, you might have a sizable network of Facebook friends or an impressive Twitter following, but if nobody has any firsthand travel experience of the kind you're seeking, you'll be barking up the wrong tree. On the other hand, on a smaller social network like LinkedIn or Pinterest, a few travel-savvy buddies can offer up a trove of useful advice. Bigger isn't always better.

Generally speaking, here's what you'll find on each network:

→ **FACEBOOK.** As a stand-alone network, Facebook isn't the first place I would turn to for travel information. However, combined with an application like GoGoBot *(gogobot.com)*, which lets you exchange vacation information and travel photos across Facebook, it can be leveraged into a powerful tool for exchanging travel tips. Facebook also allows you to search for a subject by hashtag (#), making it easier to find related posts. Try posting something using a travel-specific hashtag to get responses from others in your network.

→ **TWITTER.** Even if your network lacks travel-savvy followers, fear not. You can build a fairly quick list by following Twitter's sanctioned travel experts

---

👍**SMART** LOOK FOR INTEL THAT CAN MAKE YOUR STAY BETTER.

Say you find a hotel that everyone "loves" except one guest, who claims there's a problem with street noise. Why not use that information to request a quiet room away from the street? Or, if you're a light sleeper, use that comment to rule out a reservation at that property. Also, pay close attention to reviewer-posted photos, which are more likely to show the true look of a hotel than the glossy professional pictures on a property's own website.

(twitter.com/who_to_follow/ interests/travel), or by tracking the hashtag #travel and then following the most influential users. After a while, Twitter will begin suggesting other travel-related accounts to follow. Use a more specific hashtag to find users at your destination. So, for example, if you're visiting Orlando, try searching for and using #Orlando in your tweets.

→ **LINKEDIN.** Although LinkedIn is known as a network for professionals, it contains some valuable content for travelers, including a forum for frequent travelers *(linkedin.com/jetbiz travel).* It also has added travel-specific "influencers," including yours truly, who contribute occasional stories.

→ **GOOGLE PLUS.** Google Plus, Google's social network, is known for its travel photography. Also, check out Google's communities *(plus .google.com/communities),* which can introduce you to other travelers, no matter where you're planning to go.

→ **PINTEREST.** It's easy to get lost among the boards on this photo-heavy social network, but staying focused on the "travel" category *(pinterest.com/all/travel)* will lead you to other like-minded pinners. Pinterest is great for window shopping for a beautiful destination, but as for exchanging ideas and tips, it's probably the least useful of the major social networks.

Travel blogs

As with social networks, you don't want to base your purchasing decisions on a single blog or blog post. Instead, use the information you find online as individual data points that can, collectively, lead you to an informed decision. Although there's no shortage of destination blogs or websites that focus on a particular place, there are relatively few credible sites that cover travel from a consumer perspective. Be particularly wary of blogging networks for frequent travelers or cooperatives that host multiple bloggers, many of which are set up primarily to sell affinity credit cards that allow you to earn loyalty points with each purchase. Their advice may be tainted by commercial interests and could be misleading.

WORD-OF-MOUTH RECOMMENDATIONS

It probably goes without saying that the most credible advice often comes from a word-of-mouth recommendation from someone who knows you. But I'll say it anyway. It could come from a travel agent (a subject covered in Chapter 2) who's had a chance to get to know you based on a prior working relationship, or from a friend or relative or colleague or neighbor. This is not the same thing as advice typed into a PC or phone, and shared online (people say the darndest things on the Internet, don't they?).

Although word-of-mouth advice may have the most value when it comes to making travel-related choices—at least according to researchers—not all person-to-person advice is created equal. A few questions to ask before considering any such advice:

→ **WHEN DID THE PERSON LAST VISIT THE PLACE IN QUESTION?** Destinations change, and often the recommended restaurants and attractions of yesteryear are no longer there—or worse, they've turned into just a pale shadow of their formerly great selves. Make sure the advice you're getting isn't from the 70s.

→ **HOW WELL DOES THE PERSON KNOW YOU?** This may seem obvious, but it's worth underscoring. If it's a close relative or friend, chances are good that he or she will know what you might like and, more important, what you *dislike*. An acquaintance or

> *Although word-of-mouth advice may have the most value ... not all person-to-person advice is created equal.*

a co-worker might not know that you have a peanut allergy, don't like hot weather, or that you love spicy Chinese food. Be prepared to take some of that person's well-meaning advice with a grain of salt. Better yet, without making too much of it, briefly clue the person in on some of your interests and quirks.

NOW WHAT?

By now, you should *know* who knows the most about the place you're visiting. You've collected tips from guidebooks, the Internet, your social network, your travel agent, and your immediate circle of friends and relatives. Let's rank the advice in order of credibility.

1. Word-of-mouth advice from a close friend, relative, colleague, or trusted travel adviser.
2. Personal advice from your social network.
3. Advice from someone within your social network who lives at the destination or has recently been there.
4. Published advice, either in a guidebook or from a professional reviewer, such as AAA.
5. Advice from a blog or travel publication (in which the writer is named).
6. Anything written on a forum where anonymous posts are allowed, or anything from a user-generated review site.

PROBLEM SOLVED

HEY, THAT'S NO FOUR-STAR HOTEL!

QUESTION: I recently booked a hotel in Prague through Expedia.

Based on amenities and price, I chose an unnamed four-star hotel that was being offered for $58 a night. I paid for the three rooms I needed, and then was shown the hotel name and class.

The class was only three-star. I couldn't believe it.

Thankfully, I made screen captures of the offer and the result. I immediately sent an email to Expedia's customer service department explaining what had happened. Expedia replied with a short notice saying all sales were final. I then replied that this was not an issue of wanting money back or a change, but of getting what I paid for, namely a four-star hotel.

The next response I received was infuriating. I was told Expedia was unable to verify the change in star rating. I then responded with the screenshots. In each instance, I was told to call in to discuss the matter. I told them I wanted everything in writing.

I am very unhappy at the moment. I work at Kandahar Airfield in Afghanistan, and I take my vacation time very seriously. I want Expedia to either give me the four-star hotel I paid for or refund my money immediately. Can you help?
—Albert Muick, *Kandahar, Afghanistan*

ANSWER: If you paid for a four-star hotel, you should have received a four-star hotel booking. Problem is, no one can really agree on what a four-star hotel is — or isn't. There's no high court of hotel stars, no international governing body. As far as I can tell, if I call something a four-star hotel, it is a four-star hotel.

You made screenshots? Nice work. You insisted on conducting your correspondence by email? Even better! Keeping meticulous records on your grievance can usually ensure a fast resolution, and when it doesn't — well, that's where I come in.

I'm kind of surprised Expedia shot a form response back to you, and then, after you replied, sent another one. Come on. Is anyone reading these emails?

You might have tried a brief, polite appeal to an Expedia executive. (Contact information is listed in the Appendix and in more detail on my website, *elliott.org*.) That might — or might not — have worked.

This is a textbook case of a traveler doing almost everything right, but still finding himself unable to reach a fair resolution. I hope this is one of those rare occasions when Expedia didn't bother to carefully read your well-crafted email.

I contacted Expedia on your behalf. It reviewed your grievance and found that a "system error" occurred when you made your reservation. You've received a full refund.

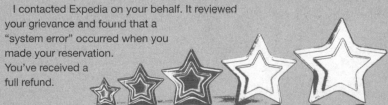

What if the advice is no good?

If you have a problem with the advice given to you by a travel agent or a friend, you can go back to that person and complain. A guidebook author (or more likely, the publisher) can be contacted and offered constructive criticism to avoid inaccurate or incomplete advice in future editions. But once you enter the domain of anonymous reviews and forums, you're on your own. You can't ask Trip-Advisor for a refund. Your only option is to leave a negative review for the hotel or restaurant, and that may be removed. If you do opt to post a negative review, try not to rant. It upsets the fraud-detection algorithm.

I'm here. Who do I believe?

So far, I've focused on the pre-trip information you need to make an informed decision. Many smaller decisions will be made on the fly, with the help of some or all of these resources, plus a few others. There's nothing quite like asking a

local to recommend a favorite bakery or restaurant. Or is there?

→ **A PERSONAL FRIEND OR A FRIEND OF A FRIEND.** A local who knows you and lives in the place you're visiting is generally the most reliable source of information. If you know someone in town who knows someone—in other words, if you have a friend of a friend—then you might be in luck. They're far less likely to offer bad advice, because they're accountable to someone.

→ **A CONVENTION AND VISITORS BUREAU OR TOURIST INFORMATION CENTER.** These visitor centers, usually located close to the major attractions, can offer reliable tips, maps, brochures, and information about attractions that may not be available online. But not always; often, they recommend only the services of "members." Also, not all information centers are official. Orlando, for example, has more than a few fake "visitor" centers that offer misleading or incomplete information to tourists. How do you tell the difference? Both Twitter and Facebook will "verify" real tourism sites with a check mark, and these in turn often list the locations where you can find more information. Fake "information" centers also practice a hard sell, hawking event tickets or theme park admissions.

→ **YOUR HOTEL CONCIERGE.** Many hotel concierges will offer unbiased advice, as well as other services, to hotel guests. But don't count on it. Concierges are sometimes offered kickbacks from establishments they recommend. How do you know they're on the take? If they give you a card that promises you a discount or a free drink or appetizer, odds are the restaurant is using it to track the referral.

What if I received misleading advice while I was at a destination?

Because you're there in person, you have more options than when you're researching a place online. You can go back to that friend and say the restaurant was awful or the museum was boring, but the feedback loop is most effective when you're dealing with a third party like a visitor center or a hotel concierge. If they point you in the wrong direction, they can be held accountable for it, and they should be. Let 'em know you're unhappy and don't be afraid to ask for a supervisor if you're dismissed.

→ **IF A VISITOR CENTER GIVES YOU BAD ADVICE:** Pay a second visit to the center and let them know you've had a negative experience. If the referral is from a member of the chamber of commerce that funds the center, then it should have the wherewithal to address your grievance—if not with an apology and a promise to do better (which is a given), then with a refund or a future discount. Remember, these centers often have a direct relationship with

the business, and if the product or service is found to be seriously lacking, the business could lose its membership.

→ **IF A CONCIERGE GIVES YOU BAD ADVICE:** First allow the employee to resolve it—again, an apology, a partial refund, or a discount on a future purchase could be offered. If that doesn't work, then reporting the concierge to a supervisor at the hotel, to the hotel chain, or to a professional concierge association like Les Clefs d'Or (lcdusa.org) may yield a desired result.

Either way, you owe it to yourself and to future visitors to warn friends and family, as well as your extended social network, when you're misled by bad advice. In fact, the only reason bogus "visitor" centers and crooked concierges can continue to mislead travelers is that those who are duped never bother to complain about their negative experiences.

Not all information centers are official.

BOTTOM LINE

Although there's more information about travel available now than perhaps at any other time in history, it's not all reliable. You may never be able to determine what is true and what isn't. But by using basic research techniques and knowing which information is most trustworthy, you can make the smartest travel choices. And if you don't, be sure to write a review so you'll warn others.

(2)

Book Your Next Trip

The real difference between an online travel agent and a person, and how to tell if you can do it yourself.

When you're planning a trip, you can do it yourself or you can let someone else do it for you. That *someone,* a travel agent, can guide you through the sometimes confusing world of travel, which includes reserving, ticketing, confirming, and then, if necessary, troubleshooting a trip. But you can also turn to an online travel agency, or click directly on a company's website, or even pick up the phone to find a deal—and still have a great trip. Confused yet? Not a problem.

When to use a travel agent:

→ **WHEN YOU WANT A PROFESSIONAL** to assist you with your travel arrangements.

→ **WHEN YOU DON'T HAVE THE TIME TO** pull together a complex itinerary and need a person to do it for you, or when you need someone to help you when you're on the road.

→ **WHEN YOU NEED THE EXPERTISE OF AN AGENT** for a special event or trip, like a destination wedding, honeymoon, or anniversary cruise. (Travel agents' rates for this type of travel can cost more than self-booked trips. Be sure to shop around and compare prices.)

When to book travel yourself:

→ **WHEN IT'S A SIMPLE TRANSACTION,** like buying a train ticket or a round-trip plane ticket, or booking a hotel room.

→ **WHEN YOU ENJOY THE CHALLENGE** of finding the best deals on your own.

→ **WHEN YOU KNOW ENOUGH** about a destination that you don't require the advice of an expert and are willing to resolve any disputes that arise directly with the airline, car rental company, cruise line, or hotel.

Mind the jargon!

Human travel agents cringe when you refer to a site like Orbitz as an "online" travel agent. They also draw distinctions between the terms *travel agent, travel adviser,* and *travel counselor.* I'm not going there. Instead, I'm sticking to the basic term *travel agent* to describe a real person, and *online travel agency,* or *OTA,* to describe a website.

A *direct self-booking* means you're dealing with the company, without an intermediary. You might still have the protection offered by your credit card, but there's no middleman handling or processing the transaction. You're flying solo.

Booking through an online travel agency means you're buying travel through a third party, usually a website like Expedia, Orbitz, or Travelocity. It's similar to a self-booking, in that it's fairly automated, but there's a company acting as an intermediary. That can be helpful.

21

TRAVEL AGENTS 101

Human travel agents remain an excellent resource for travel information, special offers, and recommendations. An agent can either work for a large, established agency, such as American Express, AAA Travel, or Travel Leaders, or can work as a freelance agent or for a smaller mom-and-pop agency. A good travel agent will offer advice, advocacy, access, and accountability.

→ **LIVE AND IN PERSON.** Many travel agents have real offices (so-called *brick-and-mortar* agencies) with real office hours. Some agencies with retail storefronts are capable of offering services like 24-hour assistance. If you like doing business with a real person whom you've personally met, a human travel agent is a smart option. Some home-based agents work remotely, but can often arrange to meet you if you need to discuss your plans in person.

→ **SPECIALIZED ADVICE.** The best travel agents spend a career honing their expertise in a particular geographic area. Look for certificates offered by accrediting organizations such as The Travel Institute *(the travelinstitute.com)*, which not only certify the agent's expertise but also refer you to an agent with the know-how you need.

→ **SPECIAL INTEREST.** Chances are, there's an agent that specializes in the kind of vacation you're hoping to book. For example, if you're into luxury travel, you'll want to check out an agent belonging to the Virtuoso agency network *(virtuoso.com)* or Signature Travel Network *(signature travelnetwork.com)*. Other agents specialize in disability travel (look for membership in the Society for Accessible Travel & Hospitality).

How do I choose the best travel agent?

→ **ASK FOR REFERENCES.** A competent travel agent should be happy to provide you with a list of other clients and their phone numbers. The agent may have to ask for permission from them before handing out their contact information. At the very least, travel agents should be able to offer credible testimonials from past clients.

→ **VERIFY PROFESSIONAL MEMBERSHIPS.** Most reputable travel agencies belong to either the American Society of Travel Agents (ASTA) or the Association of Retail Travel Agents (ARTA). These memberships signal that your travel agent pledges to adhere to certain basic ethical and business standards.

→ **LOOK FOR ACCREDITATIONS.** Two main "degrees" are used to certify travel agency expertise. The Certified Travel Associate (CTA) designation is for agents in sales, customer service, and communication, and requires little previous experience. The Certified Travel Counselor (CTC) designation is for agents with at least five years of experience and focuses on leadership, business development, and management skills. If your agent has a CTA or CTC designation, it's a good sign.

→ **AND MORE ACCREDITATIONS . . .** If you are considering a cruise, the Cruise Lines International Association (CLIA) is the primary accreditation organization. It certifies members based on years of experience, comprehensive testing, and ship visits. The Accredited Cruise Counselor (ACC) is the first step, followed by the Master Cruise Counselor (MCC), and then the Elite Cruise Counselor Scholar (ECCS). ASTA also certifies agents for specific destinations (Destination Specialists, DS) or for specific lifestyles like gay and lesbian or senior/mature adults (Lifestyle Specialists, LS).

→ **ASK TO SEE THE SELLER OF TRAVEL NUMBER.** Many states require all sellers of travel to register with the Attorney General's office and to display the registration number on all advertising. That's no guarantee that the company is reputable, but a lack of a valid registration can mean trouble.

→ **CHECK THE BBB RATING.** Individual travel agency businesses are often rated by their customers on the Better Business Bureau (BBB) site. While BBB ratings can be manipulated, and in my experience often favor the business, a low or failing grade can be a red flag. Note: Just because an agency doesn't have a BBB rating, doesn't mean it is in any way suspect. After all, you have to pay to belong to the BBB.

If you feel "off" or just disconnected from the agent, look elsewhere.

→ **CHECK YOUR GUT.** If you feel "off" or just disconnected from the agent, look elsewhere. You are preparing to spend a lot of money, and you should feel good about the agent you've chosen.

How do I know if an agent isn't right for me?

→ **NO COMPRENDO.** Some agencies cater to a specific market or niche. If the storefront is in another language, and the people at the reception don't speak your language, you've probably stumbled into one of those businesses. These niche agencies, which often cater to large immigrant communities, may offer amazing deals on "bulk" airfares to certain destinations, so don't dismiss them. Use your high school Spanish and save!

→ **THE AGENT DOESN'T LISTEN.** Travel agents work for you, so when one doesn't listen to your wants and needs and tries to book a vacation that isn't right for you, maybe it's time to look elsewhere. (See "How is my travel agent compensated?" below.)

→ **THE AGENT IS "CERTIFIED" THROUGH AN ORGANIZATION YOU DON'T RECOGNIZE.** Some unscrupulous organizations allow anyone to buy a certification without any training or knowledge. If you see a certification you don't recognize, find out if anyone can buy their way into the program. If that's the case, don't walk away—run!

Some unscrupulous organizations allow anyone to buy a certification without any training or knowledge.

→ **BY THE TRAVEL COMPANY.** Airlines, car rental companies, cruise lines, and hotels sometimes compensate your agent with various types of commissions and bonuses. They can range from an outright sales commission of anywhere between 5 and 12 percent (and sometimes higher) to an override bonus for exceeding a sales quota.

How is my travel agent compensated?

A travel agent's advice isn't free, even if you don't pay anything for it up front. It helps to understand how your travel agent is compensated.

→ **BY YOU.** When you buy something through an agent, you will probably pay a transaction fee of anywhere between $50 and $100, depending on the type of booking. This covers only a fraction of the agent's actual costs.

Is my agent telling me the truth about his or her compensation?

You can ask, and some will tell you. Others feel that their actual remuneration—at least the part that comes from a hotel or cruise line—is none of your business, and they might be offended if you bring it up. But it's important to know who pays your agent. A great agent is not a slave to commissions. That person wants happy, repeat clients who will spread the word to family and friends, leading to more business. But mediocre agents will follow the

👍 **SMART** HOW MUCH IS THAT AGENT?

Always ask about the cost of an agent's services before you start planning. Many upscale agencies charge an hourly rate or a percentage of the overall sale, and a few even require a retainer. Many will charge a "plan-to-go" fee, which is often refunded when you book your travel. Such fees ensure that "tire kickers" (people who look but don't book) don't eat up valuable agent time. Find out before you sit down to plan your dream vacation.

money—and chances are, you're not paying them enough.

Is my agent telling me the whole truth about a product?

Travel agents can be swayed in the same way you are—by ads in trade magazines, by user-generated reviews, and by word-of-mouth recommendations. Be wary of policies that may be benefiting the agent, but not you. For example, many large agencies have so-called preferred-supplier agreements, which mandate that agents always book with a certain airline or hotel. These arrangements are supposed to benefit everyone. The agents are rewarded for sending a lot of business to one company, and the company reciprocates by offering a lower rate. But it isn't always a win-win. The best agents simply ignore these policies and try to find their clients the best travel product.

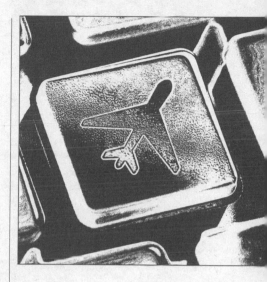

What's a FAM trip, and why should I care about it?

Travel agents are sometimes invited on familiarization trips (FAMs), or all-expenses-paid visits to a place for "familiarization" purposes. These may influence an agent's recommendations. Even if they don't go, agents can be swayed in other ways. Destinations and the suppliers of products are known to throw big parties with plenty of free food and booze in an effort to curry favor with agents. It doesn't always work; the best agents take the free shrimp and Chardonnay and then do what's best for you. But as a practical matter, FAMs and receptions can predispose less ethical agents to recommend a particular property or product.

In the end, none of this may matter. The threat of your taking your business elsewhere next time is a powerful incentive to keep an agent focused on making you happy.

What should you reasonably expect from a travel agent?

→ A COMPETENT AGENT should be available to you before, during, and after the booking to answer any questions about your trip. The agent should also be available after your trip if you have any questions.

PROBLEM SOLVED

HEY, WHAT HAPPENED TO MY TICKET REFUND?

QUESTION: My wife and I planned a trip to Antigua this summer, and in December we purchased round-trip flights, a hotel room, and a kayak excursion through Expedia.

Everything was a "go" until we received a call one day in early April from an Expedia representative informing us of a change to our American Airlines flights. American had apparently changed quite a few flights to the island, and, unfortunately, none of the changes worked for us.

After getting the rep to verify that we could cancel the hotel, excursion, and flights at no charge, I authorized them to go ahead and cancel the trip completely. The rep was able to instantly provide a refund for the hotel and kayak trip, but advised that the refund for the flights would take between four and six weeks to go through.

Six weeks later, having received no refund, I checked with Expedia. It informed me that it had already given me a refund, but it turns out it was only referring to the first refund, for the hotel and kayak trip. I emailed Expedia back to let it know that it still owed us a refund for the flight, but have not received a response yet.

It concerns me that no one can seem to tell us when we will ever get the refund.

I am at my wit's end with Expedia, Chris. Can you please help me get this resolved? My wife and I would be so grateful. —Dan Lachapelle, *Sudbury, Ontario, Canada*

ANSWER: I wouldn't be so quick to blame Expedia. Airlines are known to drag their feet when it comes to refunds, and my initial reading of your problem suggests American might have something to do with the delay, too.

This is a common problem. You buy your tickets through an agency and the agency takes your money, but if you want a refund—or something else, like a name change—then the agency defers to the airline. If you paid the agency, why can't the agency just give you a refund?

I've been covering the travel industry for years, and I still haven't heard a reasonable answer to that question. I'm told that it's technology or policy or even tradition that keeps your money from promptly flowing back in your direction. Whatever the reason, it seems the only beneficiaries are the companies that get to keep your money for two to three billing cycles. It shouldn't be that way.

Expedia should have been able to refund your entire purchase and then retrieve the money from the airline. Instead, it made you wait. Then, when you made inquiries, it told you the check was in the mail, and when you followed up, refused to answer.

For what it's worth, I think your refund would have come eventually, but you've been more than patient. You can find the names of Expedia's executives in the back of this book and appeal your case to someone higher up the food chain.

I asked Expedia about your refund. It contacted you and admitted to losing the information for your flights and refund. You received a full refund for your trip.

→ **A RELIABLE TRAVEL AGENT** should keep you posted on any deadlines for making payments and getting the necessary paperwork to travel. However, you alone are responsible for meeting all those requirements, not your agent.

→ **A GOOD TRAVEL AGENT** should support you during your trip, if not with a 24-hour phone number, then at least by phone or email during regular office hours. It's reasonable to expect an agent to help you when something goes wrong while you're traveling, instead of pushing you off on the airline or cruise line. Remember: Your agent is being compensated for this work. The top agents monitor the progress of your trip and fix problems before they happen. If you find one who does that, you've got a keeper.

How do I resolve a disagreement with a travel agent?

If you have a problem with an agent, go to the person first and try to resolve it—the sooner the better. Put your grievance in writing if it can't be fixed quickly. Some travel companies will only deal with the agent who made your reservation, so it may be impossible to fix the problem by dealing directly with the company.

A good agent should also have something called errors and omissions insurance to protect him—and you—from an incorrect name or date typed into the reservation system. Think of it as malpractice insurance for agents.

When you work with a travel agent about a dispute, you have several remedies at your disposal that you don't when you're at odds with a travel company. For example, the threat of taking an agent to small-claims court can help move your problem closer to a resolution. Some states, notably California, also require travel sellers to be licensed, so reporting an agent to state regulators can also persuade her to find a fix. As a last-ditch effort, you can dispute your credit card charge or report the agent to her trade group. Organizations such as ASTA have ethics codes that, if you can show they were violated, could result in disciplinary action being taken against the agent. Normally, ASTA doesn't remove agents for disciplinary issues; it just fails to approve the agent's membership renewal.

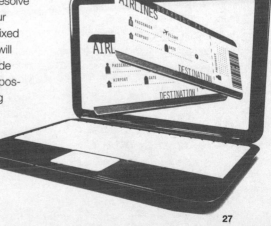

Bottom Line

Competent travel agents really *are* worth their weight in gold. They know how you like to travel and can antici- pate your needs before you ask. In the event they make a mistake, it's fixed quickly and with- out costing you anything extra. But finding a great agent can be a chal- lenge. In a world where agents are being swayed by bonuses, commissions, and free trips, some are in the business for all the wrong reasons. If you have the misfortune of working with a bad agent, it probably goes without saying that you *are* better off on your own.

> *Competent travel agents really are worth their weight in gold.*

DOING IT YOURSELF

Most travelers don't distinguish between self-booking—dealing directly with a travel company—and buying a trip through an online travel agency. Indeed, human travel agents often refer to online agencies as vend- ing machines for travel. I'm going to handle both kinds of independent bookings together in the following section because they are functionally similar. Where there are differences, I'll point them out.

What does an online travel agency offer?

Online travel agencies (OTAs) like Expedia, Orbitz, and Travelocity can be an attractive option for travelers who are comfortable booking online, even if they have a minimal level of knowledge about the travel industry. Here are some benefits:

• Access to almost-real- time airfares and hotel rates. No need to call a travel agent and ask for a quote.

• The ability to pack- age airline tickets, hotel accommodations, and car rentals in one product.

• Aggressive discounts on travel products thanks to the agencies' economies of scale. OTAs will buy blocks of rooms or flights at deep dis- counts and then resell them to you.

What are the biggest mistakes travelers make when self-booking?

Without an agent to help you through the process, you could make one of several rookie mistakes when buy- ing travel. Here are the most common ones and ways to prevent them.

→ **WRONG DATE OR TIME.** An easy mistake to make, and far too com- mon. The pull-down menus can be confusing, especially if you're dealing with a European site, which formats day-month-year instead of month- day-year. Foreign calendars also often group Saturday and Sunday at the end of the week, so it's easy to click on a square that you believe is Friday and have it actually be Saturday. Also, remember that when you're booking a hotel, you're checking in one day but spending the night, so you're staying until the *next* day. Also, DIYers frequently confuse a.m. and p.m.

→ THE FIX: Verify your times, dates, and airports before and after you click the "buy" button. You have 24 hours to cancel your airline ticket under federal rules (see Chapter 10 for more).

→ INCORRECT NAME ON A RESERVATION. Remember, the name on your airline ticket must match the one on your government-issued ID. "Frank" instead of "Francis" or "Bob" instead of "Robert" could screw up your vacation. If you're traveling internationally, the name on the ticket must match your passport exactly.

→ THE FIX: Double-check the name on your itinerary before and after you click the "buy" button.

→ NOT SHOPPING AROUND. One of the biggest benefits of using a website to buy travel is that you can compare prices. If you're pressed for time—and if you don't really care how much money you spend—then find a travel agent and let that person book the most convenient itinerary. Otherwise, you owe it to yourself to check multiple sites for the best bargain. Certainly scan the three major OTAs, but also check out a site like *Kayak.com,* which searches multiple locations for the best deal. Think of Kayak as a search engine for travel products. It allows you to cast a wide net, searching hundreds of sites for the lowest fare.

→ THE FIX: Visit at least one competing website (and preferably two) before making a booking decision.

→ BASIC TRIP RESEARCH. When you book something online, everything is up to you. That includes not only passports and visas but also your own security (see Chapters 3 and 4 for details).

→ THE FIX: If you're not prepared to at least look up your visa requirements when preparing to travel internationally and you're not likely to consult the State Department's website *(state.gov)* to help ensure

NOT SMART TRYING TO GUESS THE AIRPORT CODE.

Don't assume you know the three-letter airport code. Even professional travel agents sometimes get it wrong. For example, what's the airport code for Chicago's airport? Did you say CHG? Sorry, that belongs to Chaoyang Airport in China. It's actually ORD. No, not Orlando. Orlando's is MCO. Told ya it was confusing. Look it up, or you could end up in the wrong place.

your safety, maybe you should use an agent.

→ **FAILING TO READ THE TERMS OF YOUR PURCHASE.** If you're booking online and directly through a company, the terms will be available on its website. Airlines have a contract of carriage and cruise lines and hotels have a ticket contract, both of which can be found online. They outline your rights to a refund as well as the terms of your purchase. Similarly, your OTA has terms and conditions that outline what it will, and won't, do for you. Finally, each purchase may come with its own terms, which are displayed before you book.

→ **THE FIX:** Read *everything*. If you don't, you could be surprised by what terms you're agreeing to.

What do I need to know about booking through an online agency?

An online travel agency (OTA) is a large organization that can offer

> *If you're booking online and directly through a company, the terms will be available on its website.*

some of the benefits of a human agent, but not all. Here are a few key differences:

→ **IT'S OPTIMIZED FOR MAKING UNASSISTED ONLINE PURCHASES.** Call an OTA, and you are asking for trouble. I've handled far too many "wrong name" cases that were the result of a language barrier involving an offshore phone agent or poor phone reception. At the same time, however, the automation can be your friend. Many online agencies have superior notification systems to let you know when your reservation changes. These automated systems can notify you faster than any human agent—when they work.

→ **IT'S A BUREAUCRACY.** The major OTAs are huge companies with international presences. While that can be helpful when the company is trying to negotiate a volume discount for its customers, it can be a disadvantage when you're looking for personal attention, have a quick question, or need a quick refund.

PROBLEM SOLVED

FIRE YOUR TRAVEL AGENT

QUESTION: My husband bought airline tickets from Chicago to Puerto Vallarta on United Airlines through his travel agent, who is an old friend. My ticket was issued with my husband's surname, even though I did not change my name when I got married 18 years ago.

When I notified the agent of the error, he suggested that I get my driver's license and passport changed to reflect my husband's surname. I told him that was unacceptable. I mean, would he make the same suggestion to my husband if the tickets had been issued with my surname?

The agent says he can't change the name without buying a new ticket, which would cost $450.

I spoke with United, and it has agreed to make a notation in my record regarding the erroneous name. My travel agent says he will "try" to get this in writing, so that I will have something by the time I have to go to the airport, but I'm concerned about airport security. I have a copy of my marriage certificate. What else can I do? —Marguerite Warner, *Chicago, Illinois*

ANSWER: First of all, fire your travel agent.

Here's why. Number one, your agent assumed you shared a surname with your husband. A competent travel agent—and particularly one that you consider a friend—would make it his business to know that you have a different last name.

Second, your agent stuck you with the bill. That's highly unprofessional. It was his mistake; he should have fixed it.

Third, as a "solution," your agent recommended you change your last name to match the ticket, as if it's something you should have done, anyway. How ridiculous.

Do yourself another favor: Don't become "old friends" with your agent. Be friendly, be polite, but keep the relationship professional.

I just wrapped up a case in which a clever agent leveraged her friendship with a client and stuck the traveler with a ticket penalty that the agent should have paid. It was deeply troubling, painful, and in the end, unsolvable.

This is not to let you off the hook here. Your husband should have asked your agent to email or fax him a copy of your itinerary immediately, and he should have examined it for any possible problems. In the time between when a ticket is purchased and a ticket is issued, or "settled," your agent can make a change to your ticket without incurring any penalties. That would have solved your problem.

Your concern about being allowed on the plane is legitimate. Not only could you get stopped when you check in, but before you reach the TSA checkpoint, your ticket is checked against your ID by a private security guard. If it doesn't match, you could get turned away.

United, like every other major carrier, won't let you change a name on a ticket even if it's an honest mistake. However, as a gesture of goodwill, the airline generously agreed to fix your ticket.

→ ADDITIONAL RESTRICTIONS MAY APPLY. Don't assume that the terms of a purchase made directly through a travel company, such as an airline or hotel chain, will be the same when you book through an online travel agency. This is particularly true for so-called opaque sites that offer discounts in exchange for concealing certain details of your purchase, like Hotwire and Priceline (see Chapter 10 for details). Those purchases are nonrefundable.

So, why use an online agency? Because technically, you still have the ability to call on your OTA to advocate for you when something goes wrong. For many travelers, it's like having the best of both worlds: a large

company that can negotiate aggressive discounts and still be in your corner if something goes wrong.

What do I need to know about booking directly?

Increasingly, travel companies (airlines, car rental agencies, hotels, and cruise lines) want you to buy their product directly through their website or at a ticket counter. This reduces their expenses and gives them access to your personal information and spending data. That's worth a lot to them. Here are a few more issues you should know about before booking directly.

→ YOU'RE THE PERFECT CUSTOMER. Let's not kid ourselves: Someone who cuts out the middleman is the ideal customer. You should expect anything from bonus miles to preferred seating or room assignments for bypassing an agent.

→ THE INFORMATION COMES FROM A FIRSTHAND SOURCE. When you deal directly with a travel company, it's responsible for providing you with accurate information about your purchase. No blaming the travel agent. So, in a sense, the reservation numbers or record locators you receive from the company are slightly more reliable than when they come from a third party.

→ GOT A PROBLEM? ONLY ONE PLACE TO GO. If something goes wrong, you can't lean on your travel adviser or OTA. You'll have to go directly to the company. Failing that, you can always dispute your credit card charge. (To be fair, airlines or hotels sometimes also dump their unhappy customers on the agency that booked the trip, which basically means they refer you to the agent to solve a problem and refuse to deal with you directly—so it can cut both ways.)

> *When you deal directly with a travel company, it's responsible for providing you with accurate information about your purchase.*

How do I resolve a dispute with an online travel agency?

Online travel agencies have sophisticated customer service departments designed to send form responses or read scripted responses over the phone. Cutting through can be a challenge. Don't get me wrong: Many common problems can be resolved by phoning your OTA. For example, if you've made a booking error or if your flight has been canceled, calling your online agent is absolutely fine.

→ GET EVERYTHING IN WRITING.
OTAs do record some of their calls for "quality assurance purposes" but they don't make the recordings available to you. Get a record of your communication in writing.

→ TAKE SCREENSHOTS ON YOUR COMPUTER.
The companies do. The OTAs record every keystroke, and if necessary, can provide screenshots that show your reservation. If you want to protect yourself, you have to be vigilant, too. Record *everything*. On Windows, use the PRT SC key and on Apple, Command + Shift + 3 to make a permanent record.

→ DON'T TAKE "NO" FOR AN ANSWER.
Often, when you ask to have a problem handled by a manager, the person on the other end of the line will tell you there's no way to appeal something. That's nonsense. On my website (*elliott.org/contacts*), I list the names of the top executives for the major OTAs. If going that route fails, you can always dispute your credit card charge if you paid with a credit card. See Chapter 14 for more.

Bottom Line

An online travel agency can save you time and money, and so can a direct booking. But watch out for common mistakes that could sink your vacation. And if you're not sure you can do it yourself, hire a professional.

3

Make Sure Your Papers Are in Order

The lowdown on passports, visas, birth certificates, IDs, and anything else you need to get from here to there.

No matter where you go, or how you get there, you'll be asked at some point to show some combination of ID, passport, or visa. Having the right paperwork can mean the difference between a great trip and one that ends before it begins because you're turned around and sent home—or worse, detained overnight while you wait to be deported. Don't laugh. It happens more often than you think. But it doesn't have to happen to you.

Identification, please

→ **WHAT IT IS:** Most acceptable forms of identification are photo IDs issued by a state or federal government. The most common type of ID for domestic travelers is a driver's license issued by the motor vehicle administration in your state. Motor vehicle licensing agencies also issue non-driver photo IDs. For international travelers, the most widely used form of ID is a passport (see below).

→ **WHEN YOU NEED IT:** A driver's license is mandatory if you're planning to drive either your own car or a rental. You may also need to show a photo ID if you're staying at a hotel or catching a train.

The TSA requires an ID for passengers older than 18 flying on domestic flights. If you show up without ID, you're setting yourself up for a lot of unnecessary hassle. You'll likely get a secondary screening by the TSA and be asked to provide some additional information about yourself.

→ **WHEN YOU DON'T NEED IT:** You can make arrangements to stay in a hotel without showing an ID.

Who's responsible for my having the right paperwork?

You are, and you alone. In the end, it doesn't matter what a travel agent, cruise line, tour operator, or airline says. If you don't have the right visa, ID, passport, or transit visa, you can't go back to them and ask for a refund because they gave you the incorrect information. Nor should you rely on anyone but an official government source for accurate and up-to-date information on your paperwork requirements.

👍 **SMART** DIGITIZE YOUR WALLET BEFORE YOU GO.

It's a good idea either to photocopy your driver's license, passport, visas, and credit cards, front and back, before your trip or to scan them and store the images online. In the event your wallet is lost or stolen, you'll have the information you need, including ID and account numbers and contact information, that you'll need to cancel and replace the lost items. I recommend an app called Lemon Wallet (lemon.com), which scans your IDs and stores them in the Cloud.

PASSPORTS

→ **WHAT IT IS:** A passport is a government-issued document that certifies your nationality and identity for the purpose of international travel.

→ **WHEN YOU NEED IT:** Almost any time you cross an international border.

→ **WHEN YOU DON'T NEED IT:** When taking a "closed-loop" cruise, which is defined as a cruise beginning and ending in the U.S. (More information on closed-loop cruises later in this chapter—see page 37.)

→ **NOTE:** When entering Canada or Mexico at land border crossings, or Bermuda and Caribbean nations at seaports-of-entry, you can use the less expensive U.S. Passport Card (see below).

Should I get a passport or a passport card?

For just $55, versus $165 for a first-time passport, you can get a handy U.S. Passport Card that lets you into Canada, Mexico, and the Caribbean nations. But not so fast. The passport card can't be used for international travel by air. If you miss the boat because you had too much fun in a Caribbean port of call and want to fly home, a passport card won't work. If you're planning *any* kind of international travel, you'll probably want a regular passport.

I don't have a passport. When should I get one?

How about now? If you've booked an international trip, there's no time like the present to get your passport. It can take up to six weeks to get a passport, and during busy periods (just before the summer travel season, for example) it can take significantly longer. Considering that an adult passport lasts ten years, what's a few extra months?

I need to renew my passport soon. When should I do it?

Again, the correct answer is now. The State Department recommends that you renew your passport at least nine months before it expires. Some countries require that your passport be valid at least six months *after* the dates of your trip, and some airlines will not allow you to board a flight if that requirement isn't met.

My passport is damaged or mutilated. Do I need a new one?

Yes. When in doubt, get a replacement. I've handled cases in which a passport wasn't accepted because it was torn. One traveler had to turn around and return to the United States—from South Africa.

My cruise line says I can show a birth certificate. Can't I just save the money I'd have to pay for a passport?

No, no, no. You need a passport. Your travel agent or cruise line will likely tell you that birth certificates are an acceptable form of ID on closed-loop cruises. But you'll have to deal with others along the way who may disagree with your travel agent's or cruise line's often unreliable interpretation of what constitutes a valid birth certificate. Does it have to have a raised seal? Does it have to be an American birth certificate? Can it be reissued, or does it have to be the original? I've seen cruise passengers left at the dock because of a disagreement about a birth certificate. A valid passport trumps everything.

What about the expediting services or the expedited option for passports?

You can pay an extra $60 and get your passport in two to three weeks. (Never mind the fact that it shouldn't take that long to get a passport the regular way.) If you have a life or death emergency and must travel within the next day or two, then you can appear in person at a passport agency, provide proof of your emergency, and receive your travel documents. In addition, there are private passport expediting services that charge you an additional fee and guarantee a passport within 24 hours. You'll pay more than twice the cost of a regular passport, once fees are added.

> *The State Department recommends that you renew your passport at least nine months before it expires.*

👎 NOT SMART
LOSING FORMS YOU GET WHILE ENTERING A COUNTRY.

When you cross the border into some countries, a customs agent will give you a form. Try not to lose it. For example, Chile issues American visitors a so-called tourist card, which must be presented upon your departure. It can only be replaced at the offices of Policía Internacional by showing your passport.

waiver, including frequently visited European countries such as the U.K., France, and Italy. Check the websites or call the embassies or consulates of the countries you plan to visit for current information regarding their visa requirements.

VISAS

→ **WHAT IT IS:** A visa (not to be confused with the credit card company) is an endorsement on a passport that allows you to enter and stay for a specified period of time in a foreign country.

→ **WHEN YOU NEED IT:** If you're visiting a country with a visa requirement. You may also need a special kind of visa called a transit visa if you're stopping in a country on your way to another one.

→ **WHEN YOU DON'T NEED IT:** If you're traveling to a country with a visa

Where can I find reliable information about my passport, visa, or ID requirements?

→ **THE U.S. STATE DEPARTMENT** has a website *(state.gov)* that is widely regarded as the final authority on paperwork requirements for Americans traveling overseas. It's also a useful resource for information about security and the political climate in a foreign country.

→ **A FOREIGN EMBASSY OR CONSULATE.** If you're applying for a visa, you'll need to do so through an embassy or consulate. In the unlikely event there's a conflict between the information on the State Department site and the foreign embassy's, you should endeavor

👍SMART CUT THE LINE AT THE BORDER.

The U.S. Customs and Border Protection (CBP) Trusted Traveler Program allows preapproved, low-risk travelers access to dedicated lanes and kiosks. (See also Chapter 13.) The programs include Global Entry, a program that allows expedited clearance upon arrival in the United States; NEXUS, which allows you to use a fast lane at the U.S.-Canadian border; and SENTRI, which lets you cut the line when you're crossing into and out of Mexico. More information on applying for these programs can be found online at *cbp.gov/xp/cgov/travel/trusted_traveler*.

PROBLEM SOLVED

MY DOG ATE MY PASSPORT

QUESTION: My husband and I were scheduled to take a Spirit Airlines flight from Fort Lauderdale, Florida, to San Jose, Costa Rica. The afternoon before my flight, my dog chewed a corner off the front page of my husband's passport, and we were concerned about having proper documentation.

We arrived at the airport almost three hours early in order to have enough time to consult a ticket agent. He seemed seasoned and professional, and he assured us that there would be no problem with the passport, as the number could still be input manually.

We asked him to check with the proper authorities, as we did not want to have a problem once we arrived in Costa Rica, or when we returned from Costa Rica. We were prepared to change the flight until Monday, so we could replace the passport on an emergency basis. The ticket agent assured us that there was absolutely no reason for concern.

When we arrived in San Jose at about 2:30 a.m., we were denied admission by Costa Rican immigration and told to return. The immigration officer told us that the airline should have never boarded us. We were back in Fort Lauderdale by 5 a.m.

I called and wrote to Spirit asking for a voucher for a return trip, as I feel they were responsible under the circumstances. Had their agent not assured us, we would not have boarded the flight.

Now, we have no tickets and we wasted a lot of time and money. Spirit has declined our request, stating that proper documentation is our responsibility. That may be true, but they also have a responsibility to board only those passengers that are properly documented.

I don't think my request for a voucher that would allow us to make the trip to Costa Rica again is unreasonable. What do you think? —Olga Parra, *Boca Raton, Florida*

ANSWER: The dog ate your passport? Seriously? Maybe he didn't want you to go.

I think you're right. If Spirit assured you that your passport was acceptable and allowed you to board, it bears some responsibility for your denied entry. Its response about paperwork requirements, while true, conveniently omits that fact.

A look at the State Department's website reveals the information you need. On Costa Rica's page there's a clear warning: "Passports should be in good condition; Costa Rican Immigration may deny entry if the passport is damaged in any way."

Had either you or the Spirit representative done a little research beforehand, this could have been avoided.

I wouldn't take an airline employee's word for it unless you're talking about airline policy. The Spirit ticket agent you spoke with may have seemed experienced and his words may have sounded confident, but he didn't represent Costa Rica.

I contacted the airline on your behalf. It apologized to you, and said it would implement a new policy "for the benefit of other travelers" when it comes to documentation requirements. Spirit issued two flight vouchers to make up for the trouble.

you should be let into the country. Don't take a chance.

How do I get a visa?

For most countries, you can apply for a visa at any of their foreign embassies. Some countries require that you apply at their embassy in your country. Many visas can be processed by mail. The less touristy a destination, the more complex the process tends to be. If you're traveling somewhere exotic, you might want to contact a visa service to make sure the process goes smoothly and the paperwork is valid.

to meet *both* sets of requirements. American customs officials will follow their rules when you cross the border, while officials from the other country will follow theirs.

→ AN OFFICIAL TOURISM WEBSITE.
Some state-run tourism sites also have general information on visa and passport requirements, but they can be vague or dated. If push comes to shove at the border, it may be difficult to show someone a printout made from a tourism website as evidence

What's a transit visa? Do I need one?

Some countries issue short transit visas that let you stay in a country for a few days without applying for a regular visa. In order to get one, you have to show proof of an outbound ticket. For example, you may get a 72-hour transit visa for Russia if you arrive in St. Petersburg on some cruise tours. Again, check with the country's embassy to find out if

NOT SMART FALLING FOR AN INTERNATIONAL DRIVING PERMIT.

An International Driving Permit (IDP), available from AAA or the National Automobile Club by authorization of the Department of State, is basically a translation of your American driver's license. Generally, the permit is unnecessary unless you're traveling to a destination that uses a non-Roman alphabet (Russia, China). The IDP helps authorities in those countries decipher your license, literally. I haven't had a reader complain about being denied a rental car because of a lack of an IDP.

a transit visa is available and if it's a better option for your trip.

Do I need anything else?

Maybe. For example, some African countries and Bolivia require proof of a yellow fever vaccination. If you visit these countries, you need to have the document with you when you enter. For a complete list of health requirements, consult the Centers for Disease Control and Prevention page on health and visas: *cdc.gov/global health/visa/visatravel.htm.*

What's an entrance or exit fee?

Some countries charge a fee to either enter or exit the country. For example, Argentina requires Americans to pay a $160 "reciprocity fee" if you arrive by air. You don't have to pay it if you cross by land. Sometimes the fees are rolled into your airline ticket, sometimes not. Sometimes you have to pay in dollars, sometimes in the local currency. Check the embassy site or the State Department site for details.

TROUBLESHOOTING YOUR PAPERWORK PROBLEMS

Here are a few tips to troubleshoot issues that can pop up.

I've met all my paperwork requirements but I'm not being allowed to board. What now?

This happens infrequently with airlines and more commonly with cruises. On a cruise, the easiest way to avoid this situation is to use a passport instead of your birth certificate as an ID. Birth certificates are problematic, for many reasons.

But even when everything is seemingly in order, you can still get hung up on issues like the expiration of your passport or even the requirements for the number of blank pages within the passport. It helps to know

41

the passport and visa requirements *very* well. You may want to travel with a copy of the country's paperwork requirements that are printed from its website. Why? Well, airlines and cruise lines are held responsible for letting passengers board without the right documents, so they tend to err on the side of caution even when they're wrong. Basically, you need proof that you can travel from an official source.

What if I've lost my passport?

If you've lost your passport while you're traveling abroad, contact the nearest U.S. Embassy or consulate. You'll need to fill out Form DS-64, a statement regarding a lost or stolen passport. Then you'll have to fill out

yet another form to get a new passport, this time a DS-11, which is an application for a new passport. Once you've reported a passport missing or stolen and it does turn up, it won't work. So only report it if you're sure it's gone.

What if I've lost my driver's license, visa, or other important paperwork?

That often depends on where you live and where you are traveling. It's difficult to generalize, but one thing is certain: Storing a copy of the missing ID online makes it far easier to replace it.

BOTTOM LINE

Whether you're crossing the border into Canada or embarking on an around-the-world adventure, you have to line up your paperwork well in advance of your trip. Make sure you have a passport and all the necessary visas and permits, and be certain they're valid for the duration of your voyage. When in doubt, consult an official source and don't rely on someone who may or may not know the requirements.

SMART FULL PASSPORT? GET EXTRA PAGES.

Instead of applying for a new passport, you can legally add 24 extra pages a maximum of two times (for 48 pages total), for $82. You can add the pages outside the country at a U.S. Embassy or consulate, and it can take less than one hour to get it done. No new photo required.

PROBLEM SOLVED

WHY CAN'T I TRANSIT THROUGH LONDON?

QUESTION: I'm an Indian national residing in the United States. I was scheduled to fly from Houston to Mumbai on British Airways recently. My itinerary involved a short stopover in London.

In Houston, while checking in with British Airways, I was denied boarding because my work visa was not stamped in my passport. The original visa stamped in my passport had expired, and I was traveling to India in order to get my renewed visa stamped at the U.S. Consulate in Mumbai.

I was carrying an application that permits me to continue living and working legally in the United States and to travel abroad. However, before reentering the United States, I'm required to obtain a valid U.S. visa stamp in my passport.

I tried my best to explain this to the check-in agent; however, she was adamant in not allowing me to transit through London. This was a catch-22 situation for me—I could not go to India without my visa stamped in my passport, and I could not get my visa stamped unless I visited the consulate in India.

The British Airways check-in staff was very unsympathetic and unhelpful. I was quoted a charge of around $500 to allow me to fly on my return ticket when I said I was ready to fly out to Mumbai with a different carrier. I've tried to get a partial refund from the airline for my unused ticket, but it hasn't responded. Can you help me? —Mita Upadhyay, *Corpus Christi, Texas*

ANSWER: In order to transit in the U.K. without a visa on an Indian passport, you need one of seven types of documents, which may include a valid U.S. visa sticker in your passport or a valid U.S. permanent resident card.

"Our staff in Houston would seem to have been correct to deny this passenger boarding," said an airline spokeswoman. "There are links on *ba.com* that allow passengers to check their passport and visa requirements for their journey."

At the same time, British Airways should have been more compassionate about your situation, in the interests of good customer service. You couldn't get the required stamp without visiting the consulate in Mumbai. Given your predicament, it would have been a nice gesture of the airline to reroute you on a flight that didn't require a stopover in London. But it wasn't required to do that. Unfortunately, having all your paperwork in order is your responsibility, and yours alone, even if British Airways didn't disclose its visa requirements on its site.

Still, British Airways offered a refund of $125, and a $600 flight credit, which represents half of your airfare to Mumbai—an exceptionally generous resolution.

4

Stay Healthy and Safe

What could possibly go wrong when you're away, and how to make sure it doesn't happen to you.

Too often, your well-being on the road is an afterthought to trip planning—a hastily packed bottle of aspirin or an inattentive glance at your health insurance card to make sure you're covered. It shouldn't be. If you've read the three previous chapters, then you know how much can go wrong in just the early planning phase. But that pales in comparison to what could go wrong once you've started traveling. Fortunately, most of it is preventable.

Should I stay or should I go?

Determining whether a destination is "safe" or not isn't easy. It depends on your risk tolerance, where you're going, and what you're planning to do, but since we start most chapters with a decision matrix, here are a few basic questions.

Go:

→ **IF LARGE NUMBERS OF OTHER TOURISTS** are traveling there and there are no governmental warnings about safety conditions or health problems, such as an outbreak of a communicable disease.

→ **IF YOU'RE RETURNING TO A PLACE** that is well known to you, meeting with people you know, and following a familiar itinerary. You also know how to stay away from circumstances that may have a harmful effect on your health.

→ **IF YOU'RE GOING TO BE UNDER THE CARE** and supervision of an experienced tour operator who can keep you from harm's way.

Don't go:

→ **IF YOUR GOVERNMENT HAS WARNED ITS CITIZENS** against traveling to that destination and many people are canceling their trips to that place. (See government warnings on page 46 for details.)

→ **IF YOU HAVE REASON TO BELIEVE** your safety or health might be compromised, and you don't have any knowledge of the language, local customs, or potential dangers.

→ **IF YOU WON'T KNOW ANYONE,** aren't at all sure about what you're going to do, and have no sense of whether it's safe or not. You could be asking for trouble.

→ **IF YOUR DOCTOR** advises you to stay home.

SAFETY

Security can't be guaranteed—ever. You can take every step in the book to protect yourself and your family, but things still happen. The world is filled with wonderful but often frightening uncertainties. If you want absolute

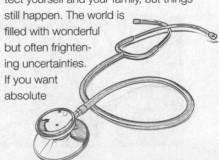

safety and you're unwilling to take any risks, maybe travel isn't for you.

When should I research a destination's safety?

Do your due diligence *before* you make your reservations. Many insurance policies won't cover political unrest or general security problems, and airlines and hotels are generally unwilling to issue refunds when you decide to cancel a trip.

Where can I get reliable safety information about my destination?

The most recommended resource for travel safety is the State Department's Bureau of Consular Affairs website *(travel.state.gov)*. It offers tips for travelers and warnings on potentially dangerous areas. It's a good starting point if you're trying to determine if your destination is safe. A travel warning is the U.S. government's way of saying, "Don't go there." A travel alert means you could run into trouble. If you see either, you might want to avoid a place.

Just as with a travel review, it's best to get another opinion. The Canadian government *(travel.gc.ca/travelling/ advisories)*, for example, issues more direct warnings, such as "AVOID ALL TRAVEL." This can be helpful when the wishy-washy wording on a State Department site leaves you confused. Other places to check include the counterpart websites of the British government *(gov.uk/foreign-travel-advice)* and the Australian government *(smartraveller.gov.au)*.

Whether or not you already have a healthy distrust for official reports, I recommend that you also do your own sleuthing. An Internet search of the destination's name alongside keywords such as "murder," "robbery," "rape," and "kidnapping" (feel free to add your own horrible event, depending on the place) should yield news and blog reports that can offer a clue as to how safe a place is or isn't. Many mainstream media outlets can be censored by governments or may practice a more troublesome act of self-censorship. You may need to read between the lines. But don't be put off by sensationalist reporting either. Otherwise you'll

---

👍SMART LOOK BOTH WAYS BEFORE CROSSING.

I know, I know. Your parents told you, and now *I'm* telling you. But I have my reasons. A colleague stepped into traffic without looking to the right on a visit to New Zealand, and she was killed. Yes, they drive on the *other* side of the road over there, as they do in many other former British colonies, the United Kingdom, and several other countries, too. Mom's right—look both ways and be patient. You'll come home alive.

probably never even venture into New York City.

Finally, a competent travel agent should know a thing or two about the place you're visiting, especially if that agent has recommended it. If you're getting answers like, "I don't know how safe it is—you should check with the State Department," then you have a clueless agent and you may need to find a new one.

What's the biggest threat to my safety when I'm traveling?

A car accident. More than 30,000 motorists die in auto accidents every year in the United States and about two million are injured, according to the National Highway Traffic Safety Administration. But in some countries where roads are less reliable, driving can be far more dangerous. Traffic accidents are the leading cause of medical evacuations. To steer clear of trouble, avoid driving after a long flight, always use safety belts and child safety seats, and rent larger vehicles if possible because they offer more protection in a crash. Make sure the car is well maintained. Also, it's better not to drive at night, but if you have to, consider hiring an experienced driver who is familiar with the destination and language and is expert at maneuvering through local traffic. Being a pedestrian can also be hazardous in certain highly populated cities in the developing world where traffic doesn't usually stop for people.

If you want to stay safer while you're on vacation, the remedy is fairly obvious: Stay off the road.

What else can make a trip dangerous?

Danger can lurk around every corner when you're traveling—sometimes literally. Here are some of the most common security problems encountered by travelers and their remedies.

→ **ROBBERIES AND PICKPOCKETS.**
No one really knows how many of these petty thefts are pulled off because they aren't always reported to authorities. The criminals are after your wallet and cell phone, and not necessarily in that order. Always carry a decoy wallet with your daily cash and an expired photo ID, but nothing that would make you want to keep the wallet in a robbery situation. This wallet should be handed over if you are robbed. Carry a credit card and additional cash in an inside pocket. Strap your pocketbook on the shoulder away from the street to deter drive-by grabs. Leave pricey jewelry and watches at home. Otherwise, you are a walking advertisement for a robbery. Also, consider a portable hotel door lock or other device that will alert you if someone is trying to break in.

→ **ANIMAL BITES AND SCRATCHES.**
Dog, cat, monkey, and bat bites are major problems for curious tourists. What's more, many locations around

the world do not have access to rabies vaccinations, meaning you might have to cut your trip short to seek medical attention. Keep your distance from animals when you're on the road, and never attempt to pet them, no matter how cute they appear to be.

> **RIOTS AND MOB VIOLENCE.** If you're visiting a place where strikes, demonstrations, or even just large crowds are common, you're better off staying away from large gatherings. Big crowds, even in a destination that isn't known for violence, can suddenly turn dangerous. If you find yourself in a mob, leave the area right away. Do not take photos to try to capture history in the making. You could become history in the process.

> **SCAMS AND SWINDLES.** Many travelers let their guard down when they're on the road. In fact, this is the time to be most vigilant. The old saying "If it sounds too good to be true, it probably is" holds fast all around the world. Cast a skeptical eye toward anything you're offered. Chances are, the scammers have pegged you as an out-of-towner and see an easy opportunity to make a quick buck. Worse, if you challenge them, they could turn violent.

HEALTH
Certainly, your health can fail at any time, but being prepared can take the

---

An easy trip is better than no trip at all.

---

sting out of most travel health issues.

Should I worry about my health when I travel?

If you have to ask, then the answer is yes. Too many travelers wait too long to take that bucket list trip, and then they try to hedge the big vacation with a travel insurance or medical evacuation policy. It is these good people from whom I hear after they slipped in the shower on their first day of a round-the-world cruise and needed to be airlifted to the nearest hospital. To them, I wish I could say a few things before they left:

> **PLEASE DON'T WAIT TOO LONG TO TAKE A VACATION OF A LIFETIME.** Too many readers want a sure thing. They wait until the kids are grown up and out of college and they've retired before embarking on that adventure of a lifetime. By then, they may already have serious health limitations.

> **EASY IS BETTER THAN NOTHING.** If you want to visit a destination that requires lots of stamina (skiing at high altitude in Colorado, for example), the time is when you are in tip-top shape. Do it when you have the endurance, and go for the cruise or all-inclusive vacation later. An easy trip is better than no trip at all.

> **DON'T PLAY GAMES WITH YOUR HEALTH.** People lose their minds

when they're on vacation, no two ways about it. They hike up Mount Vesuvius when they wouldn't even try to climb the stairs when they're at home. I have no idea why, but it happens time and again. Better to apply the same precautions when you're away as you would when you're home. Don't do anything stupid. Please.

→ DON'T FORGET TO TAKE YOUR MEDICINE. Losing or misplacing your prescription medication can significantly shorten your trip, if not end it. How do you prevent that?

• Carry a spare prescription from your physician. If your prescription medication is lost or stolen while you're away or the medication is unavailable, your vacation could be over. If your physician can write an extra prescription and you can find a pharmacy to fill it, it might save your trip.

• Keep medication in its original container with the label intact, and always pack it in your carry-on luggage. It's far more difficult to lose a carry-on, while checked luggage can get lost or pilfered.

• Don't consolidate medications in one container to save space. Security screeners don't like mystery liquids and pills. They may ask you to leave the medication behind if you can't prove its authenticity.

• Keep a list of the generic equivalents and always carry spare medication in case of an emergency.

• Be sure your medication is allowed in the destination country. Check with the foreign embassy of the country you're visiting to make sure your medicine isn't considered an illegal narcotic. A listing of foreign embassies and consulates in the United States is available on the Department of State's website at *state.gov*. If it's not allowed, find a solution before your trip—not when the medicine is confiscated at entry.

Should I see a doctor before I travel?

If you're visiting a country without modern medical facilities and standards, consider scheduling a visit to a travel medicine clinician at least one month before departure. During

SMART GET YOUR SHOTS NOW.

One critical resource is the Centers for Disease Control and Prevention travel site (*cdc.gov/travel/page/survival-guide*), which offers information about potential health problems and advice on best practices for maintaining your well-being, the most important of which is to get inoculated well in advance of your trip. Also, identify the best health care providers at your destination and their payment policies. Many health care providers in foreign countries ask for at least some payment up front.

PROBLEM SOLVED

ROUTED FROM RIO

QUESTION: My friend and I just recently traveled to Rio de Janeiro during Carnival. We had reservations at the Hotel Praia Ipanema.

On our first day in town, we went sightseeing and then headed to the beach right across the street from the hotel. We were walking along the shoreline, when we were suddenly surrounded and attacked by about a dozen teenage boys with knives. They demanded our belongings, which at the time were a beach towel, lotion, and room keys.

I managed to break free, but my male friend was held at knifepoint. Fortunately, he was also able to get free with just some minor cuts.

When we reached our hotel, the doorman stopped us. We explained to him what happened, and all he did was shrug his shoulders and roll his eyes. He offered us no help. I was still very scared. We tried getting into the hotel, so we could have the front desk call the police, but the doorman would not let us in. He was more concerned that we had sand on our feet, and he did not want us tracking it in the lobby.

The doorman then pointed to a door located in the back of the hotel where he told us to go. We did not feel safe going through that door because there was a group of kids much like the ones that attacked us standing there. We did not feel safe in our hotel any longer, so my friend and I checked out and got the first flight back home.

When we returned, we contacted our travel agency hoping for some kind of refund of the $2,500 we paid, since we were there only one day. Can you help?
—Leah Peters, *Hobart, Indiana*

ANSWER: I'd be pretty shaken up, too, if I was assaulted by a gang of teenagers and then denied entrance to my own hotel.

When I contacted the hotel, the hotel's sales manager agreed that things didn't go well, but she blames a language barrier, not incompetence, for your treatment.

For example, the doorman you dealt with doesn't speak any English. So, it wasn't the sand on your feet, but the fact that you didn't know any Portuguese, that made him stall—at least according to the manager. Her point is well taken. Then again, is it unreasonable to ask someone working at a hotel with many English-speaking visitors to learn a few useful phrases?

Other than brushing up on your Portuguese, how could you have prevented this from happening? It's always wise to check out the State Department's Consular Information Sheets before traveling. For several years these have carried warnings about crime in tourist areas in Rio, especially during Carnival.

"We are really sorry for the sequence of unfortunate facts Ms. Peters had in her travel to Rio," the sales manager told me. Although the vacation package you booked isn't refundable, the hotel views this as a "very special condition" and is offering you a free five-night stay in the future.

I think that's fair, and I would take the hotel up on its offer. Just not during Carnival, maybe.

the consultation, you'll get a risk assessment that takes into account the exact itinerary, including specific locations, types of accommodations, season, and modes of travel. Your medical conditions, medications taken on a daily basis, and allergies will also be weighed by the expert. Once a clinician has reviewed your medical history and itinerary details, you'll get an assessment with appropriate medications and vaccinations for your trip. The American Society of Tropical Medicine and Hygiene publishes an online directory of physicians who offer clinical consultative service in tropical medicine, medical parasitology, and travelers' health: *astmh .org/source/ClinicalDirectory.*

What's the biggest threat to my health when I'm traveling?

Diarrhea, and the dehydration that often results from diarrhea. It affects between 20 and 50 percent of international travelers, depending on where you visit. That means you'll probably get it at some point. Sure, you can take precautions—the adage "Boil it, peel it, cook it, or forget it" comes to mind—but even so, you may get sick. The Centers for Disease Control says using poor hygiene during food preparation is often to blame, and that boiling and peeling don't offer a fail-safe protection.

In developing countries, don't consume foods to which water has been added (such as fruit juices) or raw vegetables that have been rinsed in water.

When purchasing fruits, choose produce priced by the number and not by the weight. Water is often injected into watermelons and such to add weight and bring a higher price in markets. Use bottled water for brushing your teeth and avoid swallowing any water during showers. Check with your physician before departure about carrying an antibiotic for self-treatment of moderate to severe diarrhea or an over-the-counter medication such as Imodium.

What should I do about malaria?

Malaria, which is caused by a parasite transmitted through mosquito bites, has the potential to not only end your trip, but affect future trips. As such, it deserves a special mention. An estimated 219 million cases of malaria occurred worldwide in 2010. Some 660,000 people died, according to the CDC. Think you're the exception? Check the CDC's country-specific malaria tables before you make up your mind (*cdc.gov/malaria/travelers/ country_table/a.html*). The symptoms are flulike—fever, headache, joint pain, and fatigue—and can develop as soon as seven days after initial exposure to the *Anopheles* mosquito bite. In severe forms, seizures, mental

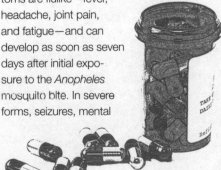

confusion, kidney failure, coma, and death may eventually occur.

Malarial mosquitoes feed during the dusk-to-dawn hours. The greatest risk of infection is in sub-Saharan Africa. You can reduce your risk by not traveling there or, once there, by avoiding contact with the mosquitoes by staying in well-screened areas, using insecticide-treated bed nets, and wearing clothes that cover most of your body. Remember, not all medications are effective in all regions. A travel medicine clinician will know what medications are effective in the areas you plan to visit.

I'm feeling a little queasy. What should I do?

Motion sickness, sometimes referred to as seasickness or car sickness, is a common disturbance of the inner ear that is caused by repeated motion. You may experience dizziness, nausea, vomiting, and cold sweats. You can avoid it or lessen its severity by staying away from alcohol before and during travel. Also, stay away from heavy, spicy, fatty, or rich foods, which may worsen symptoms, and avoid strong odors, which can ratchet up the nausea. Find a part of the plane or boat that's less bumpy, like the area over the wing on an aircraft. Low cabins near the center of ships generally have less rocking motion than cabins in higher or outer areas. Bonine tablets can help with motion sickness and are sold over-the-counter.

How about altitude sickness?

Few travelers consider the altitude of their destination until it's too late. After arriving, you have a little wine with a large dinner, and the next thing you know, you're flat on your back in bed, suffering from shortness of breath. The best advice is to climb high and sleep low—meaning you should not only consider your elevation, but also find accommodations as low as possible. Obviously, this is particularly relevant when you're skiing or visiting a high-altitude destination such as Machu Picchu. Also, avoid drinking alcohol, eat a high-carb diet, and maintain adequate hydration. For the first 48 hours at your destination, participate in only mild exercise. You can treat an altitude headache with over-the-counter analgesics. Listen to your body, don't ignore the warning signs—and never, ever ascend with symptoms, which include headaches, vomiting, and loss of appetite.

Help! I'm suffering from desynchronosis!

Desynchronosis, better known as jet lag, is usually the result of transmeridian air travel. You can minimize jet lag by staying hydrated before, during, and after your trip. Steer clear of those free drinks in first class, which can make it more difficult to adjust to a new time zone. Also, ask your physician about taking melatonin, which will help reset your internal body clock. Once you're at your destination, continue drinking lots of water, spend time outdoors in the sun if possible, and don't over-eat. Avoid the temptation to nap during the day. Instead, go to sleep when the sun goes down. In time, your body will adjust to the new zone.

A travel medicine clinician will know what medications are effective.

What's in your bag?

Here are a few must-haves for a healthy trip. Bear in mind that you can probably buy some or all of these items at your destination, so unless you're heading somewhere that doesn't have pharmacies, you may want to wait until you arrive, or until you need them, to buy them.

→ ORAL REHYDRATION SOLUTION PACKETS. These are used to treat dehydration and travelers' diarrhea, and they can be a lifesaver in the event of prolonged exposure to heat or fluid loss due to illness.

→ EPINEPHRINE AUTO-INJECTOR (EPIPEN). If you have any kind of allergy, you may want to get a couple of these, if not an antihistamine for milder reactions. Even if you don't have a known allergy, health experts recommend taking these precautions in case you're exposed to local foods, plants, stings, or bites that could trigger a deadly reaction.

→ PAIN RELIEF. Carry a bottle of acetaminophen, ibuprofen, or aspirin.

→ SAM SPLINT. Get one, along with an Ace bandage (to help secure it) for sprains and strains. It's lightweight, moldable, and has multiple uses for treating problems like arm or leg injuries or fractures.

→ ANTISEPTICS AND ANTIBIOTIC OINTMENT. For treatment of cuts, abrasions, lacerations, and bug bites. Also, don't forget the gauze, trauma pads, nonstick pads, and quick clot dressings for deep wound lacerations, and self-stick wrap to secure dressings in place. If you have no idea what I'm talking about, don't worry—it's in most small first-aid kits. Just get one of those.

→ TWEEZERS AND SCISSORS. For cutting gauze bandages and removing of ticks and leeches.

→ EMERGENCY EYEWASH. This is especially important for those facing extensive outdoor exposure or people traveling to sandy and windy environments.

→ SUNSCREEN AND LIP BALM WITH SPF AND INSECT REPELLENT WITH DEET. Mosquitoes can carry a host of diseases. Also, pick fabrics and bed nets that contain permethrin for protection against mosquito bites.

→ **POTABLE AQUA IODINE TABLETS AND FILTERS.** They're used for water purification.

→ **A HEAD SCARF OR BELT.** These can double as a tourniquet in the unlikely event that one is needed. You can also wrap coins, fishing weights, or other heavy objects in the scarf to make a handy defensive weapon (hey, you never know).

→ **A FLASHLIGHT.** In some countries, electricity isn't always available. Don't get left in the dark.

Should I consider a medical evacuation or security policy?

Companies such as International SOS *(internationalsos.com),* On Call *(oncallinternational.com),* and Frontier MEDEX *(medexassist.com)* sell policies that offer 24-hour evacuation services should medical or personal security issues arise. These are different from travel insurance and can be helpful when you're away from modern medical facilities or suffer from a medical problem that requires the attention of a specialist. A good policy should offer a 24/7 call center with physician support and emergency medical support.

The decision about whether to buy such a policy should be made in consultation with your travel agent, if you are using one, and doctor, but here are a few general guidelines:

→ **CHECK YOUR EXISTING INSURANCE COVERAGE.** Read your travel insurance coverage and medical insurance carefully. Many of the services offered by medical evacuation companies may be included in your policy. Why pay for the same thing twice?

→ **RUN A WORST-CASE SCENARIO.** Many of these companies offer a full range of services, including extracting you from countries during civil unrest and helping secure your release if you're taken hostage. You may not need that if you're going on a cruise to Alaska.

→ **KICK THE TIRES.** If you decide a medical evacuation policy is a must for your next trip, check several providers before settling on one. Some companies have a strong presence in certain areas; others try to cover it from a control center 12 time zones away. Read each policy carefully before making a purchasing decision. Bear in mind that for most of these companies, the core customer is the business traveler.

BOTTOM LINE

You can't completely control your health or safety when you're traveling, but if you take a few simple precautions, you can avoid many of the biggest dangers. The time to think about both of these important issues is long before you travel, and long before you make your reservations.

PROBLEM SOLVED

BURGLARIZED IN THE BAHAMAS

QUESTION: My friend and I prepaid through Travelocity for two nights at the Wyndham Nassau Resort & Crystal Palace Casino in the Bahamas.

On our second night, someone came into our room while we were sleeping and robbed us. The robber came in through the sliding glass door to the balcony of our seventh floor room. He took all of our money—$400 from me and $240 from my friend—and some jewelry and a cell phone.

The next morning, we didn't have a dollar between us.

After contacting the front desk to report we had been robbed, two hotel security men and then a police officer took our statements.

After more than three hours of interviews, I explained to the manager that we didn't have any money and asked for help. We were given a voucher to eat breakfast and told that we would be provided a cab ride to the airport.

I asked about dinner, and he said, "You have breakfast, go enjoy it."

To add insult to injury, we were charged a $15 resort fee for each night. We were not told about the fee by Travelocity when we booked the trip, or by the hotel when we checked in. —Nancy Miller, *Wellington, Florida*

ANSWER: You know, it doesn't get much worse than this. First the robber took your belongings, and then the hotel helped itself to a little more of your money with a surprise "resort fee." (What's a resort fee, anyway? If you ask me, it's nothing more than a meaningless room surcharge.)

This never should have happened to you. The hotel has a responsibility to protect its guests from outside threats, and it should have done better. It also failed to meet its customer service obligations to you by subjecting you to a morning of interviews and then offering you inadequate assistance after you said you were broke.

But you let yourself down, too. You were traveling with a lot of cash. That's an unfortunate decision. Credit cards are far easier to replace when they're stolen. You should only carry enough cash for tipping and incidentals. You also could have—and should have—used the hotel safe for your valuables.

So, here's what it comes down to: Wyndham has a little safety and customer-service problem. You need to do your homework next time you go on vacation. And Travelocity? It should have told you about the resort fee—in fact, it should have included the fee in the prepaid price.

I contacted Travelocity and Wyndham to see if you could be helped. Travelocity promptly refunded the resort fee. The operator of the Wyndham property, Cable Beach Resorts, is investigating the robbery. In a letter to you the company's vice president of operations acknowledged that "the manner in which our manager on duty responded to your situation failed to meet your expectations." He said "corrective action" had been taken, but offered no specifics.

As a "gesture of goodwill," he invited you to return to the Wyndham for two free nights.

5

Find the Best Travel Insurance Policy

Making sure your coverage really covers you—and what to do if it doesn't.

Travel insurance can offer peace of mind for your upcoming vacation. If something goes wrong—if your trip is interrupted or if you have to cancel—you can recover some or all of your costs. About one in three travelers buys insurance for a trip, according to the U.S. Travel Insurance Association. Should you be one of them?

Buy insurance:

→ **IF YOU'RE SPENDING MORE THAN $5,000 ON A VACATION.** That's known as a "big-ticket" purchase, and it should be insured.

→ **IF YOU'RE A NERVOUS TRAVELER** and just need the peace of mind that comes with having a policy. Even if you can't recover all of your money, you may still be able to take advantage of certain benefits.

→ **IF YOU'RE CRUISING OR TAKING A PACKAGE TOUR.** Cruise lines used to be flexible when it came to allowing passengers to rebook missed cruises. Tour operators were also more lenient in the old days. Not anymore. A policy can protect you.

→ **IF YOU HAVE A COMPLEX OR LENGTHY ITINERARY.** If you're on a tour with a lot of moving parts, then insurance could be useful. When one part doesn't go as planned, the right policy can help you make a quick recovery and avoid a domino effect.

→ **ANY TIME YOU LEAVE THE COUNTRY.** Medical providers outside the United States often ask for up-front payments for medical services that can cost thousands of dollars, and travel insurance can guarantee these payments. (This is also true for medical evacuations and repatriations, which can cost tens or even hundreds of thousands of dollars.)

→ **IF YOU'RE ON MEDICARE** and are traveling internationally. You'll want to consider a policy that includes medical expenses, since Medicare doesn't typically cover events outside the country.

Skip it:

→ **IF IT'S A SHORT,** simple, and inexpensive domestic trip.

→ **IF YOU'RE SPENDING LESS THAN $5,000,** or if you don't mind losing the value of your trip should something happen before or during your vacation. Also, if you have insurance that would cover a medical emergency or medical evacuation, you may not need a policy.

→ **IF YOUR TRIP INCLUDES COMPONENTS THAT AREN'T COVERED BY INSURANCE.** For example, say you're

staying at a friend's house, using a flight voucher, or redeeming frequent flier miles for your vacation. Travel insurance would probably be minimally useful. (Some travel insurance policies may cover the cost of redepositing miles when you need to cancel for a covered reason.)

→ **IF YOU HAVE A PREEXISTING MEDICAL CONDITION THAT WOULDN'T BE COVERED.** Read your policy carefully; some travel insurance policies do cover existing medical conditions when certain requirements are met. Normally, preexisting conditions that are controlled are covered if the policy is purchased within a certain time following initial deposit and payment of your trip.

→ **IF COVERAGE WOULD BE REDUNDANT.** For example, if your credit card or other insurance would cover the same event—then don't worry about it. Note that some cards won't cover items like medical evacuations, so if that's important, then think about insurance. See Chapter 4 for more on medical evacuations and coverage. (Most credit cards do not cover medical expenses, and almost no credit card covers for cancellation and interruption.)

How do I find a travel insurance policy?

An online search for "travel insurance" is likely to pull up a long and confusing list of travel insurance choices, but there are really just three options.

→ **BUY DIRECT.** Companies sell insurance policies directly to travelers, usually online. The big players are Allianz, CSA, and Travel Guard. A full list of other insurance companies worth checking out is on the U.S. Travel Insurance Association's website (*ustia.org*).

→ **BUY THROUGH YOUR TRAVEL COMPANY.** Many travel companies, including airlines, cruise lines, and tour operators, offer optional insurance directly to consumers. These can be a good deal, but it's worth shopping around before deciding to buy one of these policies. Also, be careful of tour operators or cruise lines that offer generic protection services. They won't cover you if the company goes belly-up.

→ **BUY THROUGH A TRAVEL AGENT OR THIRD PARTY.** Your travel agent may offer an insurance policy. More on that in a moment.

You might also consult an online company that specializes in comparing and evaluating insurance policies, such as Squaremouth, Travel

Many travel companies, including airlines, cruise lines, and tour operators, offer optional insurance directly to consumers.

Insurance Review, Trip Insurance Store, and *InsureMyTrip.com*. These can be useful resources for quickly finding the best travel insurance policy for your circumstances.

Travel insurance is extremely competitive, and by checking with multiple sources, you won't just find better terms or prices, but also avoid buying a potentially useless policy.

The two types of travel insurance you'll meet

There are two basic types of travel insurance policies. Most are what is known as named *perils policies,* and allow you to cancel or interrupt your trip if you experience a covered reason. Your policy will include a list of covered reasons for cancellation or interruption and will pay you 100 percent of your nonrefundable trip costs when you cancel for one of those reasons.

The other type of policy is often called *cancel for any reason,* which allows you to cancel a trip for almost any reason (though there may be exclusions, so read the fine print) and will pay you a percentage of your nonrefundable trip costs. Cancel for any reason coverage is generally more expensive than a named perils policy.

What should I look for in a travel insurance policy?

Here are a few coverage areas to be aware of.

→ **ACCIDENTAL DEATH OR DISMEMBERMENT.** Provides cash payment for accidental loss of life or limb while traveling.

→ **BAGGAGE.** This benefit provides reimbursement for lost, stolen, or damaged baggage or personal items. The coverage usually applies to your entire trip, not just your flight. A subset of this coverage is for baggage delay, which offers reimbursement for clothing, toiletries, and other essential items if luggage is delayed for a specified period of time.

→ **CANCEL FOR ANY REASON.** This is a subset of trip cancellation (usually available for a slightly higher premium) and provides for cancellations that aren't included in the basic coverage. You may be reimbursed up to 80 percent of your nonrefundable trip payments and deposits if a trip is canceled for a reason other than a "covered reason."

→ **DEDUCTIBLE.** The deductible is a co-pay amount that is the responsibility of the insured. Options vary by plan and can range from $0 to $2,500. Deductibles can be charged per policy, per individual, per incident, or a combination. Most medical plans require you to select a deductible

PROBLEM SOLVED

INSURANCE CLAIM DENIED AFTER BIKE ACCIDENT

QUESTION: I recently booked a trip to Colorado Springs on American Airlines. I paid for the tickets with a credit I'd received after canceling a previous flight, plus $350 in fees. I bought travel insurance from Allianz, which is offered through the American Airlines website.

I had a bicycling accident, and we could not travel to Colorado. I sent a claim to Allianz with complete documentation, including receipts from American Airlines. The receipt shows a payment of our $601 credit plus $350 in fees.

Now, Allianz says they won't pay the claim since we used the $601 credit from the earlier trip. Needless to say, I am upset because American advertises Allianz on its site and, when I rebooked, the ticket agent said to call them. Can you help me get my money back? —John Frow, *Plano, Texas*

ANSWER: Allianz should have refunded your entire ticket, regardless of how you paid for it. Period. A look at the terms and conditions of your policy on the Allianz site shows there should be no distinction between the cash and airline vouchers you used. Unfortunately, insurance claims are often denied because of a misunderstanding, and that's what appears to be happening to you.

According to the U.S. Travel Insurance Association, one in six policy purchasers files a claim, and fewer than 10 percent of claims are denied. Further, many denials are overturned on appeal. I've heard informal estimates from insurance experts that roughly 90 percent of appeals go the traveler's way, although that's hard to verify. So, you could have written back to Allianz, asking them to take a second look.

What responsibility does American Airlines have? The airline would probably argue that it has none, and that it was simply selling an insurance product from its website. I'm not sure I would agree. By selling insurance on its site, American is offering a de facto endorsement, and it bears some responsibility when you aren't compensated under the insurance company's own rules.

If your appeal had been rejected, your next step would have been to rope American into this case. Sometimes—and I've seen this happen—an airline or other travel company will step in to make things right when an insurance claim is denied.

As it turns out, none of that would be necessary. I contacted Allianz on your behalf, and it reopened your case.

"Because Mr. Frow used a previously obtained credit from American Airlines to book the flight he insured with us, we mistakenly thought that he did not incur a financial loss, and initially denied his claim on that basis," a representative told me.

After "further review," Allianz refunded you $601, which is the limit of your coverage.

option, while most travel protection plans offer a zero deductible benefit option.

→ **EMERGENCY MEDICAL AND DENTAL.** This pays for the cost of treatment associated with a medical or dental emergency incurred while traveling. This coverage may be secondary to your primary health insurance. A subset of this is emergency medical transportation, which arranges to transport a patient to an appropriate medical facility. Some policies may also cover the cost of bringing a friend or family member to the patient or getting family members home. Medical repatriation benefits may include arranging and paying for the cost of getting the patient home, including by air ambulance.

→ **EMPLOYMENT LAYOFF.** This provides reimbursement for prepaid, nonrefundable trip payments and deposits if a trip is canceled because of involuntary layoff or termination of employment. Review this paragraph carefully if you think you might make a claim. It can be highly restrictive. This is usually a named peril for a trip cancellation or interruption policy.

→ **FINANCIAL DEFAULT.** This coverage is normally offered in the event of a complete cessation of operations due to financial circumstances. The operator doesn't have to file for bankruptcy. Read this paragraph very carefully, since there's no standard language. This is a covered reason, or named peril, of a trip cancellation or interruption policy. Most travel insurance companies publish a list of travel suppliers that they either cover or exclude for financial default.

→ **LIFE INSURANCE.** This coverage provides an accidental death or dismemberment benefit while you're enrolled. Although this benefit is sometimes referred to as "life insurance," it's not technically a life insurance policy.

> *Some policies may also cover the cost of bringing a friend or family member to the patient or getting family members home.*

 SMART LOOK FOR CLAUSES THAT ADDRESS PREEXISTING OR EXISTING MEDICAL CONDITIONS.

They could affect your ability to make a successful claim. If your policy offers coverage for a preexisting medical condition, be sure that you take advantage of the waiver by meeting all of its conditions. Not meeting these requirements is one of the reasons for having an insurance claim denied.

→ **MISSED CONNECTION.** This offers reimbursement in the event of a missed flight connection or for additional costs to catch up to a cruise if the cause of delay is an accident or bad weather. It's often a subset of trip cancellation or interruption coverage. You may be required to show that you allowed sufficient time to reach your flight or cruise and were unable to reach your flight or cruise another way.

Travel insurance typically costs between 4 and 8 percent of your trip's prepaid, nonrefundable cost.

→ **RENTAL CAR DAMAGE.** This coverage offers collision loss/damage insurance for rental cars and covers the costs of damage to, or theft of, a rental car.

→ **TERRORISM.** This clause covers you in the event of a terrorist incident. Bear in mind that some plans only provide coverage if you are scheduled to arrive at your destination within 30 days of the incident while other plans only offer foreign coverage. This is a subset of a trip cancellation or interruption policy.

→ **TRAVEL DELAY.** This provides reimbursement for meals and accommodations when a trip is unexpectedly delayed for a certain amount of time. Don't forget to save your receipts when you make a travel delay claim.

→ **TRIP CANCELLATION.** This coverage reimburses you for nonrefundable trip payments and deposits if a trip is canceled for illness, injury, death, or other specific reasons, or if your destination is now in a disaster zone. Most trip cancellation language is standard, but it's worth reviewing to make sure it will cover you in the event your trip is called off.

→ **TRIP INTERRUPTION.** This coverage offers reimbursement for nonrefundable trip payments and deposits if a trip is interrupted for illness, injury, death, or other specific reasons. Again, read the language carefully to be sure you're covered.

→ **WEATHER.** Most policies include coverage if travel is canceled, delayed, or interrupted because of a hurricane or other meteorological event. Some policies offer cancellation coverage if only one part of your trip can't be taken (if, say, your hotel is closed), while others stipulate that the airport or airline has to cancel its flights.

→ **WHICH POLICY TO BUY?** Unfortunately, there's no quick and easy answer. Everyone has to carefully compare policies and find the right travel insurance policy for their needs. It can be hard work.

How much should I pay for travel insurance?

We've already talked about situations that call for travel insurance and where to find it, but how do you know if you're getting a good deal?

There's no authoritative buyer's guide that can tell you whether you're looking at a bargain or a rip-off. That's because no two travel insurance policies are exactly the same. They vary according to your age, state of residence, and types of coverage.

Travel insurance typically costs between 4 and 8 percent of your trip's prepaid, nonrefundable cost. However, a cancel for any reason policy can run you 10 percent of the nonrefundable cost, or even slightly more. Your policy may be more expensive if you're older or engaging in a risky activity that makes a claim more likely.

A word of warning: If the policy is less than 4 percent of the cost of your vacation, that should raise red flags. Too-good-to-be-true trip "protection" policies have cost travelers millions—and perhaps tens of millions—in unpaid claims. If it's really travel insurance, it will be underwritten by a reputable insurer.

At the same time, policies that cost significantly more than 10 percent of your trip's prepaid, nonrefundable cost may also be a cause for concern. Read the terms very carefully, and make sure there's a good reason why you're paying that much for your insurance. One way to check if your insurer

You can get travel insurance up until the day before you travel from some travel insurance companies.

is legit is to find out if it belongs to the U.S. Travel Insurance Association *(ustia.org)*. Its site lists every member.

When should I buy insurance?

You can get travel insurance up until the day before you travel from some travel insurance companies, but the sooner you buy your policy, the better. Why? Well, let's say your airline declares bankruptcy between the time you book your vacation and your departure date. You'll still be able to buy a policy the day before your departure, but if your airline has already filed for Chapter 11 protection, then the policy won't cover the airline in the unlikely event that it stops flying.

Another reason: Most travel insurance policies will offer coverage for preexisting medical conditions that are under control, if you buy the insurance within a couple of weeks of your first trip payment (other conditions

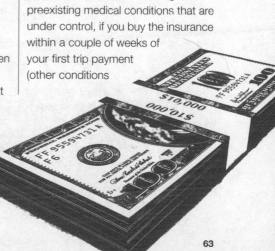

might also apply). Since up to 20 percent of claims could be traced to preexisting medical conditions, this could be an important point, and it removes another potential reason for denying a claim.

So buy the policy sooner rather than later, and keep the cost between 4 and 8 percent of your prepaid non-refundable outlay, and you're on your way.

It's better to ask about your policy— what it does and doesn't cover—before it becomes an issue.

How do I use my travel insurance policy?

Congratulations, you're the owner of a shiny new travel insurance policy. Now what?

Conventional wisdom says you wait until something goes wrong, and then file a claim, but there's a little more to it than that.

Contact your insurance company:

→ **IF YOU HAVE A QUESTION ABOUT YOUR POLICY.** It's better to ask about your policy—what it does and doesn't cover—before it becomes an issue.

For example, say your policy covers the cancellation of travel if you lose your job. If you think a pink slip is coming, this might be a good time to inquire about what's covered.

→ **IF YOUR POLICY IS WRONG.** If you see something on your policy that is incorrect, such as a misspelled name, date of birth, dates of travel, or anything else that is inaccurate, contact your insurance company immediately to get it fixed. Inaccurate information can delay your claim.

→ **WHEN SOMETHING CHANGES.** If any of the circumstances under which you purchased your policy have changed—say your travel dates have shifted several times, you've added costs or travel suppliers to your trip, or you've moved—then it's best to let the company know.

→ **WHEN SOMETHING UNEXPECTED HAPPENS.** Many travel insurance

---

👎 NOT SMART ASSUMING EVERYTHING IS COVERED.

Travelers often believe that if they're buying travel insurance, their entire trip is covered. It isn't, despite what you think your agent told you when you purchased the coverage. No policy covers everything. Rather, it covers you under certain circumstances, which are outlined in your policy. Please don't wait to read your policy until you have to file a claim. By then, it could be too late.

PROBLEM SOLVED

IS A NATURAL CAUSE A PREEXISTING CONDITION?

QUESTION: I need your help with a travel insurance problem. We booked a trip to Cancun through Orbitz last year, and when we got to the end of the online reservation process, we were offered a travel insurance policy through Allianz. We thought it would be a good idea to have insurance, so we bought it.

Afterward, we received a document with the specifics of our policy. I didn't read it because I didn't anticipate having to make a claim, but I was wrong.

Shortly before our trip, my mother died unexpectedly. I called Orbitz, which referred me to the insurance company. An Allianz representative told me to cancel the trip, and suggested that I reschedule it. They promised they would "take care" of the claim.

A few weeks later, Allianz denied my claim for $951 because my mother suffered from high blood pressure. The death certificate listed the cause of death as being from "natural causes." I didn't know a natural cause was a preexisting medical condition. —Cheryl Ellis, *Lee's Summit, Missouri*

ANSWER: My condolences on your loss. I agree with you that a "natural cause" of death isn't a preexisting condition, or that a preexisting condition may well have nothing at all to do with your mother's cause of death, and I think Allianz should have honored your claim.

This misunderstanding might have been avoided though. When you bought your insurance policy, you didn't read the terms before buying it and made the decision to insure your vacation as an afterthought. There's nothing wrong with buying travel insurance from your agent, but I always recommend doing a little research before purchasing any policy.

It's as simple as clicking on a site like *InsureMyTrip.com* or *SquareMouth.com* which are companies that compare travel insurance policies and let you buy them—and reviewing the terms and costs. Typically, travel insurance is a good idea for big-ticket purchases over $5,000, but in your case, a $951 vacation was definitely worth insuring.

At the very least, you should have reviewed the terms of your insurance policy carefully before buying it. You might have seen some of the limits about preexisting medical conditions, had second thoughts, and taken an opportunity to shop around before buying the Allianz policy.

Then again, no one expects a sudden death in the family, so you couldn't have known what was about to happen and it's unlikely you would have done anything differently. That's the thing about travel insurance: You don't know what kind of coverage you'll need until you need it.

I contacted Allianz on your behalf and asked it to take another look at your claim. "Due to the extenuating circumstances, we have made a consideration in this case, and have paid the Ellises' claim in full," a representative said.

customers are unaware that their policies cover items like trip interruption or will provide assistance when something goes wrong. So, when something that you didn't expect happens while you're traveling, get in touch with your insurance company through the emergency number that they provide. You never know; you might be covered.

Timing is important. Read your policy when you receive it, and call if you have questions. Many travel insurance companies offer a "free look" period (normally 10 to 15 days) for all of their insurance policies. If, after reviewing your policy, you decide that it doesn't meet your needs, you can cancel it (as long as you haven't departed on your trip) and receive a full refund.

> *Read your policy when you receive it, and call if you have questions.*

a necessary paper trail that you can refer to should you ever have to make a claim. If you must call, be sure to get the name of the person you spoke with. Most insurance companies record their customer service calls.

How about the travel agent or insurance agent who sells you travel insurance? They're not off the hook after they've sold you your policy. Many states require insurance agents and travel agents who sell insurance to be licensed, and if an agent has sold you a policy with promises of coverage and the insurance didn't cover you, then you need to take that up with the agent.

While a travel agent or insurance agent can act as an advocate when your claim has been denied, you should never rely on that person for authoritative information about coverage. In fact, a good agent will insist that you review your policy for yourself before buying. Bear in mind, also, that there may be some privacy restrictions that limit your agent's involvement.

Always go directly to the primary source: your insurance company. In the event of a dispute, it's the insurance company's coverage promises made through the policy—not those of your agent—that matter.

If you receive a letter from your insurance company, review it thoroughly and write or call the company

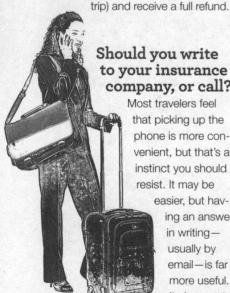

Should you write to your insurance company, or call?

Most travelers feel that picking up the phone is more convenient, but that's an instinct you should resist. It may be easier, but having an answer in writing—usually by email—is far more useful. It also creates

if you have questions. If you think you may need proof of something that was said by phone, always get it in writing.

Believe it or not, travel insurance companies want to hear from you before, during, and after your trip. Why? They are as keen as you are to avoid horror stories involving claims, and the only way to do that is to maintain an ongoing dialogue with their customers.

The most problematic travelers are the ones who purchase a policy as an afterthought—clicking a button after they've booked an airline ticket or hotel—and then forget about their insurance until they have a problem. They've probably made an uninformed purchasing decision and a boatload of assumptions that they shouldn't have.

Choosing travel insurance is as important as selecting an airline, cruise line, car rental company, or hotel. Becoming a power user of your policy is just as vital.

How do I file a travel insurance claim?

According to the U.S. Travel Insurance Association, nine out of ten travel insurance claims are honored. So, if you're thinking of filing a claim on your policy, that's the good news.

Now, the bad news: If you're among the 10 percent who have been rejected, you could face a long and ultimately unsuccessful

struggle to have your claim paid. You don't want to end up there.

→ **CALL YOUR INSURANCE COMPANY BEFORE YOU FILE A CLAIM.** Ask what it needs from you and if there are any restrictions in your policy that might make a claim unsuccessful. For example, some policies that cover medical problems require that you seek treatment within 24 hours of an incident.

→ **READ YOUR POLICY.** You should have done this before buying the insurance. Now you have to read the fine print with an eye toward answering this question: Will my claim be honored?

→ **KEEP ALL RECEIPTS.** In fact, you'll want to retain every scrap of paperwork that could even remotely relate to a claim. Don't throw anything away.

→ **ASK FOR EVERYTHING IN WRITING AS YOU TRAVEL—BILLS, INVOICES, RECEIPTS, HOTEL BILLS.** You can never have enough documentation.

→ GET THE CAUSE OF A DELAY IN WRIT-ING, IF APPLICABLE. A lot of claims are rejected because travelers can't prove a cause of delay. So if you're held up, be certain to document the cause, preferably in writing. Finding out the reason long after your trip can be difficult—if not impossible.

How long will my claim take?

Your travel insurance company will tell you how to file a claim. Claims typically take between two and four weeks to process, but some compli-cated claims that require more exten-sive research by an adjuster can test your patience. Expect to receive a form acknowledgment of your claim with a final decision within roughly a month, but no more than two months.

If you've waited longer than six weeks, contact your travel insurance company to find out about the status of your claim. You may need to refile. It's rare for paperwork to get lost, but it can happen.

A large number of the inquiries about travel insurance that I receive involve the sometimes lengthy wait

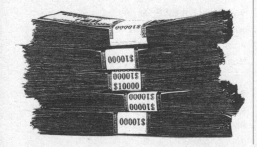

for a claim to be processed. There are two main reasons for such a delay: first, a large natural disas-ter that triggers thousands of claims; second, unusual or complicated cir-cumstances that require additional research on the part of the adjuster, or require you to send more information.

Many claims are denied because of a preexisting medical condition. As I mentioned in an earlier section, you should try to find a policy that cov-ers preexisting conditions. Also, make sure the policy covers your traveling companion, and be sure your com-panion's family members are included in the definition of "family." Some poli-cies don't cover them.

A rejection isn't the insurance com-pany's final word. It only means that based on the information it has in your claim, the company isn't going to honor the claim. A brief, polite, written appeal with any new information that you believe is relevant to your case is often the first step toward getting the company to reverse its decision. How-ever, check with your insurance com-pany to see if it requires a different method to file an appeal.

Appeals are taken seriously by most insurance companies and are typi-cally reviewed by several adjusters at a more senior level. Their goal is to make sure nothing was overlooked by the first adjuster. This review pro-cess can take as long as the pro-cess of evaluation for the initial claim did, so stay patient. In my experience, however, appeals are answered faster than initial claims are.

How do I file an additional appeal?

For most appeals, "no" is a final answer—and you're left with another decision to make: Do you accept their decision or take your appeal to the next level?

Often, a hard look at your claim by an independent third party will reveal that you don't have a case. (I'm sometimes that person, unfortunately.) Maybe the event you're making a claim for isn't a covered reason, or maybe you don't have the receipt to back your claim. Now is a good time to take another look at your claim and appeal, and decide whether it's worth continuing with your appeal.

Many claims are denied because of a preexisting medical condition.

→ **SEND A BRIEF, POLITE EMAIL TO THE INSURANCE AGENT OR TRAVEL AGENT WHO SOLD YOU THE POLICY, NOTIFYING HIM OF YOUR REJECTION.** Agents often can and do act as intermediaries when something goes wrong with a policy. Remember, your agent took a commission on your policy and he had to be licensed to sell the policy, so he has some skin in the game.

→ **CONTACT YOUR STATE INSURANCE COMMISSIONER.** Your insurance commissioner may be able to help if your claim was rejected without cause. To find your insurance commissioner, visit the National Association of Insurance Commissioners site *(naic.org)*. Many travelers have reported that their claims were honored simply by copying their state insurance commissioner on their appeal.

→ **ALERT YOUR BETTER BUSINESS BUREAU.** You'll want to copy your agent and insurance company. The BBB has been known to investigate claims of this nature, but it has little sway over the final outcome of your appeal.

→ **TAKE THE AGENT OR YOUR INSURANCE COMPANY TO SMALL CLAIMS COURT.** You don't need an attorney to go to small claims court, but there's a limit on the claim amount. So, be sure to do some homework before filing a complaint. Typically, this is your last resort. If your agent or insurance company prevails in small claims court, you are usually out of options.

BOTTOM LINE

The right travel insurance policy can protect you when something goes wrong. But the wrong coverage offers a false sense of security and, if you have to file a claim, leads to an even more disappointing end to a disappointing trip. The only way to prevent it is through careful research and an understanding of how the system works.

6

Buy the Right Luggage for Your Trip

Why one size doesn't fit every vacation, and why you don't look good in black.

They say everyone has a little baggage, and that's certainly true of most travelers you meet. Selecting the right suitcase might actually be the easy part; knowing what your rights are when the belongings are lost or misplaced isn't. If you travel enough, your luggage may eventually get lost, but a little preparation and basic knowledge will go a long way toward avoiding the unpleasantness that can follow.

Should I check my bag or carry it?

→ **AIRLINE.** You say baggage; I say luggage. You say carry-on; your airline says "no way." Luggage falls into three broad categories: a *checked bag,* or a suitcase too large to fit in the aircraft's cabin; a *carry-on bag* that can be taken with you and stowed in an overhead compartment or underneath your seat; and a *personal item* like a book, tablet computer, purse, or small briefcase.

Checking a bag used to be a relatively easy decision. Most airlines included the cost of checking a first and second suitcase in the ticket price. The checked bags could still get lost, but at least you weren't shelling out more to check them. Now, with only one or two exceptions, you pay for the privilege. That's left a lot of air travelers repacking their bags or bringing less. For most vacations or business trips (those lasting a week or less), you can usually fit everything you're likely to need into a carry-on bag. Many air travelers try to do that, instead of giving the airline an extra $25 or more per bag. (Some so-called "discount" airlines like Spirit also charge for carry-on bags, which makes this strategy more difficult to execute.)

→ **CRUISE LINE.** Most cruise lines allow you to carry one bag on board when you embark, but ask that you check the rest of your luggage, allowing it to be brought later to your quarters. There's no extra charge for checking your bags, although you'll be expected to tip your porter for the service. This system usually works reasonably well, although I would strongly recommend taking all of your valuables with you. As you'll see in a moment, your cruise

👍 SMART KEEP IT IN THE FAMILY.

Some luggage is modular, in that it's built to fit together. One piece will hook on to another, allowing you to drag all of your belongings on wheels. The catch? They can't always be used with other modular luggage. So if you're thinking of buying this kind of suitcase, make sure you buy a single brand. Mixing and matching may not work.

line may not cover all your losses if the bags are pilfered.

→ HOTEL. Bags can be left with a bellman or checked at the front desk for safekeeping, say while you're waiting for your room to become available or need to check out of your room but still have a few hours to kill in town. There's usually no charge for this service, although you may be expected to leave a tip for the employee who retrieves the luggage. Again, the hotel's liability may be limited, so you should be wary of checking anything valuable.

→ BUS AND TRAIN. Rail and motor coach operators rarely charge for checked luggage, but their liability is limited by contract or federal law. It's unusual for passengers to carry an excessive amount of luggage when traveling by bus or train, since it often involves walking longer distances within cities or between terminals. Again: Don't pack anything valuable in your bags if you leave them out of your sight.

What kind of luggage should I travel with?

Luggage comes in all shapes and sizes, and deciding which set is right for you is a personal and practical decision. This isn't a book about fashion, so I won't be able to help you choose between leather and ballistic nylon. But let's talk specifics.

> *Airline carry-on bags must fit in the overhead compartment or under the seat in front of you.*

→ EVERY INCH COUNTS. Airline carry-on bags must fit in the overhead compartment or under the seat in front of you. For most commercial aircraft (but not all), that means the maximum dimensions can't exceed 22" long x 14" wide x 9" tall. That's the largest carry-on bag you can bring on board.

However, you may not be able to take that size bag on a plane if:
• you're on a smaller aircraft, such as a regional jet.
• all the overhead compartments are already full.
• you've overpacked the bag and it won't squeeze in the overhead compartment.

If you want to avoid checking luggage, I strongly recommend that your primary bag be no larger than the maximum carry-on dimensions for the plane you'll be flying in. You can get this information online or by calling the airline. Otherwise, you're taking a chance, every time you check in, that your primary carry-on will be forcibly checked by the airline. It's just not worth it.

If you're traveling by bus or train, you may experience limitations similar to those found on a small regional jet. You may need to quickly remove the valuables from your wheeled luggage and check the larger bag, which is not an ideal situation. Check the baggage limits for your motor coach or train *before* you leave, so that you don't have to repack your bags on the fly.

→ **SOFT OR HARD LUGGAGE?** Hard-sided luggage will protect your belongings, but it comes at a cost. The luggage tends to weigh more and it's less flexible. So you won't be able to wedge the bag into an overhead bin, and it's more of a challenge to overpack

a hard-sided bag (though not impossible). Your final destination matters. In the tropics, where you might deplane onto the tarmac and pick up your luggage outside, soft-sided luggage can get soaked in a downpour before arriving at the airport carousel. Also, destinations with high humidity can cause clothes in soft-sided luggage to get damp. It isn't unusual for experienced travelers to own two sets of luggage, which they choose between depending on the likely travel conditions.

→ **DOES THE MATERIAL MATTER?** When you're buying soft-sided luggage, pay close attention to the type of fabric and its *denier,* which is a measurement of the fiber's density and can vary significantly. Ballistic or Cordura nylon is more resilient than other polyester fabrics. Look for something strong with a denier of 400 or higher.

→ **HOW CAN I TELL IF THE LUGGAGE IS MADE WELL?** Typically, the more you pay, the better the luggage. But not always. Look for covered exterior seams, lock stitches, and zippers with reinforced seams. Don't be afraid to give the bag a pull (the equivalent of kicking the tires on a car) to make sure the stitches, zippers, and handles have a solid feel. If the handle seems like it could come off with another tug, try a different set. *Consumer Reports,* in print or online *(Consumer Reports.org),* periodically tests and rates various luggage brands.

PROBLEM SOLVED

LOST LUGGAGE IN LAS VEGAS

QUESTION: I need your help. Spirit Airlines lost my luggage and won't replace it. I flew from Fort Lauderdale, Florida, to Las Vegas almost six months ago, and my checked bags disappeared.

I filed a claim when my bags didn't show up in Las Vegas. My travel insurance company, Travel Guard, also got them to send me claim forms. Spirit won't return my calls and my emails just get an automated response. Its online tracking system has no record of my luggage claim.

I finally got through to someone on the phone who told me to expect a refund soon. That was more than a month ago, and I still don't have anything. How can I get compensated for my luggage? —Michael Germano, *Palm Beach, Florida*

ANSWER: Spirit should have settled your claim quickly. The airline promises it will handle lost luggage claims two weeks to a month after receiving your claim and conducting a secondary trace.

Did it ever receive your claims? Yes and no. I checked with Spirit, and they say they got your claim, but not within 30 days of your flight, as it requires. That would explain why there was no record of your problem. The airline didn't process your paperwork.

When you filed your initial lost luggage claim at the airport, you didn't deal with a Spirit employee. Spirit outsourced some of its baggage claim operations in Las Vegas at the time of your flight. To me, that would have sent up a red flag that you needed to follow up with the airline as soon as possible—certainly within 24 hours—to ensure Spirit knew your luggage was lost.

Buying travel insurance wasn't a bad idea, but your insurance company should have done more than ask Spirit to send you another claim form. I think you could have leaned on Travel Guard a little more to get an answer from Spirit, and if the answer was "no," to process an insurance claim promptly—assuming your policy covered lost luggage.

I would have also contacted Travel Guard as soon as your luggage vanished. Every Travel Guard policy comes with a "24-hour 911 travel emergency service" to help passengers with, among other things, lost luggage tracking.

You aren't the only one who has had trouble contacting Spirit. Spirit's customer service department is described as difficult to reach by phone, fond of sending form letters to its customers, and reluctant to pay refunds or compensate its passengers for inconveniences.

I'm not as baffled by Spirit's refusal to process your claim as I am by its ability to lose your luggage—permanently—on a nonstop flight. How did it do *that?* Usually it takes a connection or two, and most lost bags are eventually recovered.

The airline isn't completely indifferent to the experiences of its passengers or their luggage. After I contacted Spirit, it agreed to make an exception to its 30-day rule and processed your claim. The airline sent you a check for $300 to cover your losses.

→ **WHEELS OR NO WHEELS?** Wheels add weight to your luggage but they can also make it much easier to haul around. I'm a firm believer in wheels, but bear in mind that not every bag must have wheels. Some of your carry-ons can rest comfortably on the wheeled luggage when you're in an airport terminal or checking into a hotel. Don't go all wheel-crazy!

→ **TWO WHEELS OR FOUR?** If your primary bag is to be wheeled, you have one more decision to make: two wheels or four? While the standard, two-wheel wheeled luggage remains the most popular among frequent travelers, spinner luggage, featuring four wheels mounted on casters, is another option. Kids love it because it moves easily in any direction, quickly. Four-wheelers also don't fall over as often as the two-wheelers, but they can roll away from you on their own.

→ **WHAT ABOUT "WEARABLE" LUGGAGE?** Several clothing manufacturers offer pants, shirts, and jackets that are advertised as "wearable" luggage. While these can hold some of your personal belongings when you travel, I don't recommend using them as your primary luggage. First, they tend to be costly novelty products that cater to techies and gadget geeks, not mainstream travelers; and second, they generally have nowhere near the

> *Wheels add weight to your luggage but they can also make it much easier to haul around.*

capacity of a standard carry-on bag. So, use it if you have it, but don't leave your conventional luggage at home.

→ **LUGGAGE SECURITY?** Would you give a total stranger your name, address, and phone number? That's what a luggage tag does without a privacy cover. Certain luggage features electromagnetic shielding compartments to protect your laptop, tablet, cell phone, and other digital devices from hacking and identity theft. You may not need this advanced protection, but if you're the neurotic type, the added peace of mind is worth it. New schemes by criminals and even some governments are developed all the time to access personal and financial data.

→ **HOW ABOUT LOCKS?** Locking your luggage or using a plastic wrapping service like Secure Wrap (securewrap .com) can make it harder for thieves to pilfer your checked luggage, but it offers no guarantees. That's because the TSA reserves the right to open all of your bags to inspect the items. Once your bag is open, anyone can help themselves to the valuables in it. You're better off leaving the luggage unlocked and not checking anything of value.

→ **DO WARRANTIES MATTER?** Absolutely. Ideally, your bag will come with an unconditional lifetime warranty. Do manufacturers cover their product?

You bet. I've talked with many travelers who were able to get their bags replaced, no questions asked. But read the fine print *very* carefully. Some warranties exclude some types of damage.

How do I pack smarter?

Ah, that's a subject for another book. But all my advice can be distilled into a few sentences:

→ **LEARN A SYSTEM.** There are various packing methods designed to fit more items into less space. Some emphasize folding clothes in the most efficient way and packing them into a suitcase, while others recommend rolling clothes. Find a system that works for you. Use it.

→ **TAKE ONLY WHAT YOU NEED.** When in doubt, leave it out. Odds are, there's a drugstore or mall at your destination, and you can buy anything you need.

→ **PLAN AHEAD TO PACK LESS.** Know the weather forecast at your destination and what your activities are and pack what works for both. Resist the temptation to add something "just in case." Think twice about any clothing that requires dry cleaning or even machine

washing. Hand-washable items will save you time, money, and general inconvenience.

→ **DON'T OVERPACK.** You'll have trouble getting it into the car or the overhead compartment and it'll stress you out. What's more, you won't be able to buy anything to take home with you. Your family will be *so* disappointed.

How to prevent your luggage from getting lost

Luggage likes to get lost, no doubt about it. Here are some ways to maximize your chances of being reunited with it.

→ **BUY A STURDY AND COLORFUL BAG TAG.** Some of the flimsier paper tags are easily ripped off in transit. If you already have a serviceable plastic or leather tag, make sure the contact information it contains is current.

→ **MAKE SURE IT'S GOING TO THE RIGHT PLACE.** Those three-letter airport codes can be counterintuitive, so if you don't recognize the one on your tag, ask the ticket agent.

→ **TELL 'EM WHERE YOU'LL BE.** Store a copy of your itinerary inside the bag or in an outside zippered pocket and make sure there's a duplicate name tag *inside* the bag. In the unlikely event your outside tag goes missing, someone will still be able to find you.

→ **TAKE A PICTURE.** Use your cell phone camera to take a snapshot of your bag before you check it. It'll be easier to track down if you can show an airline or train employee a picture of it.

→ **KEEP A PACKING LIST.** That way, you know what you put in the bag that's gone missing.

I did all those things, but my checked luggage got lost anyway. What should I do?

Lost baggage is surprisingly common. For every flight, there are usually one or two bags that are "misplaced"—an airline euphemism for "we lost it." Fortunately, most of those bags are eventually found. Luggage losses for cruise lines or trains are not reported to the government, but they are generally not as common.

→ **LOOK AROUND.** If you're at a luggage carousel or at a train station, have a look around. Sometimes, luggage arrives early and is placed next to the carousel or in a holding area. It's possible the bag is not lost, after all.

→ **FILE A CLAIM.** The sooner you let the airline, rail operator, cruise line, or hotel know of your loss, the sooner they can start looking for it. Airlines have standard forms you'll be asked to fill out. A hotel might not. Get something in writing that documents your loss. If necessary, call the police and fill out a report.

→ **ASK FOR AN ALLOWANCE.** Ask for a stipend to buy toiletries and clothes while they look for your belongings. Although this isn't written into any contracts, it is generally a policy to take care of passengers whose belongings have been lost. Details are important here. Should you save receipts? Will they simply give you a preloaded debit card? Is there a limit to the stipend? There almost always is.

→ **BE PATIENT.** It can take weeks, and sometimes months, to recover lost luggage. Sometimes it's lost forever. Good thing you didn't check anything valuable, otherwise you'd be in real trouble.

What's in the fine print?

→ **AIRLINE.** If your luggage is lost on a domestic flight, the rules are covered in your carrier's *contract of carriage,* the legal agreement between you and the airline. If it's an international flight, consult the Montreal Convention for your rights (more on this in a minute).

• **Domestic losses.** Under most airline contracts, you have to file a claim within 24 hours of the loss, but you shouldn't leave the airport before visiting the luggage counter by the baggage claim area to let them know your bag is missing in action. They have access to your reservation and can see any notations that may have been made on your checked bag. Sometimes it gets placed on another flight that's arriving soon, and you can wait for it at the airport or the airline can deliver it to your hotel. By the way, you can ask an airline to cover the costs of a change of clothes and toiletries while it searches for your bag. It's better to request an allowance before you leave the airport instead of buying the needed items and *then* billing the airline. It may or may not cover the replacements.

The contract basically makes the airline cover the cost of buying a new bag and some replacement clothes. You'll be asked for receipts, and if you can't show them, the airline may pay a nominal amount, if anything. However, there's a silver lining: Under federal regulations, it must refund the fee you paid to check your luggage if it loses the bag.

What's excluded from liability?

• **Almost everything other than clothing.** American Airlines' domestic contract excludes the following: "antiques, artifacts, artwork, books and documents, china, computers, and other electronic equipment, computer software, fragile items (including child/infant restraint devices such as strollers and car seats), eyeglasses, prescription sunglasses, non-prescription sunglasses, and all other eyewear and eye/vision devices (whether lenses are glass, plastic, or some other material), furs, heirlooms, keys, liquids, medicines, money, orthotics, surgical supports, perishable items, photographic, video and optical equipment, precious metals, stones or jewelry, securities and negotiable papers, silverware, samples, unique or irreplaceable items, or any other similar valuable items." Whew! Remind me never to check any of those!

• **International losses.** Luggage lost internationally is governed by the Montreal Convention (the Convention for the Unification of Certain Rules for International Carriage by Air). When you're dealing with a loss on an international flight, you'll want to refer directly to the convention text if you think your airline isn't compensating you appropriately. For example, Article 19 of the convention says a carrier is liable for damage occasioned by delay in the carriage by air of baggage, except to the extent that it proves that

👍 **SMART** TRACK YOUR LUGGAGE.

If your airline or cruise line is prone to losing your luggage, why not track it yourself? That's the idea behind a service like Trakdot *(trakdot.com),* a small device that accompanies your luggage and sends you a text message when it arrives at your destination. Another service called i-TRAK *(i-trak.com),* billed as a "global lost and found," will also call or email you with your bag's location. No more asking the airline where your luggage is—now you'll know.

PROBLEM SOLVED

LOST LUGGAGE, IGNORED CLAIM

QUESTION: My parents and I recently traveled between Los Angeles and Istanbul on British Airways (BA). Three of our checked bags were misplaced by the airline. We reported our loss when we arrived in Istanbul.

After two weeks, the airline said it could not find our bags and sent us a claim form. We were asked to provide receipts for all our missing items, but we didn't have the receipts for our belongings as it had been at least six months since we bought them.

British Airways told us to contact the merchants and get duplicate copies of the receipts. We did and faxed those receipts to the airline. It's been four months, and we still haven't heard a thing from BA.

The only way to contact a BA customer service representative is by email, fax, or letter. There's no phone number I can call. We have repeatedly tried to contact the airline through every available channel, but haven't received a single reply.

This has been a terrible experience for us. Would you please help?

—Izlen Umut Egeli, *Northridge, California*

ANSWER: British Airways should have delivered your luggage to you in Istanbul. When it didn't, it should have reimbursed you promptly for your lost property.

Under the Montreal Convention, BA is liable for the destruction, loss, or damage to baggage up to €1,296 per passenger.

Your case is particularly interesting in light of the airline's recent decision to charge an extra £120 per bag on international routes if you have more than two bags to check. I'm not denying that BA has the right to make you pay whatever it wants for carrying your luggage, but it seems to me that if the airline is charging passengers for luggage before they even board the plane, it should reimburse them with the same speed when it loses their luggage.

The system you describe for tracking lost baggage is a source of endless complaints about BA's North American operations. As a troubleshooter, I've heard from many exasperated passengers who have tried to navigate the airline's bureaucratic maze. Many tell me that they have given up in despair.

My best advice is to never trust an airline with your luggage if you can help it. Consider packing light and hiring an overnight delivery service to transport anything that won't fit in your carry-on luggage to your hotel.

Of course, not everyone can afford a luggage concierge. So, if you're going to hand your luggage over to an airline, how do you make sure it doesn't become another statistic? First, make sure you aren't packing anything that isn't covered by the airline's contract of carriage (the legal agreement between you and the airline). That usually includes cameras, electronics, and anything fragile. For the rest, make sure you have a receipt (or can readily find a receipt).

I contacted BA for you. It reviewed your case and mailed you a check for $2,900 to cover your loss.

it took all reasonable measures to prevent the damage, or that it was impossible to take such measures.

Article 22 sets the liability limit for damages associated with delayed passenger baggage at about $1,490 (it's calculated in something called Special Drawing Rights, a monetary unit used by the International Monetary Fund). Article 26 states that "any provision tending to relieve a carrier of liability or to fix a lower limit than that which is laid down in the Convention is null and void." By the way, violations of the Montreal Convention are forbidden under U.S. federal law. A violation would constitute an unfair or deceptive business practice and an unfair method of competition.

Under the Montreal Convention, an airline has 21 days before "misplaced" luggage is declared lost. The sooner you say something, the sooner the airline can start looking for your lost luggage. I strongly recommend making a claim within 24 hours of your loss in order to comply with your airline's own policy on lost luggage.

In the past, domestic airlines operating international flights have shortchanged passengers on compensation under the Montreal Convention, so be wary of the first offer you get for a loss on an international flight. It might not be enough.

→ **CRUISE.** Your cruise line's liability for your luggage is outlined in your ticket contract or cruise contract. Basically, you have to prove that the luggage was in the cruise line's possession, custody, or control when it was lost. A typical contract will also have an exception for wear, tear, and normal usage. Perishable items, medicine, liquor, cash, securities, or other financial instruments are also exempt.

Carnival Cruise Lines' contract, for example, stipulates that the aggregate value of your property does not exceed $50 per guest or bag, with a maximum value of $100 per stateroom regardless of the number of occupants or bags. You can get around that by declaring the value of your items in writing and paying Carnival 5 percent of the declared value. If you don't take these extra precautions in advance and your jewelry goes missing while you're on

👎 NOT SMART BUYING A BLACK BAG.

For years, to repurpose Henry Ford's words, you could buy luggage in any color, as long as it was black. At least that's how many luggage manufacturers felt. Buying a black suitcase may not have been your first choice, but now that you are stuck with it, you can give your luggage a unique, sturdy bag tag or even pull colorful duct tape around one of the handles—*anything* to set it apart. You'll thank me at the luggage carousel.

a cruise, the maximum your cruise line must pay is $100. Put differently, don't bring your jewels on your cruise or make sure your homeowner's or renter's policy covers your things. Some trip insurance policies and some credit cards also include baggage insurance.

→ **TRAIN.** In the United States, Amtrak accepts limited liability for your luggage. You have 30 days from the date of your loss to file a claim. Its terms specifically exempt items missing or stolen from inside unlocked or unsecured baggage; minor damages to baggage considered normal wear and tear (despite reasonable care when handling); baggage that was transported unaccompanied by the owner; failure to pay the applicable storage charges; loss or damage to prohibited items; items packed with prohibited items; and baggage containing prohibited items.

If you check your luggage, Amtrak's liability is limited to $50 per bag. If you check it as a parcel, it's limited to $100 per bag. Amtrak also disclaims liability for any special items carried on board or for any bicycles accepted in the baggage area that are not packed in a bicycle box.

Just as with the cruise lines, you can declare additional valuation—up to $2,500—upon payment of the applicable charges to check your bags. As a practical matter, few passengers do.

Some trip insurance policies and some credit cards also include baggage insurance.

→ **HOTEL.** If you check your luggage with a bellman and it's lost, your hotel's liability is spelled out in the state's innkeeper laws. Those tend to favor the hotel and limit the damages you can claim.

For example, California law states that in no case shall a hotel owner's liability exceed $1,000 in total. The amount of damages paid won't exceed $500 for each trunk, $250 for each valise or traveling bag and its contents, $250 for each box, bundle, or package and its contents, and $250 for all other personal property of any kind, unless the innkeeper consents in writing to assume a greater liability. Your damage claim will probably be forwarded to the hotel's insurance company for processing, and you may be asked for original receipts of all the items you're claiming. This may make it difficult, if not impossible, to file a successful claim.

BOTTOM LINE

A little knowledge of your luggage options, how to protect your bags when you travel, and your rights when they're lost can help keep your belongings safe when you're on the road. After all, your bags should make your next trip better instead of being a burden.

7

Manage Your Travel Loyalty Program

The real reason frequent flier programs
are so addictive and how
to make the most of them now.

Loyalty programs offer an irresistible incentive to travel. For every mile you fly or dollar you spend, you earn a point. Collect enough of them, and congratulations—you've just landed a "free" trip. Sometimes you don't even have to travel to earn points. Just spend money on a special credit card, buy pudding, rent DVDs, or purchase coins from the U.S. Mint for your "reward." But is this a game worth playing? Maybe, maybe not.

Who should collect miles and points:

→ **IF YOU'RE A FREQUENT TRAVELER** and regularly use the same airline, hotel, or car rental company.

→ **IF YOU TRAVEL ON BUSINESS** and your trips are managed by a travel department.

→ **IF YOU LIVE IN A CITY WITH A "HUB" AIRLINE** and you don't have a lot of choices in air travel. For example, if your home airport is in Atlanta, you'll want to consider joining Delta Air Lines' SkyMiles program and earning Medallion status.

Who should not collect miles and points:

→ **IF YOU'RE A LEISURE TRAVELER** and only fly or stay in a hotel occasionally.

→ **IF YOU'RE ALWAYS LOOKING FOR THE BEST DEAL** on a travel product.

→ **IF YOU LIVE NEAR A CITY SERVED BY COMPETING AIRLINES** that give you a real choice.

The truth about loyalty programs

For many travelers, loyalty programs are the best part of the travel experience. You can collect points by taking a flight or renting a car and, if you accumulate enough of them, you'll be rewarded with a "free" stay and elite status that offers you special perks like upgrades and access to members-only airport lounges. Talk about a win-win! Scratch the surface, and you'll see there's much more happening. Travel companies use loyalty programs for several purposes that you may find troubling.

→ **THEY WANT YOUR DATA.** Whenever you surrender your hotel or frequent flier number, a company uses it to track your spending behavior. It allows a business to know more about you than you know about yourself. When are you likely to buy something? What are your guest preferences? Your airline doesn't need to guess, because it sees what you've booked. It often shares that valuable information with its marketing "partners" without asking for your permission. If you care about your privacy and are worried about a company sharing your personal information with a third party, this may be problematic.

→ THEY WANT YOU TO SPEND MORE.

Research shows that participating in a loyalty program can increase your spending with that company by roughly 40 percent. That can easily offset the "free" ticket or 10,000 bonus miles you get for signing up. Companies know that once you're hooked on their loyalty program, you'll give them your business—even when there's a cheaper price to be found elsewhere.

→ THEY WANT TO SEGMENT YOU.

When a company understands how much you spend—which it will if every purchase is linked to a loyalty program—then it can separate the good customers from the best ones. Unless you're a *very* good customer, that probably means you'll be getting less for your travel dollar, as companies lavish more perks on their most valuable customers.

Loyalty programs can be great for you, but they can be even better for the company offering them. If you're going to start collecting miles, you need to go into the relationship with your eyes wide open. There's no such thing as a free flight or hotel room. Someone *will* pay for it. At best, you should think of it as a slightly discounted ticket or hotel room.

Don't believe everything you read

If you spend a little time online looking for information about loyalty programs, you'll stumble across blogs and websites that claim to offer expert advice. While some of them really do have a deep, encyclopedic knowledge of loyalty programs, like Tim Winship's *FrequentFlier.com,* others can be dangerous places for you—and your wallet.

→ FIRST, THESE SITES ASSUME THAT EVERYONE SHOULD PARTICIPATE IN A LOYALTY PROGRAM.

In fact, some travelers will never benefit from a loyalty program in a meaningful way. Once you factor in all of the extra trips you had to take, the higher price you paid for your flights or rooms, and the additional dollars you had to spend on a credit card, you probably would

SMART TRACK YOUR AWARD PORTFOLIO ONLINE.

Miles expire and elite levels run out if you don't travel enough. One way to prevent this is to track your points online, with a service like Using Miles *(usingmiles.com)* or AwardWallet *(awardwallet.com).* Both are free to use at the entry level and can help you manage and maximize your awards.

have been better off never signing up for the program in the first place.

→ **SECOND, THESE SITES TEND TO TAKE A NARROW VIEW OF TRAVEL, ASSUMING THAT EVERYONE TRAVELS BY PLANE.** Truth is, most Americans travel by car. You shouldn't expect reliable information about anything except an airline or hotel loyalty program. These resources also waste an inordinate amount of time revealing tricks for earning more miles or getting upgrades or exploiting fare errors made by airlines, as opposed to showing you how to have a better trip.

→ **THIRD, THESE SITES TEND TO HAVE AN UNHEALTHY AND OFTEN DYSFUNCTIONAL RELATIONSHIP WITH TRAVEL-RELATED COMPANIES.** In fact, some are literally in the business of shilling a credit card, and in most cases the reader is never made aware of the website writers' financial incentives.

→ **FINALLY—AND THIS MAY BE THE MOST OFF-PUTTING IF YOU'RE NEW TO COLLECTING AWARD MILES—THE SITES CAN BE UNFRIENDLY TO PEOPLE WITH BASIC QUESTIONS ABOUT LOYALTY PROGRAMS.** The result? There are almost no reliable sources of information about loyalty programs. Most of the biggest sites have been compromised by affiliate agreements that pay the publisher for each referral. The rest are "experts-only" terrain where you're not welcome. You'll have to do your own research and make up your own mind if you want to benefit from any loyalty program.

What's the best loyalty program for me?

Which loyalty program will be loyal back to you? Here are a few variables to consider:

→ **YOUR OWN TRAVEL NEEDS.** Are you planning to travel to cities where the hotel operates a lot of properties? Will you fly with the airline frequently enough? No? Skip this program, then.

→ **THE RULES.** Have a look at the program contract. If you see clauses that you don't understand or that veer from the norm (see more on rules below) then maybe you're considering the wrong program.

→ **THE PROGRAM'S REPUTATION.** Some loyalty programs have reputations for being generous and fair, while others are known to be exceptionally stingy. However, even the most die-hard mile age collectors regularly dis their airline or hotel when they don't get what they want.

→ **REDEMPTION RATES.** Review the actual redemption rates reported by the companies, which are usually available with a quick online search or by sifting through a company's annual report. Rates in the single digits are a sign that you may not be able to do much with your points once you've earned them.

→ **CUSTOMER SERVICE.** If the airline, car rental company, or hotel is known for its snarky employees and substandard service, then why on earth would you offer it your loyalty? You *do* have a choice.

What you need to know (and what they won't advertise)

When you sign up for your loyalty program, the terms are briefly waved in front of you. A majority of travelers either skim them (mistake) or ignore them (even bigger mistake). If you reviewed them, you'd realize how problematic award programs can be.

Here's what you'll find:

→ **YOU DON'T OWN THE MILES.** They belong to the airline or hotel. What's more, the company has the right to terminate the program or to change the rules at any time, with or without notice.

→ **YOU MAY NOT BE ABLE TO USE YOUR POINTS OR MILES.** Redemption levels can change, and award inventory may be in limited supply or might disappear.

→ **IF YOU BREAK A RULE, YOU'RE OUT.** Any failure to follow the program's convoluted rules may result in your expulsion and confiscation of all your miles. It happens.

→ **YOU COULD BE AUDITED.** If the company thinks you've been trying to game the system, it could audit your account. Your personal information, including your travel records, would be shared with a third party auditor.

→ **YOU'RE RESPONSIBLE FOR FOLLOWING THE CHANGES IN YOUR PROGRAM.** The program doesn't have to notify you when a redemption level changes or your miles expire.

→ **YOU CAN'T SELL YOUR POINTS OR MILES.** Why? Because they said so, that's why.

→ **IF YOU STOP TRAVELING, YOU COULD LOSE EVERYTHING.** Extended periods of inactivity will lead to the termination of your loyalty account.

→ **NOT ALL FLIGHTS OR HOTEL STAYS QUALIFY FOR MILEAGE.** If you think it's as simple a "fly a mile, earn a mile," you're in for an unpleasant surprise.

→ **AND PERHAPS THE BIGGEST ZINGER OF ALL: YOUR "AWARD" TICKETS AND STAYS ARE NOT "FREE."** You may have to pay taxes, airport fees, fuel surcharges, and more taxes. You may have to pay a fee to redeem the points, too. That can add hundreds or thousands of dollars to the cost of traveling.

How much is a mile *really* worth?

You might be left with the impression that a mile or point is worth $1. After all, you spend a dollar, you get a dollar's worth of miles or points, right? Not really. When companies sell each other miles, they value them at about one cent. Internally,

PROBLEM SOLVED

HELP, MY HILTON POINTS ARE GONE!

QUESTION: I used to be a very frequent business traveler. I was a regular at the Hilton chain, where I collected more than 500,000 points and became a Diamond member, their highest elite level, for a number of consecutive years. But for the past two years, I've been in a more stationary job and have not been traveling for business.

Well, this year my wife and I began to plan a summer vacation to the Pacific Northwest. We were interested in tapping into some of the Hilton points, most of which had not been used.

I found the hotel I preferred, verified availability using points, and went to book. But to my dismay, I discovered my points were no longer available. I was told by Hilton that since there was no activity on my account for a one-year period, I had "lost" all of my points. I spoke to a supervisor but he really seemed to have no sympathy for my situation, nor did he care about my prior loyalty.

The manager did offer me what he said was a very "generous" offer. If I were to have two paid stays in a Hilton I could get half my points back, and with five paid stays I could get all of my points back. So after a huge number of stays and thousands and thousands of dollars spent at Hiltons, I now have to earn all of that back again?

Needless to say I am angry and frustrated and feel used and abused. Is there anything I can do? —Ryan Sober, *Bethesda, Maryland*

ANSWER: Not really. If you read the fine print in your terms and conditions, you'll see that if you do not earn points in any consecutive 12-month period, Hilton reserves the right to remove you from its loyalty program; you forfeit all your accumulated points.

Hilton also reserves the right to "add, modify, delete or otherwise change" any of the rules, according to its contract. In other words, it's up to you as a frequent guest to keep running tabs on your program's fine print. That's convenient for Hilton, but not so convenient for you.

In fairness to Hilton, I should mention that its disclaimers are pretty much boilerplate. But is throwing the book in your face any way to repay you for all that loyalty? I don't think so. I mean, we're not talking about a couple of hundred points here.

If you ever find yourself in this situation again—sitting on a pile of points—my advice is to burn them quickly. Miles are being devalued at an alarming rate.

I contacted Hilton and asked them to take another look at your expired portfolio. I would like to say that my intervention made the difference, but it was actually your decision to apply for a Hilton American Express card that did the trick. Hilton returned all 423,170 of your forfeited points.

"Clearly," a vice president of the HHonors Customer Service Center wrote me in an email, "the man still has feelings for us."

a travel company values miles at far less—just a fraction of one cent, by some estimates.

That's not the worst of it. Airlines and hotels are constantly making award seats and stays more difficult to obtain. In other words, the value of a mile is always in decline. If you don't spend the points you earn right now, you will get less for them in a year or two. If you wait any longer, they might expire altogether.

Should I get an affinity card to collect miles?

So-called "affinity" cards are co-branded credit cards that allow you to collect miles for every purchase made. They can also allow you to avoid certain luggage fees, offer you a "free" companion ticket with the purchase of an economy class seat, and give you certain entry-level elite benefits reserved for an airline's frequent fliers. If you're a big spender, you can collect tens of thousands of miles and redeem them for multiple award trips.

But before you start using an affinity card, here are a few things to consider.

➔ **THAT FREE TICKET MAY COST MORE THAN YOU THINK.** Often, those attractive bonuses are difficult or impossible to redeem. For example, you may have to buy a full-fare economy class ticket, which costs double or triple a discounted advance-purchase fare, in order to get that "free" companion ticket.

➔ **YOU'LL PAY AN ANNUAL FEE.** While most credit cards don't have any annual fees, affinity cards generally do. The reason? There's a perception that the extra miles being generated (normally at a rate of a mile for every dollar spent) have added value. That may or may not be true. But there's a real cost to your credit card, too; it's buying the miles from the airline with which it has an affinity relationship. Not at a rate of $1 a mile, but it isn't getting them for free, either.

➔ **YOU CAN GET THE BENEFITS ELSEWHERE FOR FREE.** Look closely at the card's benefits and compare them with those offered at the elite levels of your preferred airline or hotel. They may be virtually identical. So if you qualify for silver status, why get a card that re-qualifies you? Kind of redundant, isn't it?

➔ **THE MILES PROBABLY DON'T COUNT TOWARD ELITE STATUS.** There are miles, and then there are *miles.* The miles you collect from an affinity card can be redeemed for a flight or a magazine subscription, but they may not count toward elite status (more on elite status in a moment).

What is elite status, and how do I get it?

Travel companies offer their best customers at least three levels of elite status based on the number of miles they fly, nights they stay in their hotels, or times they rent a car from their

👍SMART WHEN MILES CAN BE WORTH MUCH MORE.

First-class seats and hotel suites can cost thousands, even tens of thousands of dollars. But if you have points or miles, you may be able to use them to upgrade at a fraction of the cost. Although I'm dubious about the frequent flier community's upgrade obsession, here we are in agreement: If you can pay for a premium seat with points that have little or no actual value, you win.

company. As I mentioned before, these levels are in a state of flux, so check with your travel company on how to qualify. Elite levels are usually based on precious metals—silver, gold, platinum. There's often also an unpublished "super-elite" status that separates you as the best of the best. Elite levels have the same effect as pyramid schemes, in that they are constantly prodding you to attain the next status level. So, you'll hear a lot of frequent travelers griping about almost having made platinum status, because platinum elites get treated better than those in gold and silver levels.

The names and benefits for different elite categories vary between companies. Moreover, even *within* a single company's loyalty program, they can change at any time. Carefully comparison shop before you start betting your hard-earned travel dollar on future perks.

Don't be fooled by confusing nomenclature. For instance, entry-level elite status for many airlines is called "silver," but for American Airlines it's "gold," which is the next notch up for other airlines. Whatever you call it,

rookie-level elite status within a travel company's program may entitle you to pay for a "space available" upgrade to business or first class on a flight or to late checkouts at hotels.

Moving up the ladder a rung to intermediate status, you might enjoy access to "free" hotel room or rental car upgrades and to partner airlines' lounges while traveling overseas. At the highest published elite status level (often called "platinum"), you'll get complimentary upgrades across the board, among other benefits.

Then there are the shrouded-in-secrecy "super-elite" status levels. Basically, super-elites don't earn their status by flying, staying, or driving—they're invited to join. The criteria aren't miles, segments, or room nights; more often, it comes down to money spent. If you drop more than six figures for travel with one company, chances are you'll be invited into the inner sanctum of the super-elite.

There are stories about planes being held for these VIP customers and about employees running errands for them when they're in a pinch. Certainly, super-elites have priority for upgrades over everyone else,

👎 NOT SMART MILEAGE RUNS.

Passengers who are a few miles shy of reaching an elite level may take what's called a "mileage run"— a flight that serves only to rack up those last few miles. I'm not going to tell you *not* to do it. But in the long run, it is—pardon the pun—pointless. Soon, the airline will probably just move the goalposts again, requiring more points to get that coveted platinum card, because lots of other frequent fliers are playing the same card upgrade trick. And the only winners are—you guessed it—the airlines that collected the money for your mileage run ticket!

including the platinums who *think* they're at the top of the food chain.

It helps to put these perks into some perspective. If you're spending six figures on travel, you could probably buy your own hotel or a private jet.

How do I keep my miles from expiring?

One of the biggest loyalty program complaints—perhaps *the* biggest—is points that expire. If your account goes inactive for a certain amount of time, usually 36 months, your miles will vanish. Some programs expire in less time (Southwest's Rapid Rewards points last only 24 months). Travelers often contact me hoping they can get them reinstated. The best way to avoid that is to make sure they never expire in the first place.

→ KNOW YOUR PROGRAM RULES.
Even though these are found in a dense document filled with legalese, you should acquaint yourself with the restrictions. Knowing that *all* miles are perishable is a good start, but it helps to know *how* perishable.

→ MAKE SURE THE AIRLINE, HOTEL, OR CAR RENTAL COMPANY HAS YOUR CURRENT ADDRESS AND EMAIL. As a courtesy, most programs will send you a notice when your miles are about to expire. If you've moved or if your email address has changed, that can't happen.

→ STAY ACTIVE. In order to prevent your miles from expiring, you don't have to fly or stay. Something as small as using your miles to order a magazine subscription or flowers can be enough to keep your account active.

Remember, miles and points *depreciate* over time. Loyalty programs are meant to reward current customers, so if you haven't flown with an airline or stayed at a hotel within the last three years, an expiration isn't just inevitable— it's something you probably deserve. Think about it. You're not really a loyal customer anymore, are you?

How do you recover your expired miles or points?

The discovery that your miles are gone is never a pleasant one. It's often followed immediately by a conversation with an airline or hotel representative. This person may tell you that you have no options and may prematurely disconnect the phone call—but you *do* have options.

→ **PAY TO RECOVER.** Some companies will let you "reactivate" your miles for a fee. If you've lost hundreds of thousands of miles, that might be an option. For only a few thousand miles, the fee will almost certainly be too high. Let the miles go.

→ **APPEAL YOUR CASE.** Although companies can be rigid in their denials, here are a few things that might persuade them: You're employed by a large company that does a lot of business with the airline or hotel; you've been between jobs but were otherwise an excellent customer; you didn't have an address at which you could be contacted. What doesn't work? Drama. Telling the company you're a single mom on a fixed income with a special needs kid, while it may be true, does little to persuade even the most soft-hearted manager. They've already heard every excuse in the book. Which is too bad.

When should you stop participating in a loyalty program?

In the same way you balance your checkbook or do your finances, you should also constantly assess your continuing participation in a loyalty program. You may be giving your business to the wrong company. The sooner you know, the sooner you can make a change in your spending habits.

→ **WHEN YOU STOP TRAVELING.** If you fly less than three times a year, rent fewer than three cars a year, or stay a week or less in a hotel, participating in a program might cost more than not participating (see more on negative value of miles—that's right, *negative* value—on page 93).

→ **WHEN YOU MOVE.** If you relocate away from a place where a company you used to patronize does business—say, away from an airline hub—then being a loyal traveler will have less value. It may still benefit the company you're being loyal to, because it will still get your money, even if it doesn't deserve it.

→ **WHEN YOU'VE RECEIVED POOR CUS-TOMER SERVICE.** If a company lets you down, you should first let that company know, politely, how disappointed you are and make it aware of the fact that you're a good customer. If that company still doesn't offer to make things right or at least do better, then there must be consequences. If you don't cut up your frequent flier card, you're giving the company a license to continue abusing other customers just like you. You owe it to other passengers and guests to quit.

PROBLEM SOLVED

POOF! THERE GO MY SKYMILES

QUESTION: I've been saving my Delta Air Lines frequent flier miles for many, many years to take my wife on a 20th anniversary trip this year. I received all of my statements by regular mail. A few months ago, I asked the airline for a PIN number so I could look at my account online, and when I logged in, I was shocked to see my balance at zero miles. I had—or at least I thought I had—101,000 miles.

It turns out that even though I used to have points with no expiration date, Delta had made changes to its program and because of inactivity on my account, my points were deleted late last year. A representative also told me that since Delta had gone "green" I hadn't received any account statements, which would have informed me of my expiration dates. We asked the airline to reinstate our miles, since we have stayed at Delta partner hotels in the last year, but it refused.

I feel like our dream anniversary plans have been shattered and I am devastated since I can't afford to buy plane tickets. To quote an old movie, "Help me Obi-Wan Kenobi, you're my only hope!" —Kenneth Miller, *Albuquerque, New Mexico*

ANSWER: Delta should have told you about your expiring miles. It was wrong to deny your request. It was also wrong to underestimate the Force. (Sorry, I just had to throw in another *Star Wars* line.)

You made incorrect assumptions about your frequent flier program. You believed the terms under which you began collecting loyalty points wouldn't change—that your miles would last forever—even though, like most other airline loyalty programs, Delta's SkyMiles program allows the airline to change its terms any time for any reason. If that sounds overly broad, if not a little unfair, that's because it probably is.

I can't blame you for thinking Delta would keep its word. It's like buying a knife set with a lifetime warranty, only to discover a few years later that the guarantee has been cut to two years. If you earned non-expiring miles, then common sense tells you the miles should never expire.

You probably could have done a couple of things to increase your chances of keeping your hard-earned miles, like giving the airline a current email address and handing over your SkyMiles number to the hotels where you stayed.

I contacted Delta on your behalf. I also forwarded receipts from your hotel stays to prove that technically, you had some activity on your account, even though you never received mileage credit for it. As a gesture of goodwill, and as an exception, Delta returned your miles.

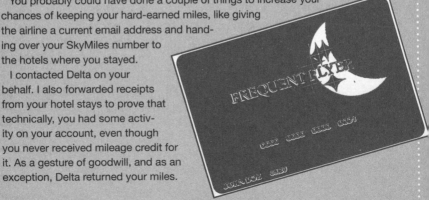

Do miles or points have a "negative" value?

I've already discussed the perceived value of a mile versus the real value, but as I've hinted, the truth is a little more complicated. Yes, a mile is almost certainly not worth $1, and probably not worth 1 cent. But did you know that many miles and points are worth less than zero?

This is one reason why loyalty programs are sometimes called the crack cocaine of the travel industry. You don't always make rational decisions when you're under the influence of a frequent flier program. You see platinum cards and upgrades and are willing to do whatever is necessary to earn a mile. Next time you're at the store, fumbling for that platinum credit card, ask yourself: Would I buy this if I wasn't earning points?

This remarkable ability to short-circuit your common sense is why loyalty programs are ridiculously profitable to most travel companies. They know you'll ignore the better deal on an airfare, a hotel chain with superior customer service, or the rental car with more bells and whistles, in exchange for a chance to get treated a little better on your next trip or for a "free" ticket.

For those customers, loyalty programs have a negative value because you're paying more and in exchange for an often empty promise. You aren't always treated better, and you have to spend hundreds or thousands of extra dollars for the "free" ticket. In other words, the program is enticing you to book the wrong product. It's leading you astray. If you're wondering which group you're in, then you're probably among them; your miles are actually worth less than nothing.

And it's not harming just you. Over the long term, when enough travelers participate in these programs, it creates a deeply divided travel experience that has no place in the 21st century. It's a caste system in which a privileged few elite travelers sit in the front of the plane and are treated like gods, while the mere mortals sit in the steerage of economy class, where there's hardly enough room to move and everything costs extra. Thanks to the game, the rich get richer and the rest of us suffer.

How do I get credit retroactively for a flight, rental, or stay?

Sometimes it happens. You're on final approach to Sydney Airport after spending the better part of the day on a plane, and you say to yourself, "I should get credit for this flight!" Guess what? You can. Most airlines will allow you to receive credit for a flight retroactively if you join a loyalty program after your trip. Likewise, many hotels will be accommodating if you inquire about their loyalty program when you're checking out.

A few things to remember:

→ **KEEP YOUR ORIGINAL BOARD-**
ING PASS OR THE RECEIPT FOR YOUR

HOTEL STAY. That's proof you were there. Travel companies are notoriously lax when it comes to maintaining records of your previous business.

You don't always make rational decisions when you're under the influence of a frequent flier program.

→ **DON'T WAIT TOO LONG.** Travel companies have a cutoff for giving credit for your flight, rental, or stay. You'll want to apply to join a program within a month, and preferably within a week. Policies vary.

→ **DON'T ASSUME YOU'LL GET CREDIT.** Some kinds of discount airline tickets aren't eligible for mileage credit, and some hotel rooms booked through certain online travel agencies can't earn points. Ask the travel company if you're eligible.

What do I need to know about partner miles and points?

Just as airlines have codeshare partners (see Chapter 10) so, too, do loyalty programs. They can be confusing, to say the least. Companies will let you earn miles through a marketing partner, which allows you to accumulate mileage or points faster. Thanks to these partnerships, you can also redeem miles through a variety of partners—so you can earn miles through an airline, but redeem them on a hotel stay.

Partnerships are so complex and change so quickly that anything I write would be obsolete by the time it hit your e-reader or bookshelf, but it helps to know a few things they won't tell you about.

→ **THE PARTNERSHIPS CAN CHANGE AT ANY TIME, FOR ANY REASON.** They don't have to tell you about changes—and they often don't bother. This can lead to an award stay being canceled because a partnership was terminated, and because you signed the program agreement, you have few if any options.

→ **THE PARTNERSHIPS ARE THERE PRIMARILY TO BENEFIT THE COMPANIES, NOT YOU.** Partnerships are presented as a "win" for you, and as a service being performed by your travel company. Basically, it appears as if the company is selflessly trying to help its customers make the most of their miles and points. In fact, it is shrewdly trying to maximize the value of its own program to shareholders. Don't be fooled. They're not doing this for you as much as they're doing it *to* you.

→ **IF SOMETHING GOES WRONG, PREPARE FOR A GAME OF FINGER-POINTING.** Just as airline codesharing agreements offer an opportunity for a carrier to play "pass the buck" with a partner, so also mileage partnerships allow a company to bounce you around between it and a partner. This can be maddening. You're almost better off paying one company for your flight or stay and dealing with it directly.

Many programs allow you to move miles from one partner to another, but the conversion rate is often terrible. Again, in 99 out of 100 cases, simply buying the product outright is a smarter move than trying to redeem points for miles or vice versa.

What to do when you quit?

Leaving a program is easier said than done. If you're a valuable customer, the company might try to lure you back. And there are all those miles to think about!

→ **DONATE YOUR UNUSED MILES.** Many charities will accept your miles and points. Give them to a good cause.

→ **STATUS MATCH, IF YOU MUST.** If you're leaving a program but intend to continue traveling, consider asking a rival airline to match your status. You'll be granted the same status on that airline, so you don't have to start from scratch when you give up your old program.

→ **DON'T LOOK BACK.** Remember, nothing lasts forever. Even "lifetime" status doesn't last a lifetime. One hotel program famously ended a generous lifetime program for some of its customers several years ago. Although many guests complained, the program was well within its rights to do so. One airline even took away several benefits that were guaranteed in writing for life to million-mile fliers. How did they rationalize it? The airline had recently reincorporated and it claimed the benefits were only guaranteed for the life of the corporation, not of the customer. And the corporation no longer existed. Pretty clever, huh?

It's only a matter of time before loyalty programs are widely recognized as the habit-forming hobby that they are, capable of blinding legions of otherwise intelligent travelers. For most people, participating in a program can be costly and unrewarding. Don't be a sucker.

BOTTOM LINE
Loyalty programs reward a travel company's best customers, but for the rest of us, collecting miles and points is a dangerous game. Because travel companies are allowed to make the rules and then change them as they go along, the house is always guaranteed to win. Unless you're constantly reevaluating your loyalties, you're probably giving your business to the wrong travel company. Pay close attention to how you're spending your money and know that the deck is probably stacked against you, and you'll come out on top.

PART TWO: GETTING THERE

8

Rent a Car

Getting the perfect wheels for your next vacation without losing your shirt.

A rental car can offer freedom of movement when you're on vacation. Or it can needlessly add to the expense of a trip and insert a layer of worry. And there's *lots* to worry about, as you'll see—everything from additional fees to frivolous damage claims—owing to a car rental industry that's sometimes on a push to squeeze every penny out of you. I'll help you steer clear of these road hazards.

When to rent:

→ WHEN THE ONLY WAY TO REACH YOUR DESTINATION IS BY CAR. That's the main reason people rent vehicles in the United States—there's just no other way to get there. Many metropolitan neighborhoods aren't served by mass transit, and if you're visiting someone in the suburbs, you really have no choice.

→ IF YOU NEED THE FLEXIBILITY AND FREEDOM OF HAVING YOUR OWN SET OF WHEELS. Bus and train schedules aren't always convenient. A car is

→ IF YOU NEED TO TRANSPORT MORE THAN JUST PASSENGERS. Mass transit isn't suited to passengers with two or more pieces of luggage, let alone a business traveler with a box of product samples to give away at a convention.

When to skip a rental:

→ WHEN YOU COULD GET THERE SAFELY AND CONVENIENTLY BY MASS TRANSIT. You could save a substantial amount of money (and the environment) by forfeiting a rental vehicle on your next trip.

→ WHEN EVERYONE ELSE IS DRIVING ON THE OTHER SIDE. A warning to anyone visiting a country where they drive on the left side of the road, including Australia, parts of Africa and Asia, India, and the United Kingdom: You're asking for trouble. Also, you may want to skip a rental in a country in which you don't speak the language or can't read the signs.

→ IF YOU'RE OF A CERTAIN AGE. Many car rental companies won't rent to you if you're younger than 25, and virtually all of them refuse to hand you the keys to a car if you're younger than 21. The most common exception is if you are renting the car for work and you're covered under your employer's insurance policy. By the way, there is such a thing as too old. American car rental companies normally don't have published age limits, but many European countries do (it's usually around 70). Check before you rent overseas.

→ IF YOU'VE HAD SEVERAL MOVING VIOLATIONS. Sometimes your driver's license will be checked against a Department of Motor Vehicles database

when you rent. If you're flagged, you might not be able to rent a car. A car rental company may also turn you down if you've damaged a rental car in the past and didn't pay for the repairs.

→ **IF YOU DON'T HAVE A CREDIT CARD.** Many car rental companies (but not all of them) will refuse to rent a car to you without a credit card. Credit cards allow the rental company to pre-authorize a certain amount for the rental and also for so-called "late" charges (billing you after you've returned the car) if you've damaged the vehicle. If you use a debit card, the rental company will place a hold of $200 or more on the account linked to your card. Think of it as a deposit that's held until you return the vehicle.

→ **IF YOU'RE JUST PLANNING TO STAY AT A HOTEL AND THERE'S A FREE VAN SERVICE TO AND FROM THE AIR-PORT.** Take some of these situations into account the next time you're planning your ground transportation arrangements. You may find that you don't need a rental car for your entire visit—or at all.

Where should I book my car?
Here are your options:

→ **ASK YOUR TRAVEL AGENT.** If you're

Car rental companies offer vehicle classes ranging from subcompact to luxury.

uncomfortable booking online or don't rent cars often, this is your best choice. Bear in mind that agents get paid a commission on rentals, so they may steer you toward a company that pays a higher commission or bonus. That doesn't necessarily mean it's a bad deal for you.

→ **BOOK DIRECTLY.** If you are partial to one brand, you'll probably want to go straight to the car rental company's website or call its 1-800 number. Car rental companies will offer bonuses and other incentives to you for dealing directly with them. You can also negotiate a discount using many membership organizations, such as AAA or AARP. The downside? You won't be able to easily compare rates and, unless you're careful, you might book a nonrefundable rate.

→ **USE AN ONLINE TRAVEL AGENCY.** Companies like Expedia, Orbitz, and Travelocity offer virtually every major car rental brand. Smaller, focused companies like *CarRentals.com* often offer particularly good deals. Note that as with full-service agencies, online agents sometimes display the cars that pay them the highest commissions or exclude the companies that pay a lower commission.

→ **VIA OPAQUE SITES.** Sites like Priceline and Hotwire sell you prepaid, deeply discounted rentals, but you don't find out the name of the car rental company until you book the car. The benefit? You can save between 20 and 40 percent, and the voucher you receive includes all mandatory taxes and fees. But there's a catch: The car is totally nonrefundable.

→ **GO LOCAL.** You'll have to do an Internet search for local car rental companies in the area you'll be staying in, and if you're coming from the airport, transportation to the car rental company can be a hassle. You may be put into an older rental unit too—so be sure to ask questions over the phone to establish the local rental company's modus operandi.

No matter how you book your car, you'll want to double-check the dates of your rental and the location before pulling the trigger on a rental vehicle. If you're using an opaque site, it may be difficult, if not impossible, to modify your reservation. Above all, read the confirmation you get by email. The last thing you want is to discover a problem on the day of your trip.

What about vehicle classes?

Car rental companies offer vehicle classes ranging from subcompact to luxury. These designations are about as meaningful as the star ratings used to grade hotels, which is to say you shouldn't give them too much weight. Your car rental agreement usually doesn't guarantee an exact car type. One car may be considered a "compact" by one company and "midsize" by another. Why? Because the car rental company says so, that's why!

Rental customers typically use one of several strategies to book the best car.

→ **RESERVE THE CAR CLASS YOU THINK YOU'LL NEED.** Most drivers do this—they take an inventory of number of passengers, luggage, and itinerary, and then book the vehicle that's best suited to them. It's a safe strategy.

→ **BOOK THE SMALLEST CAR AND HOPE THEY RUN OUT.** It's an open secret that car rental companies often run out of subcompacts because they're

Sedro-Woolley Public Library

NOT SMART MAKING DUPLICATE RESERVATIONS.

Since you can make as many reservations as you want and then cancel them without a penalty, you could play one car rental company off another. I know of some frequent business travelers who will always make a "backup" reservation just in case they can't get the car they want or in case the company runs out of vehicles. Not only does that mess up the car rental company's inventory management, but it is selfish to take more than you'll use—particularly if you're doing it just to see which rental agent will offer you the most favorable terms or upgrade.

so popular (or maybe because this strategy is so popular). The accepted industry practice is to give you a car in the next available class, which can mean a free upgrade for you. This is a risky move if you have more than two passengers and lots of luggage because the car rental company *could* have the vehicle you reserved. Worst case scenario, they'll see you need a bigger car and you'll pay for the car class you should have booked anyway.

→ A NOTE ABOUT SPECIALTY VEHICLES:

If you need something that's not on the menu on the company's website, don't assume that it's unavailable. Get the name of the location manager and call at least a week before your rental date. Ask what types of minivans, SUVs, or trucks they have in their fleet.

What about fees?

Fees are a never-ending source of frustration to travelers. A one-day rental at Orlando International Airport, for instance, included the following gems:

Energy Recovery Fee: 60 cents per day
Florida Surcharge: $2 per day
Waste Tire/Battery Fee: 2 cents per day
Vehicle License Fee: 78 cents per day
Customer Facility Fee: $2.50 per day
Concession Fee: 10 percent
And, of course, tax—to the tune of 6.5 percent.

Pretty complicated, huh? At first glance, perhaps.

Let's break it down. The *base rate* is a theoretical price, minus taxes, fees, and rental options. No one ever pays the base rate, but the car rental company wants you to see it because it makes the rental look less expensive. The number you'll want to pay attention to is the *estimated total*.

You can't negotiate your way out of the mandatory taxes and surcharges that are added on. For example, if there's an airport surcharge—which covers the car rental company's cost of operating at the airport—the only way to avoid it is by renting at an off-airport location.

Some of these fees are imposed by local municipalities, the airport, or the

SMART CONSIDER CAR SHARING.

If you need a car only for a day or less, you might want to consider a short-term car rental, available through car sharing or a car club. Companies such as Zipcar *(zipcar.com)* and Enterprise CarShare *(enterprisecarshare.com)* are commonly found in large cities. Joining one of these clubs is fairly quick and requires a valid credit card and driver's license.

state, and yes, they often fund stadiums and convention centers and all other manner of pet projects.

Note that fuel-purchase options are not part of this quote. They're optional, and you'll have to settle on them when you pick up the vehicle. More on that in a moment.

You can also add any number of optional services to your bill. These are daily charges. They might include:

Rental Options
GPS Navigation: $11.95
Roadside SafetyNet (RSN): $5.99
XM Radio: $4.99
Toll Tags: $2.95

Protections—Coverages
Loss Damage Waiver (LDW): $26.99
Personal Accident Insurance (PAI): $4.00
Personal Effects Protection (PEP): $2.95
Additional Liability Insurance (ALI): $14.43

Note that saying "yes" to all of these choices will more than double the daily rate of your car—and again, we haven't even added the fuel-purchase option or a charge for an additional driver, which some car rental companies will add.

The first set of options is more or less self-explanatory. If you need a navigation system or a SiriusXM radio, here's a chance to rent it. You can also get the equivalent of "OnStar" for roadside service, although the car rental company will also have a 24-hour, toll-free number you can call if you are in trouble. These are somewhat profitable

add-ons for the company, and I would definitely think carefully before giving them the nod. For $5 a day, you could buy a lot of new music for your iPod and simply play it through the car's stereo. Also, many phones now have navigational system apps, and don't forget the old-fashioned paper maps, which your car rental company should offer at no extra charge. When it comes to toll tags, read the deal on offer carefully: Some toll tagging systems bill you by the day once you start using them, whether you use a toll road or not. That's not exactly a bargain if your car is parked in a hotel lot most of the time.

The second set of options (protections) is not as obvious. Car rental companies offer several insurance options. You absolutely have to think about insurance before you arrive at the counter. If you don't, you may buy too much insurance, or worse, not enough.

What other add-on fees might I expect?

→ **THE FUEL PURCHASE OPTION.** This comes in several flavors, from prepaying for a tank of gas, to paying after you return for the fuel you consume, to topping off the tank yourself before you bring back the car. If you choose the latter option, keep your gas station receipt—you may have to show it as proof you refueled within a certain mileage radius of the rental location. The first and second option may work for you if you're in a hurry or on

PROBLEM SOLVED

A $481 BILL FOR DAMAGE I DIDN'T DO?

QUESTION: I'm trying to resolve an issue with Alamo and have not been able to communicate directly with anyone in the claims department. Now, they're threatening collections and legal action. I'm in the process of buying a house and can't afford a ding on my credit rating.

I rented a car from Alamo in San Francisco for three days. There was no attendant to assist me in the dimly lighted parking lot. I walked around the car for a visual inspection, noticed that it was slightly dirty in front, but I saw no dents or dings. I considered having them run it through the car wash again, but I had an appointment to get to.

I drove the car 81 miles during the weekend rental period. I parked carefully, pulling in facing a wall or building. No one could have impacted the car from the front during the time it was parked, which was most of the rental period. When I drove it, I didn't run over or hit anything.

When I returned it to the airport, the agent walked toward the car from the front and said, "What did you hit with the car?" I thought he was joking. He pointed out what appeared to be a crack in the lower portion of the front grill. I didn't see it right away—I had to get down low to view it. It would have been easily missed in the parking garage when I picked it up.

I disputed the damage on the spot, telling him I didn't hit a thing and that this damage had to have been preexisting, but I received a letter from Alamo's damage recovery unit for $481. Can you help? —Mary Dampier, *Coronado, California*

ANSWER: Alamo should have given you the keys to a clean car and offered to inspect it before you left the airport.

Always ask an employee to walk around the vehicle, noting even minor damage. If no one is available to do that, then you should make a notation of the damage and ask an employee to acknowledge the car's condition before you leave. Always take pictures of your rental car with a cell phone or digital camera.

I reviewed the correspondence with Alamo and the photos of the car you were alleged to have damaged. I posted the pictures, along with the letters, on my website and asked readers for their feedback. They noted several problems with your rental, including the amount of the damage claim (which was suspiciously close to your $500 insurance deductible) and evidence that the damage shown in the photographs wasn't from your vehicle.

Although Alamo's parent company, Enterprise Holdings, insists that damage claims such as yours are not a moneymaking scheme, stories like yours do make customers wonder. If Alamo was really concerned about the state of its cars, it would vigilantly photograph the vehicles before every rental and conduct a thorough inspection—not wait until the end to point out every little ding, dent, and scratch.

I contacted Alamo on your behalf. It dropped its claim.

an expense account; otherwise, go for door #3. Car rental companies will probably make money off of any fuel purchase option unless you return the tank bone dry.

What types of rental insurance are available?

Let's have a closer look at each type of insurance.

→ **LOSS DAMAGE WAIVER (LDW).** This is your basic insurance, and it normally covers the loss of the vehicle or damage to it, and any loss of use to the rental company. A related kind of insurance, Collision Damage Waiver (CDW), is more limited, covering the car, but not injuries or damage to other property.

→ **PERSONAL ACCIDENT INSURANCE (PAI).** Covers you and the passengers in your car if you're injured in an accident.

→ **PERSONAL EFFECTS PROTECTION (PEP).** Insures the property in the car up to a certain amount.

→ **ADDITIONAL LIABILITY INSURANCE**
(ALI). Extra protection that covers everything from bodily injury to death to property damage.

Note that the names of these insurance policies may vary based on which company you rent from.

How do I decide which policy to buy?

You need to understand a few things about car rental insurance before you buy. Some of these policies make perfect sense for you and are a good deal. Others are overpriced and unnecessary. Which is which? It depends on where you're renting and who you are.

Normally, you'll have enough coverage between your car insurance and credit card, but watch out—if you're renting a specialty vehicle like a van or SUV, or if you're renting outside the country, your policy may not apply. (Israel, Ireland, and Jamaica rentals are not covered by most major credit cards, and you'll need to purchase a separate policy when you rent a car.) Read your policy and card member agreement carefully *before* you rent. Remember, your credit card or car

NOT SMART
DON'T TAKE CHANCES WITH CAR RENTAL INSURANCE.

Don't drive a car without insurance. Ever. I shouldn't have to tell you that, but here's the sad reality: If you have no insurance and anything happens to a rental vehicle while it's in your possession, you're responsible. And yes, car rental companies won't hesitate to ask you to pay for a new car if you total one of theirs.

rental insurance may or may not cover all of the damage to a rental car. Make sure you know.

Above all, try to avoid having to make up your mind at the counter. Car rental agents are trained to sell you insurance and other extras. They are not travel agents; they're often evaluated based on how much insurance and other add-ons they can sell you when you pick up the car. You won't be able to avoid the pitch, but you can manage it.

Don't forget to read before you sign on the dotted line

Make sure the options you asked for are on the final contract you sign. Some car rental employees have been known to "accidentally" check the option for insurance, and if you sign the contract accepting it, you will be charged the full amount, and there's usually no way to get the money back. Electronic signature pads, which may or may not display your contract clearly before you sign, have made this even trickier. Only the most ethically challenged rental agents do it, but in the end you are responsible for what you've signed. If you don't

understand the contract (or if it's in another language), ask an employee to explain. If you're uncomfortable with anything at all, don't sign. Take your business elsewhere.

WHAT SHOULD I DO BEFORE I DRIVE AWAY?

Many car rental problems can be avoided by taking a few precautionary steps.

Do you know how to operate the car?

Car rental companies are now offering everything from electric vehicles to hybrids to Smart Cars (microcars), and they don't operate the same way that standard gas-operated cars do. (Don't believe me? Try starting a Toyota Prius without first reading the manual. Go on. I'll wait.) This is the time to ask. Car rental employees are trained to help you get acquainted with your car. This is especially important if you're switching from a left-hand to right-hand drive vehicle, where many of the switches are reversed. At the very least, check your glove compartment to make sure

SMART MAKE YOUR DECISION *BEFORE* YOU ARRIVE AT THE CAR RENTAL COUNTER.

Review your personal car insurance policy, credit card, and travel insurance before you leave to see if your rental car is covered. Also, if you're renting outside the United States, be sure that you are meeting that country's insurance requirements—otherwise, you may be forced to buy insurance. Bottom line: Know *before* you go.

the manual is there. You'll be glad you did.

Are you ready for your close-up?

You *must* photograph or videotape every rental car before you leave. I'm not joking. Most car rental companies do not adequately document the condition of your vehicle, and only a small fraction take photos of your car before you rent it. Whip out your digital camera or smartphone and get to work. At a bare minimum, you need shots of the front, back, and sides of the car. I would recommend two close-up shots of each side, the front and rear windshield, the front and rear of the car, and the roof. Don't forget the interior: the dashboard, front seats, back seats, and trunk. If you want to be extra careful, take snapshots of the whole and under the two bumpers. Believe it or not, motorists have been billed for damage that can't be seen by the naked eye at the time of the rental. You can't be too careful.

If you're in a garage with low light, drive the car somewhere in the parking area that's well lighted to conduct your visual inspection. Do not leave without taking these pictures. Repeat: Do not allow yourself to feel rushed and leave.

By the way, if you are videotaping, hold the camera steady and make sure it's set to the highest resolution. If you're shooting still images and you have the option to timestamp the photos, make sure that feature is activated on your camera. It is impossible to over-photograph or over-videotape the vehicle.

Download your photos and/or email them to yourself or upload them into an Internet-based storage feature (the Cloud) for safekeeping. How long should you keep these photos? At least six months after your rental ends. That's the longest I've seen a car rental company wait to file a damage claim. After that, feel free to delete these files.

Your car rental company should furnish you with a form on which you can note the condition of the vehicle. The form allows you to identify any problems you notice on a diagram of a car. Record any preexisting damage on this form and make sure a car rental employee signs it. Don't, under any circumstances, leave without a copy of the signed form.

What if you see a ding, dent, or crack?

If you spot a scratch or dent while you're photographing the vehicle, inform an attendant right away. You will either need to document the damage in writing or ask for a different vehicle. Don't let anyone tell you that a dent or scratch "the size of a golf ball or smaller" doesn't count. *Everything* counts. If the car isn't clean and free of large dents, you need to ask for another one. Not because you're being picky, but because you could be held accountable for those dents later on. Also, scratches and other imperfections are difficult to see when the car isn't clean. If you need to accept a flawed vehicle, be extra vigilant about noting the damage on your form. And again, make sure an employee signs off on it, noting every ding, dent, and scratch.

Other reasons to reject your rental:

• It's not the car you reserved, as stated on the contract.
• It appears unsafe to drive (balding tires, malfunctioning lights).
• The registration has expired, or will expire during your rental (don't forget to check).
• It has high mileage (more than 50,000 miles).
• It has a chipped windshield. You should have zero tolerance for anything irregular on the front or back windshield.
• It's the wrong color. (I'm kidding.)

After driving off the lot, don't be afraid to return if you feel the car is not working properly.

How about the sign-off?

Before you leave the airport car rental lot, you'll usually pass through a checkpoint where your rental agreement and driver's license will be checked by an employee. So, don't put those away just yet. (I leave them on the seat next to me, for easy access.) This last check is yet another opportunity to make sure your car is what it should be. Don't be shy about getting out of the car, walking around it, and mentioning to the employee if something looks wrong. Remember, this is your last chance.

These procedures will vary if you're renting from a non-airport location. For example, there may not be a gate, and pick-ups and returns—which I'll cover later—may be handled differently, but the same principles apply: Make sure you photograph your vehicle, document any damage, and know how to operate the car.

THE RETURN

The vast majority of disputed car rental damage claims happen because of little dings and dents that no one noticed before you drove off the lot. Maybe you were parked at the mall, and the SUV next to you put a little nick in your

---

👍 SMART SNAP BETTER RENTAL PICS.

Try an iPhone or Android app called **Rental Pics**, which creates a file containing all the pictures associated with each rental and allows you to make any damage notations that would support the photographic record you're making. The images are date- and time-stamped, plus they're geo-tagged—the location is recorded. A built-in email feature offers a simple way to forward a file should the need arise in the future.

side panel when the driver opened his door. The trick is to identify any minor damage when you return your set of wheels to the rental location.

What steps should I take to protect myself when I review my car?

You'll want to give yourself ten extra minutes to walk through the steps I'm outlining here. Believe me, they're worth it.

→ FIND A BRIGHT SPACE, PREFERABLY OUT IN THE OPEN. Whip out your camera and photograph the inside and the outside of the vehicle. Take as many images as possible. Note any dings, dents, or scratches. Pay close attention to the windshield; those are the number one source of damage claims.

→ ASK THE CAR RENTAL EMPLOYEE HANDLING YOUR RETURN TO WALK AROUND THE CAR WITH YOU. She will often be busy (tell her you can wait), or totally unavailable (see the next step). Walk around the car with the form you filled out when you rented the car, and then ask the employee to sign the form or give you something else in writing verifying the car's condition, in detail. If the employee says a printed receipt is sufficient, then at least note the name of the worker who assured you the receipt was sufficient. You may need it later, if it comes to a dispute.

→ IF NO ONE IS AVAILABLE, GO INSIDE. Ask for the name and email address of the branch manager, and send the manager a brief email with your name, rental number, and a few snapshots of the car as you returned it. Is that overkill? No, and especially not if you are using your own insurance, as opposed to the optional Collision Damage Waiver offered by the rental company. It signals to the rental location that filing a frivolous claim against you will be difficult.

→ KEEP YOUR PHOTOS, VIDEO, RECEIPTS, AND SIGNED DOCUMENTS FOR AT LEAST SIX MONTHS. That's how long it could take the claims process.

YOU'VE PUT A DENT IN YOUR RENTAL VEHICLE. NOW WHAT?

I've damaged a rental car (sorry, Hertz), and I've been through all the steps, but I've also helped many others, some of whom were unjustly accused of roughing up their rental.

This is a hugely controversial issue. Car rental companies are faced with hundreds of millions of dollars in damage expenses every year, and the companies say they are just pursuing the customers who harm their vehicles. Many travelers believe car rental companies are profiting from damage claims, insisting that scratches or dents for which they were charged were either preexisting or completely fictional.

Handling the dreaded claim

Let's go through the steps of a claim.

First, let's assume that the damage isn't major, which is to say, you didn't total the car. (If the car is not drivable, you'll want to call the company right away. The claims process in this situation is pretty straightforward because no one is questioning the damage.)

→ **IDEALLY, THE CAR RENTAL CLAIMS PROCESS WILL START WHEN YOU RETURN A DAMAGED VEHICLE.** An employee will ask you to fill out a claim form in which you acknowledge the damage and explicitly agree to pay for it. Recently, some rental companies have begun charging a renter's credit card a deductible even when there's been no formal damage estimate. I'm skeptical of that practice. While it may be legal, I think you're better off waiting for a bill before paying up or asking your insurance to settle the claim.

If you purchased the optional insurance, you're all done, and you shouldn't have to worry about anything else. If you're using your own insurance or, God forbid, you're not insured, you're not out of the woods yet. You're going to have to deal with your car insurance or credit card quickly (there's a time limit on filing a claim), and then negotiate with

the car rental company or an outside company that specializes in damage claims (often referred to as a *subrogation management company*).

→ **THE CLAIM BY MAIL** In some cases, a car rental company will discover damage to a vehicle after you've returned your car. If you've gone through the process of photographing your car and getting a sign-off from a real person, then this is a nonissue. Simply send your extensive documentation back to the claims department, and your case will be closed.

If you think there's a chance the car was damaged while you had it, and a car rental company can show you credible documentation to that effect, then I would urge you to accept responsibility for the bill. Car rental customers sometimes say they shouldn't be held responsible if they were not at fault in an accident or fender bender. That's incorrect. If the car was damaged while you had it, you have to pay for the repair.

What if you forgot to take pictures and simply dashed off to the airport terminal? (Hey, it happens.) Well, there's a way out of that, too.

→ **FIRST, THE BAD NEWS.** You'll get an email or letter from either the car rental company or a claims management company, alerting you to the damage. This can be unsettling because it often doesn't contain many details—it only informs you of the problem and may ask for your credit card information and your insurance information.

PROBLEM SOLVED

BROADSIDED BY MANDATORY CAR RENTAL INSURANCE

QUESTION: Recently, we booked a Budget rental car in Israel, through Expedia. When my father arrived in Tel Aviv to collect his car, Budget would not give him the vehicle without mandatory theft protection and Collision Damage Waiver. Since the policies are mandatory, shouldn't they have been included in Expedia's prices?

We had two other bookings through Expedia and Budget, which we tried to cancel. We couldn't (Expedia said we had an incorrect reservation number).

We decided to go ahead and book through Budget directly, thinking it would be sorted out at the time of car hire collection. Big mistake. We were unfortunate enough to meet one of the rudest individuals I have encountered at the Budget car rental counter, and he refused to honor the direct booking with Budget, only honoring the much more expensive, Expedia one.

Can you help us? —Marissa Barashi, *Roselle, New Jersey*

ANSWER: Expedia should have quoted an all-inclusive rate when you booked your car. When it became clear that it didn't, a quick call to the online agency should have fixed the problem.

Why? Because Expedia's wide-ranging "promise" says it will help, guaranteeing that, "Whether you have questions about your itinerary or need help resolving a problem with the trip you booked, we're here to help 24 hours a day, seven days a week."

The online agency should have been able to retrieve your reservation through your full name, address, or email. I have no idea what went wrong, but it's pretty clear that Expedia didn't keep its promise.

Some countries—and Israel is one of them—have mandatory insurance requirements. Those should have been noted when you made your reservation through Expedia. I checked the site after bringing your case to the company's attention, and the insurance requirements are not disclosed until you click on the fine print, under "certain conditional charges."

Expedia can do better.

Budget shares some of the blame for your negative car rental experience. The rude employee you dealt with should have been more understanding of the situation, and at least honored the less expensive reservation. If you're ever in a situation like that again, try appealing to a manager or phoning the corporate office to make your case.

In the end, this problem could have been averted if Expedia had given you an all-in rate on the rental. Which is to say, insurance is required, and here's the actual rate you'll have to pay.

I contacted Expedia. The company agreed to reimburse you for the additional cost of the mandatory insurance you were required to buy. It also reviewed the details of your rental with Budget and threw in a $100 coupon by way of apology.

→ **HERE'S THE PROOF.** The message will be followed by an email or letter that contains photos of the damaged car and an estimate of the repair. It could also contain two fees unrelated to the repair: *loss of use* and *diminishment of value*. These fees are exactly what they say: 1. An estimate of how many days the car will be out of commission and the average daily rate it might have earned. 2. An estimate of how much less the car is worth now that it's been banged up. Read everything carefully. Make sure the license plate matches the plate on your rental and that it's the same car. (Sometimes, it doesn't.)

→ **PAY UP . . . OR ELSE.** If you don't respond to the first or second letter, the car rental company will threaten to refer your case to a collections agency. This is probably the last time you'll hear from the agency, and it is your final opportunity to come to an agreement. By the way, if you fail to respond, you won't just have a collections agency harassing you—you may also be blacklisted from renting from the rental car agency again.

Strategies for disputing a claim

Again, assuming you are absolutely certain that you returned your car undamaged, here are the steps.

→ **POLITELY TELL THEM YOU DIDN'T DO IT.** This should be done in writing, not by phone. Resist the urge to get an immediate resolution. The process takes time. Be as detailed as you can in your explanation, but keep your initial letter tight. Most of these rebuttals are rejected, but all the same, they are a necessary part of the claims process, and you'll need to get your denial on the record.

→ **AFTER THE DENIAL, SEND A MORE STRONGLY WORDED EMAIL TO THE CAR RENTAL COMPANY,** restating your position. Copy your insurance company. By now, you should have received a repair estimate. Feel free to challenge some of the items, including loss of use and diminishment charges, which can be as inflated as your repair bill. With a little prodding, I've seen these charges lowered or deleted.

→ **IF THAT DOESN'T WORK, APPEAL TO A MANAGER,** a customer service vice president, or the CEO. This is a good time to loop in your attorney, if you have one, and the insurance commissioner in the state in which the car was rented. I've spoken with damage claim companies who say that if it gets to this point and the damage is less than $500, they will drop the claim as a matter of policy. If none of those strategies work, call me.

Is this a scam?

Your scam radar should be on full alert if you see any of the following:

→ **A CLAIM THAT'S A FEW DOLLARS SHORT OF $500, WHICH IS THE STAN-DARD CAR INSURANCE DEDUCTIBLE.** This may be a sign that the car rental company is trying to ding you for a trumped-up damage claim. It doesn't want to go over $500 and invite the scrutiny of an insurance company.

→ **A DAMAGE CLAIM FOR NORMAL WEAR AND TEAR.** If an essential part of the car stopped working on your watch and it was due to a maintenance problem, then it's not your fault. A car rental company is responsible for changing the oil in its cars and keeping the fluid levels where they ought to be.

→ **DAMAGE TO A PART OF THE CAR THAT IS UNSEEN TO A NORMAL PERSON.** That would include the roof and the undercarriage. Almost no one checks the roof before they rent a car, and no one crawls under the car. It's really their word against yours.

→ **A CLEANING FEE FOR SMOKING OR PETS**—especially if you don't smoke or didn't bring your dog or cat on your trip.

Can you ask for an independent review of your repair bill?

Generally, the answer is no. Car rental companies can't be bothered with getting a second opinion when they're processing thousands of claims, but that shouldn't stop you from questioning the bill or doing your own research in order to determine if you're being billed the right amount.

WHAT ABOUT MOVING VIOLATIONS?

If you've run through a tollbooth or a red light, there's nothing you can do. Your car rental company will forward the paperwork to you, and in many cases it will furnish you with photos that establish your guilt. At the very least, it should document the time and place of the alleged violation. Review this information carefully. I've dealt with many tickets where the driver was out of state and couldn't have possibly run the red light, or where the wrong car was billed for a moving violation.

BOTTOM LINE

If you rent a car while you're on vacation, treat it as if it's your own. Read your rental contract, carry enough insurance, drive it carefully, and don't forget: Your car loves to be photographed before *and* after your rental. Happy trails!

9

Take a Road Trip

Navigating the world of car trips, buses, and trains—and getting to your destination safely.

When it comes to travel, ground transportation rules. The automobile remains the preeminent way to reach your vacation destination in the United States. The great American road trip is all but fused into our national DNA. On some trips, notably California's Highway One and historical Route 66, to *not* drive would seem almost, well, unpatriotic. In most of Europe, trains are the preferred way to travel, and in other parts of the world, everyone goes by bus. But the road ahead can be full of unexpected hazards. I'll help you avoid them.

Take the car:

→ **IF IT'S A SHORT TRIP,** usually less than 200 miles.

→ **IF NO MASS TRANSIT IS AVAILABLE** (I'll discuss mass transit later in this chapter).

→ **IF YOU HAVE THE TIME** and want the freedom to explore off the beaten path.

→ **IF YOU ARE TRAVELING WITH TWO OR MORE FRIENDS** or family members with the same agenda.

→ **IF YOU NEED THE MOBILITY OF A CAR** at your destination and can't afford to rent one.

Consider leaving the car at home:

→ **FOR POINT-TO-POINT TRAVEL** involving more than a day's worth of driving.

→ **IF THERE'S A REASONABLE MASS-TRANSIT ALTERNATIVE.**

→ **IF YOU'RE IN A HURRY.**

→ **IF YOU'RE VISITING A PLACE** where you don't need your own car or can rent one.

→ **IF THE AREA IS KNOWN** for bad traffic or bad driving.

CAR TRIPS

Many travel writers are enamored of things with wings and bored by road travel. You deserve better. The drive may turn out to be the most important part of your trip.

By the way, that's also true overseas. Sure, gas is ridiculously expensive in Europe and the tolls can be outrageous, but the sense of discovery and adventure is electric. If you're only planning on using a car to move

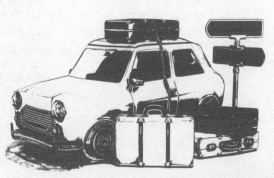

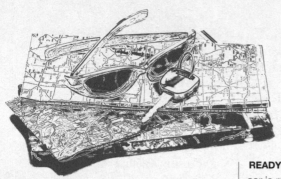

A high-mileage trip might push the mileage of your car above a certain threshold, and if you're trying to sell your vehicle it could cost you a lot more than just the gas.

→ **DO YOU DRIVE A ROAD TRIP–READY CAR?** Let's face it: Not every car is ready for a road trip. If you drive a vintage automobile and it happens to break down (as vintage cars are prone to do from time to time), good luck finding spare parts. A rental might be a better option. Plus, the air-conditioning will likely work every time.

→ **CAN I DEDUCT THIS?** If the trip is a business expense or if you're mixing business with pleasure, you'll want to figure out if you can deduct the rental or if it's better to use your own car. The Internal Revenue Service offers a helpful and exhaustive guide on mileage expenses (*irs.gov/publications/ p463/ch04.html*).

between major cities, a train might work best for you, but for a group of three travelers (and often even two travelers), a rental car is almost always a better deal.

Should I drive my own car or rent?

If you're going to take a domestic road trip, one of the first questions you'll want to answer is *whose* car? This may seem like a no-brainer—after all, all you have to pay for with your own car is the gas. Not so fast.

→ **IS YOUR VEHICLE SUITED TO THE ROAD CONDITIONS?** It's one thing to drive your car a few hours to see Grandma, but what if you're going skiing, or someplace where some of the roads are unpaved? A four-wheel-drive, if you don't already own one, may be a better vehicle, but if it's a rental, watch out—most rental contracts specifically forbid you from taking the vehicle off-roading. Ask before you go mudding.

→ **WOULD A LONGER ROAD TRIP DIMINISH THE VALUE OF YOUR CAR?**

Now that I'm on the road, how do I find the cheapest gas?

With a lot of research, you can find a gas station that charges a few pennies per gallon less, but how practical is that? Usually, the answer is "not at all." So, here are a few general tips that can be used to help you decide.

→ **GAS "APPS" ARE HELPFUL, BUT DON'T LET THEM RULE YOUR ITINERARY.** If you have a smartphone, an app like GasBuddy (gasbuddy.com) can help you track down a lower price, but you have to solve the cost-benefit equation of following the app to a remote gas station. I don't just mean the cost of the fuel to get to the cheaper gas station—I mean the cost of the time and effort to find the less expensive gas. Is it *really* worth it?

→ **IF YOU *REALLY* WANT TO SAVE ON GAS, DRIVE RIGHT.** Speeding can reduce your car's fuel efficiency, and so can improper maintenance, including under-inflated tires. If you really want to save on your fuel bill, drive your car correctly and responsibly.

→ **TYPICALLY, THE CLOSER TO THE AIRPORT, THE MORE EXPENSIVE THE GAS.** Fill up away from the airport. Gas prices are often higher near an airport, where desperate car rental customers try to refill their tanks before returning the car. Don't be a victim.

What's the half-tank rule?
If you're driving across the country east to west, the distance between gas stations grows and the opportunities to fill your tank shrink. My rule is that any time you're west of the Mississippi River, have less than half a tank of gas, and see an opportunity to refuel, take it. That's especially true if you're not traveling along a major interstate highway. You might run out of fuel if you disregard the half-tank rule.

How long should I drive?
If you're driving with someone else, I recommend driving no more than three hours at a time before switching, and no more than three three-hour shifts before resting for the night. That's a total of 18 hours on the road, which is enough to get you through a few time zones.

If you're driving solo, I wouldn't recommend anything more than two four-hour shifts separated by an hour-long break. That's a total of eight hours of driving before resting for the night. You can push it to 10 hours, but I wouldn't go beyond that. Anything beyond 12 hours and you're endangering the lives of your passengers, yourself, and your fellow motorists.

What's the best time of day to drive?
Actually, the question is, "What's the best time of night?" Unless you're driving somewhere to see the sights along the way, the best time to drive is during the night. That's especially true for weekends and holidays, when traffic can turn a three-hour drive into an all-day affair. The most trouble-free drive starts in the late evening after a power nap and extends to the early morning hours, just before rush hour. That's when you'll find a lot of the professionals on the road, too. If you require eight hours of sleep *at night,* this strategy isn't for you. It's not foolproof, either. Some roads are closed at night for construction, which means you could be waiting in traffic at 2 a.m.

Research the road conditions with an app like INRIX *(inrix.com)* or Waze *(waze.com)* to avoid problem areas.

How do I avoid speed traps?

Smartphone-based apps like Trapster *(trapster.com)* let you share the location of so-called "speed traps" with other motorists. You can also buy a radar detector (where legal) to detect highway patrol officers lurking around a corner, but the best way to avoid a speeding ticket is—wait for it!—to obey the traffic laws.

Do I need a AAA membership?

The American Automobile Association (AAA) offers maps, guidebooks, and emergency roadside assistance to its members. If you're planning more than one road trip in the upcoming year, the annual fee may be a worthwhile investment. (AAA also offers discounted insurance and other travel services.) A cautionary note or two about your membership: First, it's under *your* name, not your car. So, if

someone else is driving your car, it's not covered. And second, depending on where you are, AAA may take a while to reach you. I recently phoned AAA when I had a flat tire, and two hours later, with no sign of the tow, I managed to swap out the spare tire and get to the nearest garage.

When should I delay or cancel my road trip?

Any weather conditions that significantly impair visibility—snow, rain, or fog—should obviously make you think twice about starting or continuing your road trip if you are driving. There are other factors to consider, too.

→ **IFFY ROAD CONDITIONS.** Damaged or poorly maintained roads can make your trip a nightmare. Inclement weather, and particularly freak storms or hurricanes, can destroy roads and bridges. State transportation departments will update road conditions via a 511 telephone service or online, through their websites.

→ **TRAFFIC.** Almost every mapping app now has a built-in traffic function

SMART YOU MAY ALREADY HAVE ROADSIDE ASSISTANCE.

Some credit cards offer an emergency roadside services benefit, and car rental companies offer roadside assistance (but you often have to pay for it). So, if you don't own your own car and only take occasional road trips in a rental car, your credit card may be enough. Also, if you take out travel insurance, you may have some coverage. Check your policy before you invest in a membership.

that warns you when roads get congested. When you see the roads turn red with gridlock, you might want to either reroute or delay your trip. If you absolutely have to be there and you can't find a way around the traffic, consider mass transit.

Should I rely on GPS?

GPS (global positioning system) mapping applications for your smartphone use satellites to pinpoint your precise location. They can offer a convenient way to find your way around a new place. But don't depend on them. Gadgets can run out of batteries, and the latest mapping apps can also lead you astray, thanks to buggy coding. Experienced travelers may use a GPS system, but they always carry a map for redundancy.

Troubleshooting your drive

My readers almost never complain about their road trips. One possible reason is that their expectations are realistic. When a tire blows out, we don't ask Subaru to pay for a missed day of vacation. When we run out of gas, we have only ourselves to blame. Bad service at a rest area? We shrug it off, usually. Almost every potential problem you face while driving can be easily avoided with careful planning. Also, maintain your car properly. It's common sense, but for some drivers, it's easily forgotten or overlooked.

A warning about traffic tickets in Europe

Of all the recurring complaints I get from readers about road trips, the most vexing one is about traffic tickets in Europe, usually Italy. Tickets issued thanks to a traffic camera are received via your car rental company—months, and sometimes more than a year, after you return home. They're almost impossible for the average American visitor to decipher because they're in a foreign language and in legalese, to boot. There's no easy way to appeal them, through either a car rental company or the government, so most visitors pay up. The only way to avoid them is to obey all traffic laws carefully. What if you don't settle? I'm told it won't affect your ability to return to Italy, but it could affect your eligibility to rent another car from the company. (For more on car rental company blacklists, see the previous chapter on rental cars.) Why take chances?

ALL ABOARD!

Like car trips, travel by bus and train in the United States is the subject of relatively few complaints, at least in comparison to air travel. On some routes, Amtrak is the most efficient way, if not the cheapest, to get from one city center to another (Washington to New York being a prime example). Other routes (the California *Zephyr* from Chicago to San Francisco, for instance) slice through some of the continent's loveliest scenery. The *Auto Train*, between Lorton, Virginia, and Sanford,

PROBLEM SOLVED

NO REFUND FOR DERAILED AMTRAK TRIP

QUESTION: We recently traveled on Amtrak's California *Zephyr* from Chicago to Sacramento. It was not a good experience.

When we entered our sleeper room, it was readily apparent that the visual depiction on the Amtrak website was a gross exaggeration. The condition of the car was very poor.

We soon realized that the latch on the bathroom door had a problem. When my wife tried to operate the latch from inside the bathroom, she found that she was trapped. The door could only be opened from the outside.

We discussed this with the attendant, and she said she could move us to the only remaining sleeper room available. We decided that would be for the best but the new room was no better. The carpet was soaked. An attendant told us that a drink was spilled in that room and gave us towels to put on the floor as a second carpet. It didn't work too well. We had to keep our shoes on or suffer wet feet whenever we were in the room.

Both sleeper rooms were decrepit. They looked totally worn out and unclean. We were told when we booked that we would have to change cars in Denver, so we decided that we could suffer through one night.

Our bedroom in Denver was even worse. The stench inside the car was almost unbearable. I secured a hotel room for the night in Salt Lake City. I also booked a flight for the next day. When we arrived at Salt Lake City around midnight, we left the train and continued with our trip.

I've written to Amtrak, asking for a refund. It sent me two vouchers for $400. I want my money back. Can you help? —David Battas, *Indianapolis, Indiana*

ANSWER: Amtrak knows that the first-class service on its *Zephyr* needs work. Amtrak's refund policy on unused tickets can be found on its website. The company is technically right: Your accommodation charge wouldn't have been refundable in your situation since you canceled your trip less than seven days before your departure. There's no mention of partial refunds for passengers who disembark before the end of their trip.

That's beside the point. Amtrak promises a "more luxurious experience" on the *Zephyr,* which it calls "one of the most beautiful train trips in all of North America." Maybe it's just referring to the outdoor scenery.

Clearly, you were sold a bill of goods. Amtrak's terms don't apply because it breached its own contract, giving you a substandard product for your first-class fare. I think you're owed a full refund. I contacted Amtrak on your behalf, and it agreed. It refunded your entire train ticket.

Florida, transports both you and your vehicle to sunny Florida, offering a practical alternative to a tedious drive south on I-95.

Why travel by train in the United States? Maybe you like to take it slow. Maybe you don't like to fly. In Europe, however, the national train infrastructure tends to be considerably more robust and it is often heavily subsidized by the government. The train might be your first choice there, but do your research. Some low-cost airlines may offer a faster and cheaper way of reaching your destination.

Traveling with class

Bear in mind that there are various classes of service on Amtrak trains. Business class and coach service are available on most trains, but the high-speed *Acela Express,* which operates between Boston and Washington, D.C., has only business class and first class.

Paying more brings amenities such as additional legroom and complimentary food and beverage service. *Acela* is so fast and convenient that it competes against airlines in some markets, and in some cases it outperforms the plane. After all, when's the last time your airline dropped you off in downtown Manhattan or Washington?

As in the case of the corridor trains, overnight services usually stop in city centers, often with some scheduled suburban stops. But many routes also travel far from major roads or through remote areas where few people other than adventurers or mountain goats

tread. These trains have sleeping cars with compartments of various types and sizes, as well as reclining coach seats that may make airline or bus passengers envious. Meals and soft drinks in the dining car are included in the charge for the sleeping car accommodation, and coach passengers can use the dining car at menu prices, or buy snack bar–style food in the lounge car.

Amtrak makes almost all of its money in the northeastern United States, where it operates reasonably good facilities. Outside of the Northeast, Chicago, and Los Angeles, stations are usually modest—sometimes one-room buildings with no meaningful facilities. Amtrak's operations can reflect political whim. If politicians in a state want train service to the beach, they may get train service to the beach.

Most of the gripes about train travel in the United States focus on the infrastructure used by Amtrak, which it sometimes doesn't own, or on slow service. These are difficult to address from a customer service point of view. Amtrak typically doesn't offer refunds when amenities don't meet expectations, or when a train is late, but you do have some significant passenger rights.

Troubleshooting your train trip

Although Amtrak publishes its terms of transportation online *(amtrak.com/ terms-of-transportation),* you need to review its full set of policies in order to understand your rights *(amtrak.com/policies)*. Let's review the highlights.

→ BAGS RIDE ALMOST FREE. You can carry two small bags and check up to four bags (the first two at no additional charge) on Amtrak. Some trains allow no checked luggage, however. Reports of lost or misplaced items left on trains or in stations must be submitted within 30 days of travel.

→ LIMITED LIABILITY FOR CHECKED LUGGAGE. Amtrak disclaims all liability for missing or stolen items inside unlocked or unsecured baggage, minor damages to baggage considered normal wear and tear, and baggage that was transported without the owner of the items via Amtrak, or payment of the applicable storage charges. Liability is limited. See the Amtrak site *(amtrak.com)* for details.

→ WE DO REFUNDS. Refund rules vary by ticket, but in comparison to airlines, they are far more customer friendly. For example, a sleeper compartment ticket is refundable, less a nominal processing fee, if you cancel 15 days before your departure, and after that you can get a ticket credit; a first-class fare is refundable up until the time of your departure. Even if you're a no-show,

the ticket is refundable, less a processing fee.

→ WE'RE NOT RESPONSIBLE FOR OUR SCHEDULE—OR YOURS. Unfortunately, Amtrak's lawyers had a field day with its terms. Its contract specifically disclaims liability for "inconvenience, expense, or damages, incidental, consequential, punitive, lost profits, loss [sic] business or otherwise, resulting from errors in its timetable, shortages of equipment, or due to delayed trains, except when such delays cause a passenger to miss an Amtrak guaranteed connection." These blanket statements mean you can't go to Amtrak for restitution if you missed an appointment or a dinner reservation at a restaurant. Not that you would.

The truth about Amtrak's rules and fares

Every Amtrak ticket is governed by a set of rules and enforced by computer software. But rules can be broken. Some agents have the ability to override the program in order to rebook entire trains of people when a train is canceled. But they can do it for a single passenger, too. It doesn't hurt to ask for an exception.

Amtrak fares can be as confusing as airfares, and vary based on when a fare is available for purchase, when it can be used for travel, the inventory it can use, if it can be discounted, its refundability, and its changeability. In other words, just as with an airline ticket, you can get different prices for a ticket to the same destination on the same day and in the same class of service.

Discounts can be difficult to understand, as well. To make matters even more confusing, the definitions used are based upon who owns the service. For example, Amtrak can sell New Jersey Transit tickets, but New Jersey Transit has different definitions for "children" and "senior citizens" than Amtrak does.

As you navigate the sometimes confounding world of train fares, remember once again that some agents can break almost any rule. So ask.

Contacting Amtrak

As a practical matter, Amtrak is easy to reach through its website (amtrak .com/contact-us) when you run into problems, but remember to keep a paper trail of your correspondence. Customer service problems should be referred to the railroad itself. The National Railroad Passenger Corporations Board of Directors, 60 Massachusetts Ave., NE, Washington, DC 20002, is your highest level of appeal when it comes to a customer service issue. Safety problems should be sent to the Federal Railroad Administration (www.fra.dot.gov). If you run into problems, you can appeal to the government, which owns Amtrak. You may also want to contact your elected

federal representative, since Amtrak receives a substantial amount of funding from the government.

GOING GREYHOUND

Bus-related complaints are rare, and although I would like to believe it's because most motor coach operators provide great service, it is also because when you're selling $1 fares, as some bus companies are known to do, passengers don't set the bar very high. That's understandable. Still, you have rights when you travel by bus.

Troubleshooting your bus ride

Greyhound offers a nationwide bus network and is the largest motor coach operator in the country. Details of your rights are found in the relatively simple terms and conditions on its website (greyhound.com/en/termsandconditions.aspx). Let's hit a few highlights.

→ **TICKETS ARE GOOD FOR A YEAR.** Unrestricted tickets are typically good for one year from date of sale.

→ **FARES ARE SUBJECT TO CHANGE.** Prices may be higher during some holiday periods, and additional restrictions may apply during various times of the year.

→ **NO BULK SALES.** Greyhound doesn't sell more than five tickets at a time to a single purchaser.

➔ **SOME TICKETS ARE REFUND-ABLE.** The refund value of unused one-way and round-trip walk-up fare tickets is generally calculated as the amount paid by the passenger minus a penalty for cancellation.

➔ **TICKETS CAN BE CHANGED.** If you have a refundable, walk-up fare, you can change your ticket without paying a fee. If the ticket is nonrefundable or an advance purchase ticket, departure date and time may be changed for a fee of $15 per ticket.

➔ **THEY'RE NOT RESPONSIBLE.** Greyhound isn't responsible for delays caused by breakdowns, weather, or other conditions outside its control.

➔ **TICKETS CAN'T BE TRANSFERRED.** If you try, Greyhound will cancel the ticket.

As with Amtrak's rules, these are fairly commonsensical and nowhere near as convoluted and confusing as those imposed by the average airline, but there's still enough wiggle room that Greyhound could get away with delivering some pretty awful customer service—for instance, leaving you in the middle of nowhere, with no way to get home, after one of its buses breaks down. Greyhound is fairly easy to contact by phone or email *(grey hound.com/en/contactus.aspx),* and it's highly unusual for me to receive a complaint about an unresolved issue. Appeals can be made to Greyhound's owner, the British transportation conglomerate FirstGroup plc. (For more

information, consult the Appendix or *elliott.org.*)

Other U.S. bus companies

The other major bus companies in the United States, including BoltBus and Megabus, have similar contracts with passengers, and complaints about them are equally rare. Check their websites *(boltbus.com* and *us.megabus.com)* for details. The contacts are usually listed under "terms and conditions."

Some of the deeply discounted bus carriers operate from curbsides—even in big cities—without restrooms or shelters. If waiting outside for a bus under a blazing summer sun or in a blizzard or spring rain shower strikes you as uncomfortable, it could be worth the extra money to choose another travel mode.

The U.S. Department of Transportation's Federal Motor Carrier Safety Administration regulates commercial motor coach transportation in the United States. It can be a powerful ally when you've exhausted all of your options with a bus operator. You can contact it online *(nccdb.fmcsa.dot .gov)* or by phone at 1-888-368-7238.

BOTTOM LINE

If you're traveling somewhere, chances are you'll be making part of your trip, if not most of it, by road or rail. Choose your method of travel carefully, and consider every possible option.

PROBLEM SOLVED

WHERE ARE MY GREYHOUND REWARDS?

QUESTION: A few days ago, I received a notice from Greyhound that a ticket I had earned as part of its rewards program was about to expire.

I tried to resolve this at the Greyhound station in Philadelphia, but they said their computers couldn't handle an awards redemption. I called the customer service number they gave me, but they said they do not process award tickets anymore, and they gave me another number. The person at that number was extremely rude and refused to help me. I was told to go to a Greyhound station in some other city that had the computer capability.

I sent an email to Greyhound and received a reply that they'd reimburse me for half a ticket if I paid for it.

This is a classic example of bait-and-switch. I am thoroughly disgusted with Greyhound. —Lois Shestack, *Philadelphia, Pennsylvania*

ANSWER: Are you sure you weren't flying? The kind of behavior you're describing—the silly rules, the endless runaround, the rude customer service—is typically associated with airlines, not Greyhound.

Greyhound's Road Rewards program *(greyhound.com/roadrewards)* is relatively straightforward. It entitles you to discounts, companion passes, and free tickets, with a minimum of fine print, but you still have to read the terms carefully: Many of the rewards expire or can be used only in conjunction with other offers.

I couldn't find any restrictions about award redemption that apply to your situation. On the contrary, the Greyhound site is clear about where to redeem your reward ticket. You can cash in your points at the terminal or by phone, it says. All you have to do is to print your reward voucher and bring it to the bus terminal.

What went wrong? In the email you received back from Greyhound, a company representative blamed the problem on "a lack of knowledge regarding the program in the field." Greyhound also promised to forward your concern to a program manager so that it could be addressed, but as far as I could tell, it didn't actually resolve your problem. Instead, it warned that you only had a few weeks left to use your voucher, but offered no meaningful information on how to redeem it.

Once you received the apparent form response from Greyhound, you could have searched for a supervisor, but I had some trouble finding anyone at the company in charge of customer service. Greyhound does, however, have a Twitter account that seems pretty responsive. That might be one way to escalate your grievance.

Ultimately, I think you might want to reconsider your participation in any loyalty program that makes it difficult to cash in your points (see Chapter 7 for more on this). Make that any loyalty program, period. I believe so-called "rewards" programs invariably benefit the travel company more than they do the traveler.

I contacted Greyhound on your behalf. A representative called you and made arrangements to issue your ticket at the Philadelphia terminal. Greyhound also offered you a $50 certificate to make up for the trouble.

10

Make Sense of the World of Air Travel

Deciphering the fascinating, frustrating world of air travel.

Commercial flight is one of the greatest inventions of the 20th century—fast, convenient, and relatively affordable, when things are running smoothly. Still, many travelers view air travel as a major frustration, and it's a leading source of reader complaints. Pull back the curtain on the aviation industry to find out why and to learn how to gain a fair advantage whenever you fly.

Should you fly?

Of course you'll fly—it's faster and often cheaper than other forms of transportation. But hang on. You may be overlooking other ways of getting there that are more suited to your travel needs.

When to book a flight:

→ WHEN YOU NEED TO GET THERE NOW. There's no faster way to cover long distances. A coast-to-coast drive in the United States takes at least four days, but with a good tailwind you can fly the distance in about five hours, sometimes for the same cost as gas. Plus, there are more nonstops than ever before.

→ WHEN YOU HAVE TO CROSS AN OCEAN OR THE NORTH POLE. No matter where you're flying, you'll find more international airlines than ever that can get you there. Transpolar routes have made travel much faster from cities like Chicago and New York to Beijing,

Shanghai, and Hong Kong. Many of those international carriers offer great service and are worth considering.

→ IF YOU LOVE TO FLY. If you get a little jolt of adrenaline during takeoffs and landings (I admit, I do) and love the view from 36,000 feet, then flying is definitely for you. If you have the travel bug, spotting lakes and cities from seven miles up can be a wonderful game to experience with your family.

When to skip a flight:

→ IF YOU WANT TO TAKE YOUR TIME. Road trips are one of the best ways to see a place or what's *between* places. You can go anywhere, stop when you want to, eat where you want, and get as close to the scenery as you want. What could be more memorable than seeing the largest prairie dog in the world as you drive through Kansas? There's no way to truly experience a place when you're flying over it at 550 miles an hour.

→ IF YOU'RE TRAVELING A SHORT DISTANCE. Commuter flights and puddle jumpers can sometimes take longer than other travel options, particularly when you

factor in the time to get through security, and they may be less convenient. For example, Amtrak's *Acela* service between Washington and New York will often get you to your destination faster than flying would if your end point is Manhattan. However, a small aircraft from Denver to Helena, Montana, can be half a day faster than the 800-mile drive over mountains.

→ IF YOU SUFFER FROM AEROPHOBIA.

Fear of flying is probably the best reason to remain grounded. If you can drive or take the train, you should. By the way, you can enroll in classes to overcome this phobia if you want to. Some flight training schools also offer "discovery" flights to introduce people to flying, and many people take these classes to help overcome their fears.

→ IF YOU WANT TO AVOID THE TRANSPORTATION SECURITY ADMINISTRATION.

If you're put off by having to either walk through a full-body scanner or get patted down, you may want to stick to driving. (See Chapter 13 on travel security and the TSA for details.)

Don't think of a fly/no-fly decision as a no-brainer. You may be able to reach your destination as quickly if you choose another form of transportation. Flying isn't for everyone, and it isn't even the dominant form of transportation, at least not in the United States. Statistics show that for every mile Americans fly, they drive nearly ten, but thanks to stories in travel magazines and on TV that assume the only way to get anywhere is to board a plane, there's a common misperception that Americans fly everywhere. Don't believe everything you read. Ground transportation is still a great choice.

If I do fly, where should I book my ticket?

Here are your options:

→ USE A TRAVEL AGENT.

Typically, travel agents don't receive a commission for booking airfare, so many prefer to buy a ticket as part of a package. Some fares—complex multi-stop or multi-airline flights, or around-the-world tickets—are best left to a professional. Agents also have access to wholesale fares that you might not find online, but be warned that some of these fares come with significant restrictions. For a simple point-to-point itinerary, you may be better off booking it yourself.

→ BOOK DIRECTLY.

Airlines will happily sell you a ticket through their websites or by phone. If you go that route first, you'll lose the ability to run a side-by-side price comparison with a competing airline. An airline may also charge a fee to buy a ticket by phone, and it may quote you a higher fare than the one you'd find online. You'll also receive some benefits, such as the ability to customize your fare with optional items like the ability to check a bag or get a confirmed seat reservation. Airlines sometimes offer direct-booking customers a mileage bonus. On the other hand, you don't have a travel agent to call for help if you need to change the ticket, and you'll be bound to that airline's policies for changes.

> *An airline may also charge a fee to buy a ticket by phone, and it may quote you a higher fare than the one you'd find online.*

→ THROUGH AN ONLINE TRAVEL AGENCY OR AGGREGATOR. Online agencies such as Expedia, Orbitz, and Travelocity, and aggregator sites like Kayak and Hipmunk display most available airfares, allowing you to quickly compare fares for the most convenient routing and the most affordable ticket price. What's more, if something goes wrong you can call the online agency for help with everything from rebooking a flight to obtaining a refund. Online agencies are excellent research tools—they allow you to search for the lowest available fare and then book wherever you want—but these sites will not display every airline, every fare combination, or every route. Instead, they might show fares from airlines with which they have a preferred relationship—which results in fare bias (for more on fare displays, please see Chapter 2 about online travel agencies). Southwest Airlines, the biggest domestic U.S. carrier, does not make its fares available to Expedia, Orbitz, and other online travel sites. You'll need to visit *Southwest.com* to find its fares.

NOT SMART BOOKING OPAQUE WHEN YOU SHOULDN'T.

Sites like Priceline and Hotwire are called "opaque" because they lack transparency: They conceal, either partially or totally, the price, company, and exact itinerary you'll get until you've put down money. You can save a lot, but there's a big catch. Whether you're booking an airline ticket, car rental, or hotel, an opaque site will bill your credit card immediately and the purchase is 100 percent nonrefundable. So don't go opaque unless you're sure. For a leg up on making an informed bid, check out Bidding Traveler (*biddingtraveler .com*) or the Bidding for Travel forum (*biddingfortravel.yuku.com*).

→ BOOK OPAQUE. Sites such as Priceline and Hotwire, which allow you to "bid" for a seat, offer discounts of between 20 and 40 percent on some routes. In exchange, you give up certain important benefits, which can include the ability to choose your exact departure time, airline, and precise routing, or to reserve a seat, collect frequent flier miles, or change a ticket. Opaque sites are a sensible option for leisure travelers who are flexible or who are willing to fly somewhere without being on a specific schedule. Most airlines charge more for fares booked at the last minute, so when you need to fly in the next seven days, the opaque option may work best.

> *Airlines use sophisticated algorithms to calculate demand for their seats.*

How do I find the lowest fare?

Airlines use sophisticated algorithms to calculate demand for their seats. These so-called yield management systems mean that the price you're being quoted for a flight may not be the lowest one. It's based on demand for that flight taken from historical averages. What's more, if you don't push the "buy" button now, the fare may be gone in a few minutes. Air travelers often find these systems frustrating and unfair, but remember, if you buy, U.S. carriers are required to give you a full refund within the first 24 hours if you change your mind. So you're not stuck.

Unfortunately, fixing the system sounds a lot simpler than it is. For example, if you've ever tried to buy a ticket and had the site tell you that the fare was "unavailable" (though a more expensive one was) then you've probably felt like the victim of a bait and switch. Truth is, you were probably a casualty of caching—the practice of storing data on a site so that it can be retrieved quickly. The website just failed to refresh the data, so when you tried to buy the ticket, it was already gone because someone else had booked it.

Fortunately, there are systems that can help you ferret out the best fare.

👍 SMART HOW TO FIND OUT IF YOU REALLY HAVE A TICKET.

Most airline tickets are what are known as e-tickets: travel documents stored in a database from which they can be retrieved when needed. So if you're not getting a piece of paper, how do you know if the ticket is any good? Right after your travel agent sends you your reservation number, go to the website of the relevant airline and check the status of your ticket. A valid ticket will show as "issued" and open for use. It will remain open for use until you check in. If it isn't, call your agent.

If you want to know what people paid for the same flight in the past, you can run a fare history search of the U.S. Department of Transportation's consumer fares database. The database can be searched at FareReport *(farereport.com)*, a commercial site. This is particularly helpful if you're making a bid on an airfare through an opaque site.

A *fare predictor,* such as Bing *(bing.com/travel),* can also help you determine if prices are still too high and if they're likely to fall. Again, don't wait too long; airfares usually rise 14 days before the scheduled flight, and then again seven days before the flight departs. If you wait too long, you can pay a lot more than you anticipated. If you're flying six months from now, it might be wise to wait for a fare sale, but don't expect ticket prices to drop significantly less than 30 days from departure.

Once you've purchased your fare, you can also use a free fare tracker like Yapta *(yapta.com),* which helps secure a refund of the fare difference if the price of your ticket drops. Most major airlines will not refund a fare difference unless it's more

than $200, the cost of a change fee, so don't get too excited.

→ THE TRUTH ABOUT CHEAP AIRFARES.

Your airfare probably represents no more than a third of your trip expenses. You'll save yourself lots of time and misery by taking a deep breath and following this advice: If you see an airfare you can afford, book it now, and don't look back. You might be able to find a less expensive ticket, but I can practically guarantee that you'll waste hours trying to find it—hours that could be better spent doing something more productive.

Airlines have spent a small fortune on yield management technology, but foiling it by subscribing to every fare alert newsletter, reading every airfare blog, and using every tool at your

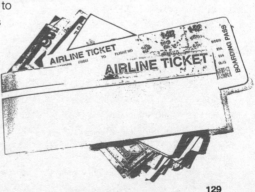

PROBLEM SOLVED

HELP, MY AMERICAN AIRLINES TICKET CREDIT DISAPPEARED

QUESTION: We had to cancel a cruise recently because my husband needed surgery. I called American Airlines to cancel the flight and was told that the tickets would be good for one year from the day they were purchased.

But when I called the airline to rebook, I was told the tickets were worthless because I was a no-show.

I've called American Airlines several times and they keep insisting that we have lost the tickets. I called Expedia, the online travel agency through which we booked the tickets, and they show that the tickets were canceled.

I don't want my money back—I just want to use the tickets for another trip in two months. I would appreciate anything you could do to help.
—Miriam Bustamonte, *San Francisco, California*

ANSWER: Your credit should still be good. But how can you know if it is?

Normally, when a business cancels a service, it offers you a cancellation number. If you get a cancellation number, be sure to keep it for future reference, just in case someone questions your order. If you didn't receive one, then you need to get one. A business should be able to offer some kind of proof in writing that you forfeited a product or service.

And what if it doesn't? Well, then it's your word against its word. Businesses—and specifically airlines—have a way of believing their own version of events.

I can understand why American would want to keep your money if you were a no-show. It didn't have the opportunity to resell your seats, so it lost money. Still, if you tried to cancel, there should be some record of it, somewhere.

I would have handled this cancellation differently. Since you booked your tickets through Expedia, I would have canceled my tickets directly through the online travel agency and insisted that it provide evidence of the cancellation in writing. Expedia would have been able to let American know of your change in plans.

After that, you needed to get a paper trail going: written proof that your flight reservations were canceled—preferably including a cancellation number of some kind—and then, when American denied credit, use those back-and-forth emails between you and the airline. (These emails can easily be forwarded to a supervisor, if necessary.)

Calling American or Expedia wasn't the best idea. There's no evidence of these conversations, so they're not even worth having when it comes to a grievance like yours.

I contacted American on your behalf and it restored your credit.

disposal in order to save $10 on your next flight is a meaningless victory.

What do I need to know about air travel?

If you only fly occasionally, you might be in for a surprise the next time you board a plane. Here are a few of the recent changes:

→ AIR TRAVEL IS "COMMODITIZED." There's virtually no difference among airlines if you're flying in economy class. This reflects commoditization, or the idea that all economy class seats are the same— a "commodity"—and it's perhaps the biggest change since the industry was deregulated in 1978 during the Carter Administration. As far as passengers are concerned, a seat is a seat. Unfortunately, this removes some of the motivation to create a better economy class section. In the minds of many air travelers, it's a race to the bottom, with narrow, uncomfortable seats that have no legroom as the industry standard. Today,

Airlines sell unrestricted tickets, but they are often two to three times more expensive than a restricted ticket.

while the planes are usually the same, Delta or JetBlue tend to have slightly more space in economy class than budget carriers. Some airlines have begun trying to market on-board features such as more legroom and early boarding to de-commoditize economy class and squeeze even more revenue out of you.

→ MOST TICKETS COME WITH *LOTS* OF LIMITATIONS. Most airline tickets are super-restrictive. If you want to make a change, you'll pay a fee of $100 to $200 *plus* any fare differential. You can't easily correct the name on a reservation, sometimes even to fix a typographical error. If you miss your flight, the airline will offer to put you on the next flight—if you buy a new ticket. These restrictions are bound to get even tighter as airlines come up with new ways to increase revenue. Airlines sell unrestricted tickets, but they are often two to three times more expensive than a restricted ticket. Typically, the only folks who can afford them are business travelers.

→ **THERE'S A FEE FOR ALMOST EVERY-THING.** Airlines used to earn most of their revenue from the sale of tickets. But today, in part because of competition, higher fuel prices, and changing business models, airlines generate a sizable portion of their profits through fees. You'll probably pay extra to check your bags and maybe for an advance seat assignment. Meals are also extra if you're sitting in economy class on a domestic flight. You should assume that everything will cost extra.

Your preflight checklist

Before you fly, here's an essential checklist.

→ **IS YOUR NAME SPELLED CORRECTLY?**

→ **ARE THE DATES RIGHT?**

→ **DO YOU HAVE A CONFIRMATION NUMBER** and/or have you confirmed the flight with your agent or airline?

→ **DO THE AIRLINE AND TRAVEL AGENT** have your most up-to-date contact information?

→ **DO YOU KNOW WHERE YOUR FLIGHT IS LEAVING FROM AND WHICH AIRLINE IS OPERATING IT?** (Some flights are codeshare flights operated by another airline, often out of a different terminal.)

What's a contract of carriage, and why should I care about it?

A contract of carriage, sometimes also referred to as the conditions of carriage, is the legal agreement between you and the airline. It is by far the most important reference point when it comes to your rights as an air traveler. The contract usually comes in at least two flavors: the domestic contract, which regulates U.S. flights, and an international contract. These are legally binding contracts. The U.S. government requires airlines to follow them, although it doesn't set them. In other words, if an airline says it will offer a hotel room to passengers on a delayed flight, then the carrier must do so, although the government doesn't say it must put that provision in the contract. You can find the contract of carriage on the websites of

NOT SMART MISSING A LEG.

Some airlines will automatically cancel all flight bookings in your itinerary if you miss one flight segment, even if it was not your fault that you couldn't catch the flight. If you miss one segment, let the airline know immediately so it can rebook you. If you don't let them know, you may have to pay for a new full-fare ticket to get home. For more on connections, see Chapters 10 and 11.

all major U.S. airlines. Additionally, a ticket tariff—that's the fine print in the actual ticket—informs you of other restrictions, and federal laws and regulations may also apply.

What you need to know about your contract:

From the perspective of someone who has mediated thousands of air travel complaints, most passengers run into trouble with the rules, which are constantly changing, and not always in the passenger's favor. Keeping abreast of these restrictions is becoming increasingly difficult. When someone runs afoul of one of them, they usually don't even know if they have any recourse; often, sadly, they don't. So, I'll give it to you straight: What you *don't* know can hurt you.

→ **IT'S AN "ADHESION" CONTRACT THAT APPLIES ONLY TO YOU.** The contract of carriage is one-sided—it binds passengers, but not the airline. So, for example, if you cancel your flight before you leave, you may lose some or all of the value of your ticket. If an airline cancels the same, it may be able to do so without offering you any compensation.

→ **YOU CAN'T NEGOTIATE IT.** Think you can make revisions and send it back to the airline? Not a chance. You agree to it when you buy your ticket. In fact, you agreed to it without knowing that you agreed to it.

→ **IT CAN CHANGE ANYTIME WITHOUT WARNING.** Airlines often revise their contracts, and when they do, they often don't tell their customers. So the terms you see now may not be the same terms as when you fly. For what it's worth, most contract revisions are fairly minor, but it's still worth noting that they can change.

What's in the contract of carriage?

Here's what you'll find in a typical contract. Bear in mind that this can change without notice.

→ **CHANGES IN FARES AND SCHEDULES.** Most contracts say that you can't count on a refund if your fare drops. At best, you'll probably get a ticket credit—and only after the airline deducts a change fee. If your flight's delayed because of weather or Air Traffic Control (basically, a traffic jam in the sky), an airline will do its best to get you out on the next one. If your plane can't take off because of a mechanical problem, it might pick up your meal and hotel expenses. Any time you experience a mechanical delay that lasts longer than two hours, it's best to consult your contract to figure out your rights. Your airline might not volunteer this information.

→ **OVERSALES.** When there are too many passengers and not enough seats, an airline will ask for volunteers to take a later flight. Those passengers are first offered a flight voucher in exchange for agreeing to fly later. Beware of vouchers. They can come with significant restrictions, including which flights you can redeem them for and time limits for use. They will almost certainly expire within a year. Also, a voucher can be a bad deal unless you regularly fly alone. If you fly with a friend or spouse, you'll have to book a ticket on the airline on which you have a voucher, which may be more expensive than another carrier. What if no one volunteers to give up a seat during an oversale? The airline selects passengers and is required to pay those travelers cash

compensation in accordance with federal regulations and rebook them on another flight.

→ **BAGGAGE.** While the government sets the limit on the kind of compensation a passenger can expect to receive when luggage is lost, the fact is, your airline does not want to be responsible for your checked luggage in any way. Pay attention to the long list of liability exceptions, which include electronics, jewelry, strollers, and other valuables. Even if you can prove those items were pilfered, the airline won't cover them when they're misplaced or lost. Just as you wouldn't leave valuables laying around in a hotel room, don't put them in your luggage. If the airline runs out of space in overhead bins before you board, make sure to take the time to remove valuable items before gate checking your carry-on.

→ **MINIMUM CHECK-IN TIMES.** If you don't check in an hour before your flight, you could lose your seat. At the very least, your checked baggage

👎NOT SMART GAMING THE SYSTEM.

Consider this scenario: You need to fly from New York to Chicago for two days, without a Saturday night stayover. The fares are ridiculously expensive. But you *can* buy two round-trip tickets and throw away one portion of each—a practice called "throwaway ticketing"— and pay less than you would for that

first option. Though legal, this violates the airline's rules, which, oddly, stipulate that you must use the entire ticket as issued. My advice? Don't go for option two, because the airline has sophisticated tracking software that will bust you, confiscate your frequent flier miles, or even bill you the fare difference.

may not be accepted. In order to facilitate an on-time take-off, aircraft doors are usually closed ten minutes in advance of the scheduled departure. Be sure to check the minimum check-in time for your specific airport on your airline's website. Some smaller airports may have longer minimum check-in times than you would expect.

If you miss your flight, you lose everything, unless an airline is sympathetic.

→ **UNACCOMPANIED MINORS.** An unaccompanied minor (UM) fee is charged for young children flying alone. Normally, airlines won't accept a child under the age of five flying alone, and some airlines don't accept children on complicated or multi-stop itineraries. The UM fee is typically required of any passenger younger than 12, but it varies. When you pay this fee, the flight attendants will be made aware that your child is traveling alone and the airline will escort your child during any connections. This may include having them in a UM club during any stopovers.

→ **REFUNDS.** If your flight is canceled, you can get a full refund. If your plans change, you'll get a ticket credit. If you miss your flight, you lose everything, unless an airline is sympathetic. Don't bet on it, though.

→ **DELAYS AND CANCELLATIONS.** If it's the airline's fault that your flight is delayed or canceled—if, say, a plane

can't take off because of a broken engine—you have more rights than if it's an event beyond the airline's control, often called a *force majeure* event. Even if the delay is the airline's fault, your rights rarely extend beyond a meal, a hotel room, and a ticket on the next flight out—if there's room.

→ **AUTHORITY TO CHANGE CONTRACT.** The airline can change the contract at any time, for any reason, and it doesn't really have to tell you.

What does *nonrefundable* mean?

Is a *nonrefundable* airline ticket really nonrefundable? Yes—and no. Airlines will always refund a nonrefundable ticket if you die before your flight, sending the money to your next of kin. (Real helpful, I know.) They'll refund a ticket if your flight is canceled. (How nice of them.) Sometimes they'll refund your ticket or waive their change fee if a close relative dies (as long as you can show a death certificate), or (even more rarely) they'll offer a refund if you fall ill and can't make the flight. You get bonus points for a highly contagious illness that might have infected other passengers.

There's a good reason why airline tickets are nonrefundable. Every empty seat is a missed opportunity to make money, and most passengers understand that. An airline doesn't get paid when a seat flies empty. But at the same time, airlines delay or cancel flights for all kinds of reasons, including the weather, acts of God, and mechanical problems—often suffering few or no penalties as a consequence. Shouldn't the airlines show a little flexibility from time to time? Also, airlines are allowed to re-sell your seat when you change your plans or miss your flight. When that happens, why shouldn't you get a full refund?

In the years immediately after airline deregulation, many airlines would allow you to talk your way into almost anything—including, sometimes, a full refund for a nonrefundable ticket. It was costing them real money. After 9/11, the pendulum swung in the other direction—perhaps *too* far in the other direction. It resulted in policies despised by both airline employees and passengers, including one called "No Waivers, No Favors" that forced employees to stick to the published rules, no matter how onerous. Airlines softened their rules a little after their business stabilized, but they're still likely to stick to their post-9/11 playbook, unless you happen to be one of their favorite elite-level customers.

Things you should read before you book:

→ **THE FARE RESTRICTIONS ON YOUR TICKET,** which is also called the ticket tariff.

→ **YOUR AIRLINE'S CONTRACT OF CARRIAGE** (see pages 132–135).

→ **THE AIRLINE'S CUSTOMER COMMITMENT OR CUSTOMER SERVICE COMMITMENT,** which is a nonbinding pledge to maintain minimum service standards. It's on your airline's site.

→ **THE ACTUAL LAWS GOVERNING AIR TRAVEL ARE LISTED IN SECTION 14 OF THE CODE OF FEDERAL REGULATIONS.** But you can find a nice summary in the pamphlet called "Fly-Rights" published by the federal government. It's online at *airconsumer .dot.gov/publications/flyrights.htm.*

Whom should I contact when I have a problem?

Ideally, you won't experience any trouble with your flight. Roughly 75 percent of all flights are on time. Your plane will probably leave as scheduled, and you'll almost certainly arrive safely. (You can find your flight's on-time record online, using a search tool like FlightStats [*flightstats.com/go/ FlightRating/flightRatingByRoute.do*]). But if you experience a problem, your first step should be to contact the airline right then and there. Don't wait.

For example, say you have a problem with your in-flight entertainment system; the best time to speak up is *now*. A flight attendant may be able to reseat you or offer you a drink voucher to make up for the trouble. That's far more meaningful than holding in the anger for the entire

PROBLEM SOLVED

I'M STILL WAITING FOR MY REFUND ... AND WAITING ... AND WAITING

QUESTION: Last year I had to cancel a Lufthansa flight I had booked through Expedia because of a death in my family. The ticket cost $303. When I told my travel agency the reason for canceling the trip, it gave me a list of documentation necessary for a refund.

I called Lufthansa and a representative told me they wouldn't process a refund by phone. So I sent the necessary paperwork to both Lufthansa and Expedia.

Since then, I've followed up several times online and have re-faxed the documents to Lufthansa. To date, I have never received any response from Lufthansa—not even to acknowledge receipt of the documentation. Any advice?
—Megan Gallardo, *Podgorica, Montenegro*

ANSWER: You've been more than patient with Lufthansa. The airline should either send you a refund or refuse to return your money. Not responding is unacceptable.

Most airline tickets are nonrefundable, but airlines sometimes make exceptions when there's a death in the family. Your online agent should have recommended that you send a death certificate and a letter to the airline, explaining your circumstances.

Refunds can take a while. Airlines usually advise customers to wait two to three credit card billing cycles, but a year isn't unheard of. I've seen that a time or two.

Why the foot-dragging? Of all the explanations I've been offered—slow accountants, obsolete technology, or just corporate policy—the one that rings truest is this: Airlines don't want to part with the money.

I'm not sure that's what happened in your case. Maybe Lufthansa didn't have all of your paperwork. Maybe your letter went to the wrong department. Either way, the airline kept you waiting for a year. It shouldn't have.

Was this preventable? Absolutely. You bought your ticket through an online travel agency, which should have done more than just give you an address for refunds. You might have applied a little pressure to Expedia to nudge Lufthansa about the status of your refund.

After a few months, you might have also considered sending a polite follow-up email to Expedia and Lufthansa. An online inquiry is fine, but if you aren't getting through to anyone, I recommend escalating your case to a manager or an executive. Their email addresses are not difficult to find.

If neither the agency nor the airline responded, you might have contacted your credit card company to initiate a dispute. (If your ticket was fully refundable and your credit card company believed your airline was simply holding on to your money, it might have been an open-and-shut case.)

At my suggestion, you emailed Expedia one last time. It responded, saying, "Your request for refund is still in progress as of this time" and that there were no further updates on whether the request had been approved.

So I contacted the airline. Initially, the airline deferred to Expedia. But eventually it came through. After nearly a year and a half, Lufthansa issued a $303 refund.

flight and then firing off an invective-filled letter to the airline—an email that will likely be replied to with a form response and a meaningless certificate that must be used on a future flight.

Many air travelers get in touch with me because they have a problem with an airline rule, specifically one of the rules relating to ticket changes or fares. Airlines sometimes waive their rules during special circumstances. For example, if there's a major winter storm approaching that affects their flight operations, they'll relax their rules and allow you to reschedule your flight. But it doesn't necessarily go both ways. If you can't make a flight because of a natural disaster in your area that affected a small number of people, an airline may or may not extend the same courtesy.

Many air travelers send their complaints about rules to the U.S. Department of Transportation (US DOT), which oversees domestic airlines. You can also send a complaint to the DOT's Aviation Consumer Protection Division. The best way to get in touch with DOT is in writing, through its website—*dot.gov/airconsumer/file-consumer-complaint*.

While DOT doesn't mediate disputes, at least not officially, if you can show that an airline violated its own contract or federal law, then it will contact the carrier on your behalf. Nothing makes an airline move faster than an email ending in dot.gov. Even if it turns out that the airline was following the law, it will elicit a lightning-fast response.

How do I get DOT to review my case?

→ **PUT YOUR COMPLAINT IN WRITING.** You can call DOT, but you will have more success writing and creating a paper trail, which will be easier to track.

→ **KEEP IT BRIEF.**

→ **FIND THE EXACT RULE OR REGULATION THAT HAS BEEN VIOLATED.** If possible, point to a previous DOT advisory that sets a precedent. They can be found on the DOT site, *www.dot.gov*.

→ **BE POLITE.** Like all government agencies, the Aviation Consumer Protection Division is stretched to the limit. It can't take every case. Your good manners will set you apart from the other, sometimes shrill, complaints received by the agency.

How do I get the airline to review my case?

Airlines operate call centers with thousands of employees whose job it is to quickly process your questions. About half the customer queries come by phone, and the rest are by email, snail mail, or some form of social media like Twitter or Facebook. Unless you're in a situation that requires an immediate, real-time resolution— for example, your flight has been canceled and you need to rebook—I'd recommend sending something to the airline in writing. Why? Because it creates a paper trail that can be saved if necessary. This will show the airline that you've gone through all the right channels to get your problem resolved, in the event that you need to appeal to a manager. While it's true that customer service calls are logged and sometimes recorded, you're not going to have access to those files, which puts you at a serious disadvantage when you're trying to fix something.

You can call DOT, but you will have more success writing and creating a paper trail, which will be easier to track.

→ **ALWAYS START AT THE FRONT DOOR.** Send a short, polite email to the airline through its website. Every airline offers a "contact us" section. It may seem silly, but you'll see why this is important in a minute. Offer a brief description of your problem and a desired resolution. Don't forget to include your name, flight dates, and record locator, the alphanumeric code associated with your reservation.

→ **OFFER A CONCISE, REASONED REBUTTAL.** Most airline systems create a tracking number based on the query. This guarantees that no customer inquiry slips through the cracks. Be sure to include your case number in every reply. If the airline sends you a scripted "no" response acknowledging your initial complaint, you'll want to follow up with a polite rebuttal. Include any relevant documentation, such as a doctor's note, death certificate, or a photo of damaged luggage (with a date stamp).

→ **APPEAL TO A HIGHER AUTHORITY, IF NECESSARY.** The names, numbers, and email addresses of many travel company customer service VPs can be found on my website *(elliott.org/contacts)*. While it's rare for executives to become personally involved in a case, your well-reasoned appeal will ensure that a senior customer service

Which rules are negotiable?

On one level, every rule the airline sets can be changed . . . if you're an airline. From a passenger's perspective, some are more negotiable than others.

→ I MISSED A FLIGHT. NOW THEY WANT ME TO PAY FOR A NEW TICKET. Most airlines have an informal policy called the "flat tire" rule. It means that if you get stuck in traffic on the way to the airport and miss your plane, the airline will put you on the next available flight at no extra charge. They are well within their rights to charge you for a new ticket, since technically you're a no-show, so be polite when invoking this rule.

→ THE NAME ON MY TICKET IS MISSPELLED. Airlines claim they can't change the name on your ticket for security reasons. That's more or less true 24 hours before departure, when all passenger lists are scanned by the U.S. Department of Homeland Security for terror risk, but before that, the real reason is that they are protecting their revenues; they don't want to transfer the ticket to someone else and lose the money they would have pocketed for a new ticket. As long as the change is minor—two or fewer letters—a misspelling should be fixed at no charge. Remember that, by law, airlines must allow cancellations at no charge within 24 hours of ticket purchase. If you booked the wrong name just

employee will review your request.

What works? Generally, complaints that are tight and polite get the fastest resolutions. If you include all of your specifics and suggest a reasonable resolution, chances are you'll never have to write an appeal. If you send a lengthy, emotional email and don't suggest a resolution, or if you make an unreasonable demand, like "two first-class tickets anywhere your airline flies" or to have a flight attendant fired for being rude to you, your complaint will likely end in your frustration.

Can I sue an airline?

Yes and no. Because of a federal preemption provision in the Federal Aviation Act, you must sue an airline in federal court in most cases. But for lesser complaints (damage limits vary by states), you can take an airline to small claims court, where you can represent yourself, and where the odds are fairly good that an airline won't bother to send a representative, allowing you to win by default.

after hitting "buy," then cancel it immediately by calling the airline.

→ **YOU'RE STUCK WITH A "JUNK" FEE.** Airlines have added a series of fees that passengers find highly annoying. These include fees for advance seat reservations, for special seat assignments in economy class, or for the first piece of luggage. These can be negotiated. For example, you can sometimes avoid the luggage fee by bringing your regulation-size bag to the gate and carrying it on the plane and, if there's no room in the overhead bins, getting a complimentary gate check. (A better solution, however, would be to pack light.)

Which rules are nonnegotiable?

Airlines would like you to believe that all of their rules are strict, and some actually are.

→ **YOU WANT TO CHANGE THE DATE**

> *Generally, complaints that are tight and polite get the fastest resolutions.*

ON A TICKET. Almost every airline will hit you with a change fee plus a fare differential if you change your travel plans. Waiving that is next to impossible.

→ **YOU MISS YOUR FLIGHT BECAUSE YOU HAD THE WRONG DATES OR FORGOT TO CHECK.** Once the plane takes off and you're classified as a no-show, the best you can hope for is a refund of your government fees and taxes.

→ **YOUR FLIGHT WAS DELAYED AND YOU MISSED A DAY OF YOUR VACATION OR WORK.** If you want your airline to compensate you for missing a day of vacation or work or to pay for a hotel stay that you missed, forget it. The airline's automatic answer is "no."

→ **YOUR MILES EXPIRED.** Airline miles are a highly perishable commodity. When they're gone, you can't usually get them back. Sometimes an airline will let you pay a fee to

---

NOT SMART
CHANGING YOUR NAME BEFORE THE HONEYMOON.

Attention new brides! Can't wait to take your husband's last name? Well, it's worth the wait. I've lost count of the number of times a devastated newlywed contacted me, asking for help changing the name on her ticket back to her maiden name in order to match her old ID, so she could catch a flight to her honeymoon. Some airlines will change the last name as a courtesy, if you can show a marriage license—but don't count on it.

reactivate the miles, but it's rare. Understand your mile expiration dates, which vary from 12 months for some airlines to "never" for others. Usually the expiration date starts over every time there is activity on your account, so using 2,000 miles to subscribe to a magazine could give you another year to use the rest of your miles. (See Chapter 7 on managing your loyalty program for more tips on how to get around the expiration.)

In order to wade through the red tape and obscure rules and find the best flight and fare, you'll need a little patience and a good sense of humor.

How long should I wait for a response?

Airlines offer an immediate response if you email through a website, but it's nothing more than a polite auto-responder with a tracking number. For simple requests, expect to hear back within seven business days. For more complex queries, a four- to six-week time frame is fairly standard.

One of the most common airline questions involves refunds. How long should they take? Well, it depends.

As a general rule, airlines take their sweet time returning your money. Wait at least two credit card billing cycles before panicking. I've had cases that dragged on for one or even two years. If you're asking for a refund on flights that are part of a package vacation tour, the request will go through your travel agent or tour operator, which could test your patience. Hang in there, and if the money doesn't show up, contact me.

What is code-sharing, and why should I care about it?

Codesharing is an agreement that allows two or more airlines to "share" a flight. So between New York and London, British Airways can fly a British Airways aircraft, but it's also serving as an American Airlines flight, "operated" by British Airways. Codesharing can be confusing to passengers and allows airlines to shrug off their customer service responsibilities—which is why you need to know about it.

→ **ALWAYS PAY ATTENTION TO THE FLIGHT DETAILS.** The DOT requires that every codeshare flight be disclosed at the time you buy it. So, look for "Airline X operated by Airline Y" when you're making your reservation. Mostly, these are "Express" airlines operating shorter flights for a larger airline, but for long-haul international trips, it's not uncommon to see three different airlines listed under one ticket.

→ MANY OF THE RULES OF THE FIRST CARRIER APPLY TO THE ENTIRE FLIGHT. Airlines have different rules for luggage, refunds, and miles, but remember: The rules of the first airline, which is known as the operating carrier, should apply to your entire flight. The government holds airlines to these agreements, so if you're hit with a luggage fee on a codeshare flight and the airline on which you're ticketed won't refund the fee, then let DOT know about it.

→ IF SOMETHING GOES WRONG, ASK THE OPERATING CARRIER FOR HELP FIRST. The airline that sold you the ticket should take responsibility when something goes wrong, even if your ticket was issued by a different airline, sometimes also called the marketing carrier.

→ TAKE ADVANTAGE OF HAVING MULTIPLE AIRLINE CONTACTS. If your ticket covers multiple airlines and you're far from home, codesharing can be helpful. You can turn to any of the airlines

listed on your ticket for help. Most airports have multilingual help desks and they are usually well-versed in the intricacies of codesharing.

→ DON'T GET CAUGHT IN THE MIDDLE. Codeshare alliances allow for an infinite game of finger-pointing among the operating and marketing carriers. Don't put up with it. Contact DOT, which will help sort things out. After all, airlines rely on the government for approval to jointly operate these flights.

BOTTOM LINE

The airline world is endlessly fascinating—and frustrating. In order to wade through the red tape and obscure rules and find the best flight and fare, you'll need a little patience and a good sense of humor. But it's worth it.

11

Make the Most of a Terminal Visit

Strategies for making your stopover and layover more productive and comfortable.

Even if you didn't catch the Tom Hanks movie *The Terminal,* you probably wouldn't rank an airport, train station, or bus terminal among your favorite places to hang out. There's no comfortable place to sleep in the waiting areas, and food options are limited and expensive. But not all terminals are the same, and you can take steps to minimize the hassles that often come with the territory. I'll show you how.

What's the difference between an airport stopover and a layover?

The terms *stopover* and *layover* are sometimes used interchangeably by air travelers, but they don't mean the same thing. Stopover is a technical term found universally in airlines' contracts of carriage. It refers to a scheduled, deliberate stop on your journey that occurs at a point between your original place of departure and your final destination. For U.S. domestic travel, a stopover must exceed four hours; internationally it must be for a minimum period of 24 hours.

Layover is a loosely defined term (not generally included in contract boilerplate) that typically refers to the period of time you'll spend somewhere between flights. For instance, Delta's website will often show "layover time" at intermediate, or connecting, stops as a number of hours and minutes; a layover can also involve an overnight stay.

In more general terms, a stopover is something you want and intentionally build into your travel plans, while a layover is something you have to put up with on your way to your final destination.

What's a "legal" connection time?

Do you have enough time to catch a connecting flight, train, or bus? Computer reservations systems show an allowable minimum connection time that warns your travel or reservations agent or online travel site and travel reservation system when a connection is too tight. Some systems won't allow a connection to be booked when there's insufficient time between travel segments.

As a rule of thumb, you should have at least one hour to make a connection on a domestic flight and two hours for an international flight, but some experienced air travelers add a half hour to each of those times, depending on the airport or the time of year they're traveling. Connecting times for buses and trains vary, but are generally shorter.

If you miss your connection, you'll be spending a lot more time in the terminal. Here are a few ways to help avoid that.

145

→ BOOK YOUR TICKETS AT THE SAME TIME FROM THE SAME SOURCE.

If you book your flight from point A to point B through one agency, and from point B to point C through another, then airline one doesn't know about the itinerary on airline two. The two bookings should be connected through the same reservation number in order for a minimum connection time to apply. They also need to be connected in order for your luggage to be routed to your final destination.

→ JUST BECAUSE YOU CAN DOESN'T MEAN YOU SHOULD.

Whether you're booking online or offline, you need to keep your own limits in mind. For example, if you need to get through customs at an airport that's known for long lines, like Miami or New York's JFK airport, you may want to add an extra hour or two to your connection, if possible.

Whether you're booking online or offline, you need to keep your own limits in mind.

→ A CONNECTED ITINERARY MEANS YOU'RE TAKEN CARE OF.

Generally, if your itinerary is connected by the same reservation number, that means if you miss your connection you won't have to pay for a new ticket. Often, airlines will also take care of your hotel and meals while you wait. Amtrak may offer hotel accommodations and meals to connecting passengers delayed overnight. Read your contract of carriage for details.

AIRPORTS

The ins and outs of everyone's favorite waiting areas.

What's an airport hub?

Airports come in all shapes and sizes, from small, one-terminal regional airports to enormous complexes. Most major airlines are part of an airline's so-called hub-and-spoke system, which means all flights go through one or more airports (the hubs) to outlying smaller airports (the spokes). So, if you're flying on United Airlines through the middle of the United States, your hub airport will probably be Chicago, because you'll make your connection there. If you're flying on Delta, you'll probably get to know its hub in Atlanta.

PROBLEM SOLVED

A LAYOVER WITHOUT A ROOM

QUESTION: My wife and I were booked on an American Eagle flight from Little Rock, Arkansas, to Chicago, where we were scheduled to connect to a flight to Norfolk, Virginia.

The first flight was canceled because of mechanical problems, and we were told to go to the main ticket counter to get rebooked. We asked for a rental car to drive to Norfolk, but were told this was not allowed.

Instead, an airline agent told us that a bus would take us to Dallas for a flight to Norfolk the following morning. We arrived in Dallas after midnight but there was no one at the American Airlines terminal to help us.

We had to take matters into our own hands. We got a room at the Hyatt and were able to get a few hours of sleep before our 6 a.m. flight the following morning.

According to a Dallas operations manager I talked to later, a ticket agent who had been on duty the night in question reported that she did not receive word from Little Rock until after 1:30 a.m. that a bus was being sent or had arrived.

I would like a refund on our hotel room, reimbursement for our parking bill at Norfolk, and a voucher for a future flight on American. I also want an upgrade on my next flight plus 50,000 frequent flier miles in my account.
—David Zerbian, *Virginia Beach, Virginia*

ANSWER: There's no doubt that you were inconvenienced because of American Eagle's mechanical delay, which is, of course, covered under the airline's contract of carriage. Without question, you deserve some kind of compensation, and telling American what you want to make things right is important.

The next time you encounter a mechanical delay, don't wait for someone at the airport to offer an update. Call the airline and find out what options you have. (Thanks to cell phones, you can stand in line and call the reservations phone number at the same time, which basically doubles your chance of getting on the next flight.)

Always think ahead. If it looks as if you're going to be stuck overnight, get a ticket agent or a supervisor to authorize a hotel or meal voucher before you board the plane or bus, or to at least make a call on your behalf to the airline station manager.

I contacted American Airlines, and it acknowledged that your trip hadn't gone "smoothly" (talk about an understatement). American refunded your hotel and offered a $400 transportation voucher. It declined to cover your parking, cover your future ticket, upgrade you, or issue 50,000 miles to your mileage account.

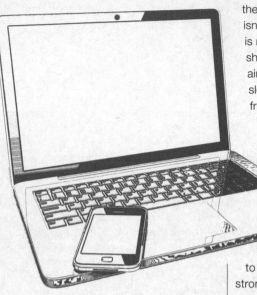

the best solution—one that, sadly, isn't available to many Americans—is mass transit. Taking a train, bus, shuttle van, or even a taxi to the airport can save you a *lot* of hassle and money. Or you could ask a friend for a ride.

How do I get connected at an airport?

When you're at a large hub airport, where passengers are likely to be stuck for many hours, a strong wireless signal can be a godsend. Some airports offer "free" Wi-Fi access to guests. (It's not really free, since you're paying airport fees with your ticket.) Others charge by the hour or day. As always, you get what you pay for. The "free" signal may force you to watch an ad or agree to onerous service terms, and in the end, it might be so slow that you can do little more than check email. The premium service may be overpriced, and you still might not escape the slow connection or the ads. Some other tips:

→ **SURF SECURE.** Public Wi-Fi means sharing the virtual highway with some pretty unsavory characters, including hackers. Avoid logging on to your bank's website or other important sites from nonsecure locations.

What's a regional airport?

A regional airport is a smaller airport with limited facilities and amenities for passengers. It serves a smaller geographical area and rarely has customs and immigration facilities and may not have a significant TSA presence. Normally, the planes operating out of a regional airport are smaller—either regional jets or turboprops.

What's the biggest problem I'll run in to at the airport?

Apart from the TSA (see Chapter 13) and airlines (see Chapter 10), the number one problem is parking. For some airports, the biggest generator of revenue is parking. Perhaps

→ **CONSIDER A PREMIUM SUBSCRIPTION TO A THIRD-PARTY WI-FI SERVICE.** Companies like Boingo *(boingo.com)*, which specialize in serving airport locations, offer reliable and reasonably priced services. If you take more than three flights a year and expect a longer stopover or layover, it's worth considering.

→ **FIND A "FREE" SIGNAL AT AN AIRPORT.** Many airline lounges offer their customers "free" wireless access. Again, it's not necessarily free, since you're paying for lounge access. Many intrepid travelers park in front of the lounge and enjoy a strong signal at no additional charge.

→ **TETHER YOUR PHONE.** A lot of wireless carriers will allow you to connect your PC or tablet computer to your mobile phone. This is known as tethering, and it can give you a relatively fast connection. (You may have to "jailbreak" your phone, meaning that you modify it in violation of your user agreement. While this isn't illegal, it will probably void your warranty.)

Bring an extension cord if you plan to use your laptop or charge your phone. Most airports have power outlets that can be accessed by passengers, but they are usually in inconvenient places. That's why you often see laptop users squatting in corners—because that's where the power outlets are. It also helps to come prepared with a miniature three-plug power strip. These strips are small enough to fit in the tiniest of backpack pockets, and most people are willing to unplug from the outlet for a second as long as you let them plug into your mini power strip. Remember: Sharing is caring!

What's the deal with airport food?

Airport food has a well-deserved reputation for being expensive and awful. But some airports now offer better restaurants and try to keep prices in check through "street pricing," which contractually requires their food vendors to keep prices in line with those in the nearby city. That's eliminated some of the food absurdities, like $6 cups of coffee, for the most part. Still, I get a fair amount of gripes about airport fare.

→ **BRING WHAT YOU'RE ABLE.** That's possible, even with liquid and gel restrictions in place. One of my favorite rules of the road is "Pack twice the food and half the clothes." You'll eat the food and have plenty of room for gifts and trinkets.

→ **THE CLOSER TO THE GATE, THE MORE YOU'LL PAY.** Unless you're at a small regional airport, competition for your business in the main terminal is intense. But as you get closer to your gate, the options become more limited, the quality diminishes, and the prices spike (um, $5 day-old plastic-wrapped cookies, anyone?). Don't let it get to that point.

PROBLEM SOLVED

A MISSED CONNECTION TO HAWAII

QUESTION: I'm trying to get reimbursed for an extra night at a hotel caused by an airline schedule change, but my travel agency and airline have been giving me the cold shoulder. Here's what happened: My husband and I recently booked a trip from Dallas to Kauai via Phoenix on US Airways. When we arrived in Phoenix, we learned our scheduled flight had departed for Kauai two hours earlier. Neither the airline nor our travel agent, *Cheaptickets.com,* had notified us of any flight changes.

US Airways sent us to Los Angeles that afternoon. We had to get a hotel room until the next flight to Honolulu departed the following morning. From there, we were on our own. Fortunately, we were able to catch a standby flight to Kauai and were reunited with our luggage later that night.

We're trying to get our money back for the night of lodging in Kauai we weren't able to use, for the hotel at Los Angeles International Airport that we had to stay in, and for the toiletries we needed to buy when we were separated from our luggage. I called US Airways and they blew me off, suggesting that I had gotten what I deserved because I booked my flight through *Cheaptickets.com.* Can you help us? —Marlene Kelley, *Lake Kiowa, Texas*

ANSWER: Both your online travel agent and your airline should have notified you of the schedule change and offered to rebook your flight. When they failed to do that, they should have covered your expenses—the extra night at the LAX hotel, the missed night in Hawaii, and your incidentals.

But you could have easily prevented this from happening by phoning your airline and agency to confirm your flight. Flight schedules can change, and the systems used to notify passengers are unreliable. Still, it is highly unusual for an airline to reschedule flights without trying to rebook a passenger's missing connection, and at the very least informing the travel agent about the change. Something obviously went terribly wrong.

When you found out about the flight schedule change in Phoenix, you should have spoken with a supervisor, who could have authorized a hotel voucher and given you permission to buy incidentals, such as toothpaste and shampoo, at US Airways' expense. Although a connection problem such as this one isn't specifically addressed in the airline's contract of carriage, it's clear that the airline was responsible for creating this situation and should have covered your costs.

You shouldn't have paid for a hotel and assumed that either US Airways or *Cheaptickets.com* would pay for it. Unfortunately, that's not how it works. Travel companies go to considerable lengths to make sure that requests like yours are met with a polite but firm "no"—no matter how legitimate. (Although I think US Airways' answer that you "got what you deserved" might need some work.)

I contacted both your agency and airline. After months of stonewalling, US Airways agreed to send you $500 worth of flight coupons and *Cheaptickets.com* issued two $200 vouchers, which more than covers your expenses.

Help, I've lost something at the airport. Now what?

Don't panic. Airports are usually required by law to collect, log, and keep your property for no less than 30 days, and sometimes longer. Even if you're half-way around the world by the time you realize something is missing, you may be able to retrieve it through the airport's website, which will list instructions for being reunited with your valuables. Train stations and bus terminals also have established lost-and-found procedures. Best way to make sure something doesn't get lost? *Label it.* (See Chapter 6 for more on how to label your luggage.)

Should I make a call from a pay phone in the terminal?

Pay phones may be an endangered species, but they can still scam you. One air traveler used a public phone after her cell phone ran out of battery power. She discovered later that she'd been billed a $10 fee for "operator assistance" and $1.29 per minute for the call. An expensive lesson learned. Next time, carry a spare battery or at least have a charger handy. At the

very least, consider buying a prepaid phone card.

How about security?

Airport security is not to be confused with the TSA. Some security-related duties, such as patrolling the curb-side passenger pick-up areas, may be handled by private security personnel. But most larger airports also have police forces that have law enforcement authority. (The TSA does not have the power to arrest you; see Chapter 13.) If you see someone break the law or have an emergency, call the police.

BUS AND TRAIN TERMINALS

In the United States, travel by bus or train doesn't enjoy the same status as it does, say, in Europe. Terminals tend to be older and often lack many of the amenities you would find in an airport.

What do I need to know about bus terminals and train terminals?

→ **DON'T ASSUME A MINIMUM SERVICE LEVEL.** Unfortunately, Amtrak is chronically underfunded and bus

companies usually offer little more than basic transportation. I receive very few complaints from passengers about the state of their stations and terminals because they don't expect much.

→ **SECURITY IS NOT A GIVEN.** Anyone can walk into a bus or train terminal, and generally speaking, most parts except the platforms are fully accessible to non-ticketholders.

→ **PERSONAL SPACE AND PRVACY MAY NOT BE READILY AVAILABLE.** Since almost anyone can go in and out of a station or bus terminal, and most are located in readily accessible and densely populated areas, you may contend with people who are between homes, pickpockets, loiterers, and other nonpassengers. (Upscale boors are more often found in airports.)

→ **TRAIN AND BUS STATIONS HANDLE LAW ENFORCEMENT IN A SIMILAR WAY TO AIRPORTS.** Amtrak has its own police department, and you can find security tips for rail travel at *police.Amtrak.com.* Bus terminals may have private security or may be patrolled by transit police officers as part of their regular beat, depending on the size of the station.

Whether you're at an airport, train station, or bus terminal, you may be screened by the TSA's little-known VIPR team. VIPR, which is shorthand for Visible Intermodal Prevention and Response, is the TSA's mobile unit. It's frequently sighted at bus, subway, and rail terminals. Often, a VIPR checkpoint can simply be avoided by walking through another entrance of the train station.

That said, it's always better to comply with screening of any kind at a terminal. If you have a problem with the way you're being screened, you can complain to the TSA and you can vote for a political candidate who may pass a law to change the way the TSA searches passengers.

An airport, train station, or bus terminal isn't the place to take a stand if you want to continue your trip.

What's a lockout and how do I avoid it?

Some bus and train terminals may not always be open, and even some airport terminals may also close at night, so it's imperative to check before your trip to make sure you'll have access if you have an extended layover without a hotel booking. It's especially important when you're making a bus connection and you are using an interline provider (a subcontractor, which is the bus equivalent of an airline codeshare). I've heard from many passengers who were literally left standing in the cold after a bus dropped them off at a station that wasn't open. Greyhound has pledged to keep its terminals open during operating hours, which is to say, when buses are running, but the best way to avoid a lockout is to steer clear of connections that happen during off-hours. In other words, travel by day.

Make sure you've given yourself enough time to connect to your flight, train, or bus, but prepare for the inevitable delay.

BOTTOM LINE

Although some terminals are so safe and comfortable that they can easily be confused for shopping malls, you'll want to do everything you can to avoid a lengthy stay in any waiting area. Make sure you've given yourself enough time to connect to your flight, train, or bus, but prepare for the inevitable delay.

If you have a problem with airport terminal infrastructure not directly related to your airline, you need to take it up with the airport authority, which is usually run by a local government. But many service problems are simply referred back to the company providing the transportation—either the airline, bus company, or Amtrak.

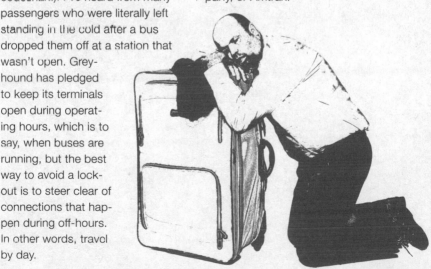

12

Plan a Cruise

---

*Hitting the seven seas like a pro
(and how to not get soaked at the end).*

Admit it, there's just *something* about cruising. Maybe it's that smell of saltwater spray and the stunning vastness of the ocean unfolding from your balcony. Maybe it's the food, from the gourmet restaurants to the all-you-can-eat ice cream sundae buffet. What's not to love about a cruise? Not much—until there is. Things can go wrong. What happens when they do? I've got you covered.

Consider a cruise vacation:

→ **IF YOU LIKE TO BE AT SEA.** Obviously, you'll love a cruise if you enjoy being near the ocean and like ships. That's probably the best reason to cruise.

→ **IF YOU'RE IN THE CRUISE DEMO-GRAPHIC.** Cruising was long thought to be the preferred vacation for the newlywed, overfed, and nearly dead. Although it's changing, the stereotypes still often hold true. You're likely to find a lot of honeymooners, folks who hit the midnight buffet and every buffet that follows it, and members of the AARP set.

→ **IF YOU DON'T LIKE TO PLAN.** Once you're on a ship, your biggest worry is where to have dinner, unless you want to take an optional shore excursion. Even shore excursions are meticulously planned, so that everything—including bathroom breaks—is built into them.

→ **IF YOU LIKE TO PLAN BUT NEED A REST FROM DOING ALL THE WORK.** A cruise is programmed to offer as much entertainment or as little as you might want, without any effort on your part after handing over your payment.

→ **IF YOU LIKE EXOTIC PORTS OF CALL.** Once you get away from the touristy Caribbean ports, you'll find yourself making stops in places with minimal tourism infrastructure, but with maximum appeal to visitors with a taste for the exotic. If you don't believe me, look up some of the round-the-world cruise itineraries. Pretty awesome, huh?

Don't cruise:

→ **IF YOU GET SEASICK.** Look, there's no point torturing yourself by popping Dramamine and pretending you like being at sea. Do yourself a favor, and stay on land.

→ **IF YOU'RE PREGNANT AND YOU'RE CLOSE TO YOUR DUE DATE,** or have a medical condition that could affect your cruise. Cruise ticket contracts prohibit women past their 24th week

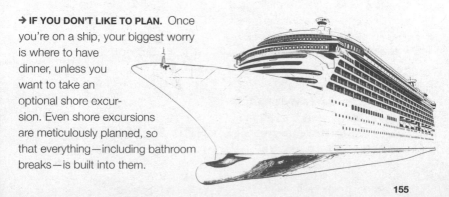

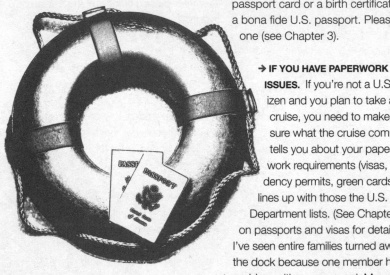

passport card or a birth certificate—a bona fide U.S. passport. Please get one (see Chapter 3).

→ **IF YOU HAVE PAPERWORK ISSUES.** If you're not a U.S. citizen and you plan to take a cruise, you need to make sure what the cruise company tells you about your paperwork requirements (visas, residency permits, green cards, etc.) lines up with those the U.S. State Department lists. (See Chapter 3 on passports and visas for details.) I've seen entire families turned away at the dock because one member had a problem with a green card. My advice? Find a travel agent who knows the ins and outs of your paperwork requirements, and bring all your documentation and supporting paperwork with you. If you're not sure about your ability to leave the country, don't risk it.

→ **IF YOU LIKE TO BE IN CONTROL OF YOUR VACATION.** If you're a free spirit, a cruise might make you feel like you're on a prison barge.

If you're concerned about your cruise ship sinking like the Costa *Concordia,* I would probably look for something else to worry about. Cruising isn't entirely safe (I'll cover that in more detail soon), but sinking isn't a rational fear.

of pregnancy from sailing. But I would also advise you to be in reasonably good health before embarking on a cruise. If you have significant mobility challenges or chronic health issues, check with your doctor before booking a cruise.

→ **IF YOUR FAMILY INCLUDES VERY YOUNG CHILDREN.** Even the most family-friendly cruise ships are not ideal for kids who are not toilet-trained. Childcare is usually restricted to kids who don't use diapers. Your children have to be old enough to understand that the railings are *not* for climbing, too.

→ **IF YOU DON'T HAVE A PASSPORT.** No matter what the cruise lines tell you about a birth certificate being enough, I wouldn't dream of boarding a ship without a valid passport. Not a

HOW TO BUY A CRUISE
You can turn to a full-service "bricks-and-mortar" travel agency, an online

agency, or, in many instances, you can deal directly with the cruise line. But which option is right for you?

The case for a full-service agent

Some travel agents are cruise specialists who spend a career developing their expertise, and the best ones have actually cruised on the itineraries they recommend.

→ BENEFITS OF AN AGENT:

• One-on-one service and attention to detail. A good agent will make sure the cruise matches your personality type. The odds of a devoutly religious family onding up on a rambunctious singles cruise under this scenario? Virtually zero.

• Special access to agent-only discounts. If the agency is a member of a larger group, like AAA, you'll get deals no one else has, and they may be unbeatable.

• Access to possible upgrades and onboard credits. Again, these offers come by way of the relationships cruise agents have through their company.

• Knowledge of individual ships—to help you find staterooms that are preferred over others for value or motion while at sea, for instance. A good agent will also educate you about the distinct personalities and reputations of different cruise lines.

→ DRAWBACKS:

• If it's a small shop, you may not have 24/7 support. So, if something goes wrong while you're overseas, you'll have to wait until business hours for help. (See Chapter 2 on travel agents for more on your options.)

• Agents are not free. You may be charged a fee to book airfare and make other arrangements, although the cruise booking itself is "free."

• Agents are often incentivized by commissions and bonuses called *overrides*, whereby cruise lines reward agents for booking a lot of itineraries with the same company. (Think of it as a kind of rewards program.) First and foremost, an ethical agent will make sure the cruise is the right one for you, but some agents, sadly, go straight for the highest commission. Travel agents can make 10 percent or more in commissions and other bonuses from your cruise. I've heard of these payments rising as high as 14 percent. It's difficult to determine if an agent is recommending a cruise because it's good for him or her—or for you.

> *Travel agents can make 10 percent or more in commissions and other bonuses from your cruise.*

PROBLEM SOLVED

HELP! I CAN'T MAKE MY CRUISE BECAUSE OF A HURRICANE

QUESTION: We booked a cruise to Alaska on Norwegian Cruise Line (NCL) last summer. First, NCL notified us that we would be sailing a day after our scheduled departure because they had to fix a propeller on the ship. This meant that the ship would not be stopping in Juneau for a scheduled excursion.

Then we had to cancel the cruise because a hurricane made it impossible for us to fly to Seattle, our port of embarkation. We had purchased a travel insurance policy through the cruise line.

Our airline gave us a full refund on our tickets, but NCL said we were only entitled to a 75 percent insurance credit that could be used for a future cruise. That isn't in line with what other cruise lines did. For example, Princess offered a 75 percent credit for passengers who had insurance and an additional 25 percent credit that could be used for a future cruise.

Norwegian Cruise Line says I should have taken the 90 percent insurance plan. But the representative never offered that choice when I booked the cruise. If I had known about the 90 percent plan, I would have bought it.
—Debra Weissman, *Hartford, Connecticut*

ANSWER: If you booked your vacation directly through the cruise line, I don't see any reason why it shouldn't offer a full credit.

But that's not how it works; cruise lines sell expensive and often highly restrictive insurance policies as add-ons that give you a credit if you have to cancel a cruise—and only under certain circumstances.

I think special conditions applied to your cruise. First, NCL already inconvenienced you by changing the date of your sailing. You were very understanding of that and didn't ask for any consideration in return.

Second, you booked this cruise directly with NCL. You bought the only insurance it offered. (For future reference, I would recommend shopping around instead of buying the first policy you're presented with. You could have found insurance that covered your entire cruise through another company.)

And finally, this event had nothing to do with you. It was a natural disaster that affected a lot of NCL passengers. While it may be true that NCL only had to offer you a 75 percent credit, I think they could have done better.

Your case shows how careful you have to be when you're shopping for cruise insurance, but it also shows how vigilantly cruise lines protect their revenues.

I contacted NCL on your behalf. As a "special courtesy" it extended an additional 25 percent of your cruise fare as a credit.

The case for an online agent

Today's travel websites try to combine the best aspects of a full-service agency with the conveniences of modern technology. Often, they succeed.

→ BENEFITS OF AN ONLINE AGENT:

• You're in control. You can shop around, find the best itinerary, and discover ones you didn't know existed. You can also book the cruise whenever you want to.

• You have 24/7 phone support through most of the online agencies. When something goes wrong, someone should always be there for you.

• Because of their size, online agencies can negotiate ridiculously good volume discounts, which they pass along to you.

→ DRAWBACKS:

• It's an online travel agency. Many of their phone agents are located in overseas call centers. They read scripts and sometimes seem as if they really don't care if you're having a good vacation. No wonder offline agents call these operations "vending machines." Also, they may try to steer you to the highest commission cruises by displaying *their* favorite cruises first.

• Service, when it does come, can be slow and impersonal. It's not uncommon to hear of people waiting upward of an hour for help before being hung up on.

• You may feel like a number. That's because you *are* a number. You're one of a million, literally. Online agencies are a volume business, so if you like to feel special and appreciated, you might want to book elsewhere.

The case for a direct booking

Cruise lines have always been cautious about offering their products directly to consumers, fearful that they might offend the travel agency community on which they depend for distributing their product. But in recent years, they have become bolder, offering cruises through their websites and, while you are onboard, offering special rates on future cruises.

→ BENEFITS OF A DIRECT BOOKING:

• You'll probably get the deepest discounts and, in some cases, price protection that assures you that if the fare drops, you'll get a refund. However, cruise lines are reluctant to undercut an agency with a lower fare.

• You're dealing directly with the cruise line, so the company can't

> *Because of their size, online agencies can negotiate ridiculously good volume discounts, which they pass along to you.*

blame an intermediary for anything that goes wrong. By the way, you can transfer your "direct" booking to your favorite travel agent if you want, giving you the best of both worlds.

• You might get an incentive like a shore excursion, other discounts, or a credit on a current or future cruise. Cruise lines are nothing if not creative with these offers.

→ **DRAWBACKS:**
• You have no one to turn to when something goes wrong except the cruise line—unless, of course, you transfer the booking to an agent.

• The aggressive onboard sales agents sometimes force you to make a decision about a future vacation before you're ready. It's a high-pressure sales pitch on the high seas.

How do you buy a cruise, then? In the end, there may be no correct answer for everyone. If, for example,

you're taking your extended family on an anniversary cruise, you'll probably want to find a cruise specialist who has some experience with large groups. On the other hand, if you're just traveling with your sweetie and you're flexible, online might be the best option.

How do I book a shore excursion?

Shore excursions come in all flavors, from all-day snorkeling trips to guided tours of local historical sites. For years, the conventional wisdom was that you should only book your shore excursions through the cruise line because if, for some reason, the excursion were to run late, the cruise line wouldn't leave you behind. That's still more or less true, although some new, credible excursion companies promise to fly you to the next port if your shore excursion isn't back before the ship leaves. Shore excursions offered

Shore excursions offered by a cruise line will almost always be more expensive than independent ones.

by a cruise line will almost always be more expensive than independent ones. That's because cruise lines are adding their commission to the price of the day trip.

Do your homework before going with the cruise line's shore excursion. You can scout out shore excursions with these resources:

→ **CRUISE LINE WEBSITES.** Even though you may not be interested in booking directly with the cruise lines, their shore excursion sections are always a good place to start.

→ **SHORE EXCURSION COMPANIES.** Well-known companies like Viator offer shore excursions that offer rates up to 30 percent lower than the cruise lines' price.

→ **ONLINE REVIEW BOARDS.** The online review boards aren't always accurate. Check out Cruise Critic (cruisecritic.com) for cruise line–specific reviews on excursions and to find the best deals.

→ **LOCAL TOURISM ORGANIZATIONS.** Tourist board sites often recommend a list of tours available in a port. It's a good place to find a second opinion on worthwhile activities.

WHAT TO DO IF SOMETHING GOES WRONG

So much can go wrong on a cruise, I hardly know where to begin. Maybe here: Informed consumers don't usually get ripped off. They know what

they're buying, where to book it, and the pitfalls that await.

The more you know about cruising, the less you have to worry about having a negative experience.

What's the international cruise line passenger bill of rights?

After a series of high-profile customer service incidents in 2012 and 2013, the cruise industry adopted a voluntary "bill of rights" to clearly communicate to passengers their rights regarding comfort and care. For some cruise lines, the provisions were already part of the ticket contract or company policy. But it was the industry's way of saying it could do better. Among the provisions:

→ YOU HAVE THE RIGHT TO DISEMBARK A DOCKED SHIP if essential provisions such as food, water, restroom facilities, and access to medical care can't "adequately be provided onboard."

→ YOU HAVE THE RIGHT TO A FULL REFUND FOR A TRIP THAT IS CANCELED because of a mechanical failure, or a partial refund for voyages that are terminated early.

→ YOU HAVE THE RIGHT TO "PROFESSIONAL EMERGENCY MEDICAL ATTENTION" ONBOARD.

→ YOU HAVE THE RIGHT TO TIMELY INFORMATION UPDATES regarding any adjustments in the itinerary of the ship in the event of a mechanical failure or emergency.

→ YOU HAVE THE RIGHT TO TRANSPORTATION TO THE SHIP'S SCHEDULED PORT OF DISEMBARKATION, or your home city, in the event a cruise is terminated early because of mechanical failures.

→ YOU HAVE THE RIGHT TO LODGING if disembarkation and an overnight stay in an unscheduled port are required when a cruise is terminated early because of mechanical failures.

If you're at sea and you encounter a problem, you may want to invoke your bill of rights. Chances are, your cruise line has already agreed to these rights. But it's unclear how this bill will be implemented—it was introduced as this book was being written.

Help, I've booked the wrong cruise!

Many of my cruise-related cases involve buyer's remorse, which is to say, a traveler was booked on the wrong ship, in the wrong cabin, or on the wrong sailing. Wrong sailing? Oh, yes. It usually involves a family with young kids being stuck on a special theme cruise where folks let it all hang out. Do you want me to go into details? No.

Do your homework, kids, and this won't happen to you. But what if it

---

👍SMART AVOID CHOPPY SEAS.

If you're a little prone to seasickness—and who among us isn't?—then choose your cruise carefully. On my first Alaska cruise, our ship churned through nine-foot swells in early September. The Caribbean is known to have some of the smoothest waters. But be mindful of hurricane season, from June to November, which can disrupt your journey.

PROBLEM SOLVED

CAN THIS CRUISE BE SALVAGED?

QUESTION: We need your help with a Carnival cruise that went nowhere. Earlier this year, we booked a Western Caribbean cruise directly through Carnival; the package included airfare and shore excursions.

On the day we were supposed to travel, our nightmare began. Our plane was delayed because of mechanical problems. So was the next flight. We missed the boat in Miami.

We wanted to reschedule the cruise, but Carnival suggested that we catch up with the ship in the Cayman Islands. We had to pay for new tickets to the Caymans. But when we arrived in Miami, a Carnival representative asked us for passports—and we only had passport cards.

We had to turn back to Cleveland. There were more mechanical delays. We made a claim through our travel insurance carrier, but were only reimbursed $500 per person. Carnival says they should be able to give us something for the missed cruise but says we first have to fill out the insurance claim.

We booked the cruise, shore excursions, balcony upgrade, and the missed flight through Carnival. We want a vacation and we don't have the money because Carnival is holding us hostage. Could you help us? —Denise Frantz, *Cleveland, Ohio*

ANSWER: This cruise just wasn't meant to be. But it might have been — if you'd gotten a passport instead of a passport card.

Carnival doesn't mince words when it comes to your paperwork requirements. On its site, it clearly recommends that all guests travel with a passport that's valid for at least six months beyond completion of travel.

Your passport cards would have been fine if you'd boarded the ship in Miami. But you need a passport to fly to the Cayman Islands.

You would think that by booking your cruise directly through Carnival, as well as buying its recommended insurance, you'd be fully covered. The fine print on the cruise line's website specifically says it's not responsible for an incident like yours.

So why book your plane tickets through Carnival? I have no idea.

You might have considered buying your cruise through a travel agent. An agent wouldn't have let you board a plane for Miami without proper paperwork and might have been able to get you on a flight that ensured you didn't miss the ship in Miami. Also, a competent travel professional would have helped you choose travel insurance that would have fully covered you. Still, you alone are responsible for having proper documentation for your trip.

I contacted Carnival on your behalf. It initially offered you two $1,000 vouchers, but then also agreed to cover the $489 in shore excursions and $444 for your extra flights to Grand Cayman. It looks as if your cruise has been salvaged.

does? Well, if you discover the problem beforehand, call your agent or cruise line and ask to move your sailing date to a more suitable cruise. I have yet to come across someone who asked to be moved for that reason and was declined. If you find that you're on the wrong cruise after you board, it's really probably too late. A young couple looking forward to a restful week at sea who accidentally booked a Disney cruise? Not much to be done about that. You're partying with Mickey!

HOW DO I DECIPHER MY CRUISE FARE, AND OTHER MONEY MATTERS?

Here's a sample cruise fare on a Caribbean sailing for a recent cruise.

Total 2 Travelers: $738.00
Gov't Fees/Taxes: $147.50
Grand total: $885.50

The $738 is not important to you, but it is to your travel agent. That's the number on which your agent's commission is based. I don't think cruise lines should quote the fare before fees and taxes quite as prominently as they tend to because it's a meaningless number that makes your cruise look cheaper than it is.

The government taxes and fees, on the other hand, *are* relevant. Those fees are refundable if you cancel your cruise, even if the fare is nonrefundable. Of course, the real charge you should pay attention to is the grand total—that's what the cruise will cost. Probably.

Beware of additional "opt-in" charges later in the booking. Those can include optional insurance, automatic tipping, and shore excursions. If you think your agent can guide you through what's worthwhile and what isn't, don't be so sure. I've heard of unscrupulous agents telling their clients that insurance is required on a cruise (it isn't) and employing other hard-sell tactics ("Oh, it'll be a wasted cruise if you don't go snorkeling on the reef!") to make more money from a booking.

Point is, that $885 is just the beginning. It isn't unusual for the final bill to double, and even triple, once you've added all the extras. I'm not kidding.

Where did all of these fees come from?

Cruising used to be billed as an "all-inclusive" experience. With the exception of some luxury cruise lines, it isn't anymore. Cruise lines make a significant portion of their revenue from ancillary fees, of which there are many. From the "welcome" drink (it's not always free) to a special request at dinner (I'm not making this up—a fee for the end piece of a roast, which is an extreme example), your cruise line is trying to monetize your vacation in ways you probably can't imagine.

How do I avoid fees?

There's only one way to make sure you don't get caught by these fees: Learn the word "no," and use it often. Want a picture of you and your beautiful family? No. Care for a soda? No. Lunch in one of our specialty restaurants? No, no, no. Not that these things aren't fun to have while you're on a cruise, but in many cases, they're ridiculously overpriced. Try getting wireless Internet access or making a ship-to-shore phone call if you don't believe me.

Also, it helps to know another phrase: "How much?"

If you want to see how much the cruise lines' ancillary revenue pursuit can hurt, wake up early on the last day of the cruise and head downstairs to the front desk. The friendly faces that greeted you when you arrived are gone, replaced by stone-faced dudes maintaining their unflappable demeanor while one passenger

Cruising used to be billed as an "all-inclusive" experience. With the exception of some luxury cruise lines, it isn't anymore.

after another tries—and usually fails—to argue his way out of a surcharge. How pathetic.

By the way, one of the worst money traps is your magnetic room key. By default, it doubles as a charge card on many ships. Make sure you deauthorize it before handing it to your kids—especially teenagers—otherwise you will hear a giant sucking sound from your bank account when you check out. One reader contacted me trying to get my help in removing a $400 charge her grandchildren had run up at the ship's arcade. Kids!

I lost money at the tables!

Those slot machines are nice to look at while you're in port, but once

165

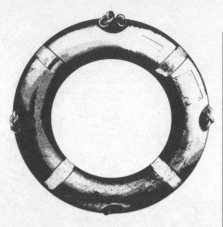

you're in international waters and the velvet rope to the gambling area falls, they morph into a money trap. Stay away. The money is as green at sea as it is on land, and there are no refunds when you lose big at the tables. If you think you may have a problem avoiding the floating casino, book a cruise without one or ask for a magnetic card that won't allow you to access your shipboard account.

TROUBLESHOOTING YOUR CRUISE

Your actual rights on a cruise are governed by a ticket contract, which is available on your cruise line's website, and which you are required to sign—even if you don't read it—before you sail. It can be a problematic document.

Here are some of the lesser known "gotchas":

→ **YOUR LAWS AREN'T OUR LAWS.** The rules governing cruises have nothing to do with where you live or buy your ticket. Instead, federal maritime law, international law, or the laws of the country where the cruise ship is registered—typically the Bahamas, Liberia, or Panama—will govern your rights.

→ **DON'T HOLD US TO THE BRO-CHURE.** The ship may or may not keep to the promised schedule. This is perhaps the most frustrating contract provision for passengers. Here's Royal Caribbean's: "Carrier may for any reason at any time and without prior notice, cancel, advance, postpone or deviate from any scheduled sailing, port of call, destination, lodging or any activity on or off the vessel, or substitute another vessel or port of call, destination, lodging or activity." What's more, it owes you nothing if it does.

→ **THE QUACK WHO TREATED YOU ISN'T OUR PROBLEM.** Most medical care on cruise ships is perfectly adequate. But just in case it isn't, cruise lines have a clause that say they aren't responsible for the malpractice of the ship's doctors. Have a look at paragraph 13 of Princess's passage contract: "Doctors, nurses or other medical or service personnel work directly for Passenger and shall not be considered to be acting under the control or supervision of Carrier, since Carrier is not a medical provider. Similarly, and without limitation, all spa personnel, photographers, instructors, guest lecturers and entertainers and other service personnel shall be considered independent contractors who work directly for the Passenger." In other words, when a doctor's negligence leads to the death of a family member, the cruise line is off the hook.

→ **TIME IS SHORT.** There's a one-year limitation period to file a claim, and a six-month period to write a letter to the cruise line when the passenger has been injured. That's a relatively short period of time, compared to the statute of limitations of most states. What if you miss your deadline? You're outta luck.

With careful planning and diligent comparison-shopping, a cruise can be an adventure of a lifetime.

Approaching a cruise line with a complaint

Most cruise grievances fall under the "laundry list" complaint category—which is to say, they aren't one big problem, but a lot of little ones. When those complaints cross my desk, it suggests either the guest's expectations were too high or she didn't plan her floating vacation carefully.

Laundry list complaints to cruise lines tend to generate form responses, if any. It's important to focus on one grievance and tell the cruise line what it can do to fix the problem, preferably as soon as it occurs. Many passengers wait, allowing one problem to pile on top of another until they blow their top

and then send a rambling, angry email to the cruise line. That rarely works. A cruise line can fix a service problem quickly in a variety of ways (an upgrade to a better cabin, a room credit, or a free spa treatment). All you have to do is ask.

For more serious problems, see Chapter 14 on complaint resolution, which will take you through all the right steps. Remember to keep your expectations realistic. A cruise line won't offer a full refund on a sailing if your cabin had a leaky toilet or a crew member was rude to you, although sometimes I wish they would.

BOTTOM LINE

With careful planning and diligent comparison-shopping, a cruise can be an adventure of a lifetime. But inattention to detail can also turn your floating vacation into a nightmare, a drain on your finances, or both, if you aren't careful. So be careful.

13

Handle the TSA and Travel Security

Dealing with checkpoints, scanners, and other security screenings you might encounter on the road.

If you fly commercially—and possibly, if you drive or take mass transit—you'll encounter the Transportation Security Administration. The federal screeners, in their blue uniforms, may ask you to unpack bags, remove shoes, and submit to a scan or a pat-down. It's for your own safety, and you know it, but it can also be disconcerting. If you learn a little about the TSA before your trip, then your next checkpoint encounter may be a little easier on your nerves.

Where will you find the TSA?

The TSA's job is to protect America's transportation systems and "to ensure freedom of movement for people and commerce." As a practical matter, the agency can't police every highway, airport, or waterway, and it never will. Instead, you'll find the TSA in the following places:

→ **AT MAJOR AIRPORTS AND SOME REGIONAL AIRPORTS WITH COMMERCIAL SERVICE.** If you're using a major airport, you'll have to be screened by the TSA. You may be able to avoid the TSA by flying on certain charter flights or noncommercial private aircraft

You're less likely to see the TSA in these places:

→ **ON THE ROAD.** TSA is deploying its mobile VIPR teams (that's shorthand for Visible Intermodal Prevention and Response) on some roadways, but you're probably more likely to see a UFO than to be stopped by a VIPR team.

→ **AT SEA.** If you're cruising, you probably won't see any TSA agents. Screenings and passport control are handled by customs agents and cruise personnel.

→ **ON THE TRAIN.** Although some VIPR teams have been spotted on subways, light rail, and Amtrak, their presence is random and sporadic. Your odds of seeing an A-list celebrity on the train are greater than being searched and questioned by a TSA agent.

Do you have to comply with the TSA?

Once the screening process at the airport has begun, you're required by law and by the TSA to go through the screening. But it's important to note

that TSA screeners, also referred to as Transportation Security Officers, do not typically have law enforcement authority. In other words, they usually can't arrest you. They have to call airport police to do that.

If you're not at the airport, the rules are different. If you approach a VIPR checkpoint, you can make a U-turn or walk away, and there is no legal requirement that you allow your vehicle or your belongings to be searched. In addition, you can deny permission to the agents to search you or your car by saying, "I do not consent to a search." A law enforcement officer can't search your car without probable cause—in other words, unless he or she sees something suspicious. So technically, it's possible to pass through a VIPR checkpoint and deny agents the right to search your vehicle. But you are probably better off just leaving or complying.

Should I try to avoid the TSA?

Probably not. A vast majority of TSA airport searches are problem-free. The agents are polite, efficient, and helpful. But some aren't. There are disagreements at the checkpoints over the safety of the TSA's body scanners, misunderstandings over prohibited items, and, of course,

A pat-down is typically used when you refuse to go through a full-body scanner or if a scan sets off an alarm.

altercations over pat-downs. I know some travelers who believe the TSA is doing a great job protecting us from terrorism. Others flat-out refuse to fly.

Travelers with disabilities and especially passengers with mobility problems tend to have a higher-than-average incident rate with the agency and its screenings: These travelers endure more complex logistics to begin with at checkpoints, and perhaps, inspections by agents inadequately trained to screen them appropriately, as well. The agency also seems to dislike shutterbugs, even though taking pictures of a TSA screening is generally allowed, but may be restricted by local law. (For more on this, see: *tsa .gov/traveler-information/ taking-pictures-checkpoint*.)

Also, if you're skittish about being touched, poked, and prodded, then some TSA screening methods might bother you. As this book goes to press, the TSA still uses what's called an "enhanced" pat-down to investigate any screening anomalies or initial findings that trigger suspicion. A pat-down is typically used when you refuse to go through a full-body scanner or if a scan sets off an alarm (more on that in a moment). That means an agent will touch your arms, legs, torso, and other parts of your body, including possibly your head, with a gloved hand. The TSA says only a small percentage of screenings require a pat-down.

How to get around the TSA

The best way to steer clear of the agency is to plan a trip that avoids a scheduled airline. If you have to fly, take a chartered flight on a small aircraft or use a smaller, noncommercial airfield that isn't likely to have a TSA presence. Most business and leisure trips take place by car, so you would be in good company if you simply decided to drive. A cruise is another way to travel TSA-free. But none of these methods is a guarantee; the agency, if it could, would probably screen every method of travel, in accordance with its mission statement.

Are you approved for expedited screening?

Certain passengers don't need to be screened or are given access to expedited screening procedures. They include the following:
- Some working pilots.
- Flight attendants on duty.
- Members of the military and their children (under the age of 12).
- Police officers on duty.
- Cargo loaders, baggage handlers, fuelers, cabin cleaners, and caterers who work at the airport, have airport IDs issued

after undergoing background checks and training, and are on duty.
- Airport volunteers who have airport-issued IDs as a result of passing background checks and training.
- Members of TSA's Pre-Check (trusted traveler) program. (The program, however, is relatively new and is not available at all airports.)

Mythbusting the TSA screening experience

With the possible exception of fares, no aspect of air travel is more misunderstood than the TSA checkpoint. Here are a few common myths about TSA screening.

→ **MYTH:** There's a "good" and a "bad" time to be flying, in terms of getting through the TSA screening area faster.
REALITY: TSA scales back its staffing during slow times and ramps up its checkpoints with employees during busy times. Predicting a better time to go through security is difficult. You go when you need to fly, and if you're traveling at a busy time of day, give yourself an extra 15 minutes or so on top of the hour that the TSA recommends to get through security—just to be safe.

→ **MYTH:** The TSA mobile application *(tsa.gov/traveler-information/my-tsa-mobile-application),* which uses crowdsourcing for airport wait times and conditions, is the best way to know how long you'll have to wait.

REALITY: Not necessarily true. The mobile app relies on passengers to report their wait times, and the content is controlled by the TSA, which hosts the app. It shouldn't be your only source of information. Check the TSA Status website *(tsastatus.net),* which specializes in screening area conditions and reports on the location of body scanners and whether they are currently being used.

→ **MYTH:** Everyone you encounter in the screening area is a TSA "officer" whose instructions must be followed to the letter.

REALITY: No. Some of the uniformed employees you'll meet prior to reaching the security checkpoint are contracted out by the airlines for queue management and are not trained or authorized to conduct inspections. Either way,

If the questions are too personal, you can refuse to answer.

none of the TSA workers have actual law enforcement authority, even though they refer to themselves as "officers."

If they need to make an arrest, they typically have to call airport police. If a TSA employee gives you instructions that you are uncomfortable with, you can politely refuse. The worst that can happen is that the agent will call the police and you will get to explain the problem to a third party.

→ **MYTH:** You can be selected for a secondary security screening for any reason, and it might even be random.

REALITY: It's been years since someone complained to me about randomly getting the legendary "SSSS" (Secondary Security Screening Selection) marked on a boarding pass, which instructs agents to give you a secondary screening—a second look to make sure you're not carrying any contraband. And, while the TSA won't comment either way, many frequent travelers agree that triggers for getting the ol' once-over can include paying for your tickets with cash, flying one way, and, of course, having a

👍 **SMART** GET-SCREENED BEFORE YOU LEAVE YOUR HOME.

If you're a frequent traveler, you may want to consider joining the Pre-Check program in order to avoid some screening procedures. Bear in mind that while the program may expedite your screening, it can't promise that you'll avoid a scan or pat-down. For more information on joining Pre-Check, consult the TSA's site: *tsa.gov/tsa-precheck.*

name that matches one on the terrorist watch list. You can also set off the magnetometer or body scanner.

→ **MYTH:** American passengers love to bring guns and other dangerous weapons on the plane. Thank goodness the TSA is there to stop them!
REALITY: TSA likes to brag about weapons confiscations, but the truth is, virtually all of the "dangerous" weapons it confiscates are brought through the screening area by accident.

→ **MYTH:** TSA agents have access to extensive information about you at their fingertips.
REALITY: Hardly. Agents can't ping the DMV database for speeding tickets or pull up your criminal record. They do vet travelers against terrorist watch lists. For more information on what the government has on you, see its Secure Flight page at *tsa.gov/es/node/718*.

→ **MYTH:** If you have a disagreement with a TSA agent, you'll be added to some kind of no-fly list.
REALITY: As of now, it isn't a crime to disagree with the TSA, or even to be a critic (I should know). You'll only be added to the terrorist watch list if, as the name suggests, you are a suspected terrorist. The TSA doesn't keep the watch list; it's actually maintained by the Terrorist Screening Center, an arm of the Federal Bureau of Investigation *(fbi.gov/about-us/nsb/tsc/tsc)*.

→ **MYTH:** You must answer a TSA agent's questions if he or she engages you in a "chat down."
REALITY: If the questions are too personal, you can refuse to answer. You will be subjected to a secondary screening, which you can endure in silence.

→ **MYTH:** Behavior Detection Officers are mind readers. They know if you are harboring unpatriotic thoughts.
REALITY: Nope. These specially trained agents (part of the Screening of Passengers by Observation Techniques, or SPOT, program) can tell if you're nervous, at best. Nothing more.

PROBLEM SOLVED

TWO LETTERS ON MY TICKET COST $300

QUESTION: I recently booked two tickets through an online travel agency for my husband and me to fly to the Philippines. When I got his ticket, I noticed that "Jr" was missing from his name. I went back to the site and discovered that there was no "space" provided where I could put a "Jr."

I called the agency and a representative told me it was "not a big deal" and that I should not worry about it. They suggested I call Delta Air Lines, the airline I was flying on, to give them a heads-up.

This weekend, I called Delta and asked them about the name issue. Delta told me that the name on the ticket should match the one on the passport. Delta said that my husband may not have a problem checking in with the airline but that he may have some problems with security, immigration, and even entry to and exit from the country we are visiting.

This set me into a panic mode. Delta also told me that, to ensure that my husband not have any trouble at all, I call my travel agent and request a name change. My agency says Delta doesn't allow name changes and that they need to issue a new ticket. I persisted, and they finally agreed to change the name for $300—that's $200 for Delta and a $100 fee the agency charges. I find this ridiculous and expensive. Please help us. —Agnes Lednum, *Henderson, Maryland*

ANSWER: Your travel agency was both wrong—and right.

Wrong, in the sense that it should have offered a section for "Jr" or "Sr." Given how particular TSA, customs, and immigration officials can be, they ought to allow you to input your full, legal name.

But your agency was correct about this not being a big deal. I've never heard of someone being denied boarding because they were listed as "II" instead of "III" or "Jr" rather than "Sr."

It's difficult to tell if this is an airline hang-up or a TSA issue. But in a situation like this, I just follow the money. No terrorist has ever slipped aboard a plane by hiding behind a suffix. Airlines like Delta, however, collect billions of dollars a year in ticket change fees and other ancillary surcharges.

Airlines need to adopt a more flexible, customer-friendly ticket change policy. That way, a little problem like this wouldn't get turned into a federal case. I contacted Delta on your behalf. It reviewed your record and agreed to fix your husband's ticket as a goodwill gesture.

> Security Check
> Point
> Boarding Pass
> or
> Security Documents
> Required

How do I prepare for screening?

Want to get through the TSA screening process as quickly and painlessly as possible? Here are a few tried and true ways to make your checkpoint experience a smoother one.

→ **PACK LIGHT.** The more you have to screen, the longer it takes. Bring a small carry-on bag if possible.

→ **LEAVE THE HIKING BOOTS AT HOME.** Taking your shoes on and off can slow down the process. Wear shoes you can slip out of—and back into—quickly.

→ **DIVEST.** You've been through a metal detector before, so you probably already know what sets it off. Don't wear anything that might make it beep. If you do, you'll have to undergo a dreaded secondary screening. Pay attention to belt buckles and jewelry, which tend to make the machine scream. Also, remove your belt and all items from your pockets when going through full-body scanners.

→ **NO JACKET REQUIRED.** If you can avoid wearing a jacket, do it. Jackets usually have to be removed, and that's another step that slows down the process.

→ **DON'T FORGET TO BREATHE.** The screening area is the most stressful part of the airport. Slow down, take deep breaths, and don't let them see you sweat. No, seriously. If you look too nervous, you could get a secondary screening.

How do the experts do it?

Frequent fliers are often members of Pre-Check or have access to the special first-class lines run by the airlines, so they move through the system much faster than we ordinary mortals

---

👍 **SMART** ARE YOU READY FOR YOUR "CHAT DOWN"?

The TSA's Behavior Detection Officers sometimes conduct brief interviews, called "chat downs," with passengers who are being screened. The interview process usually takes less than five minutes and includes basic questions, like where you're going, the purpose of your trip, and how long you will be gone. You don't have to answer the questions, but if you refuse, you may face a scan or a pat-down.

IBODY WASH

ISHAMPOO

ICONDITIONER

IBODY LOTION

Toothpaste

→ **BUY A DECENT CARRY-ON BAG.** Get something that's easy to open and, if you're traveling with a laptop, make sure it's in a TSA-approved laptop case (that way, you shouldn't have to take your laptop out of your bag, which can also cause delays). You'll also look like you know what you're doing, which counts for something.

→ **DOUBLE-CHECK YOUR BAG BEFORE YOU LEAVE HOME.** Make sure you didn't pack any knives, firearms, or other prohibited items such as liquids (see below). They may be discovered by the TSA screeners, which is your best-case scenario. Trust me, the last thing you want is to be on the plane when you find the loaded revolver you accidentally packed. That could lead to a series of unfortunate misunderstandings, civil penalties, detention, arrest, or incarceration . . . and a very serious delay.

do. Even when their preferred lines aren't available, they know how to get around the masses.

→ **LOOK FOR THE LINE WITHOUT THE SCANNER.** Those lines tend to move faster because the body scanner adds anywhere between 30 seconds to a minute of screening time per passenger. You can choose the line you stand in most of the time, at least in my experience. Check the TSA Status site to find the exact locations of the scanners. It's a good idea to stay as far away from them as possible, as I'll explain in a minute.

→ **SHOES FIRST.** You'll want to remove your shoes first and put them on the conveyor belt before the rest of your luggage. Why? Because after you pass through the magnetometer, it's the first thing you'll be looking for and the first thing you should do—put your shoes back on. If you reverse the process, you'll be standing around in your socks.

Do my liquids and gels really need to go in a plastic bag on the conveyor belt?

Enforcement of the TSA's 3-1-1 rule is sometimes erratic. I've personally seen agents allow large containers of liquid to pass through the x-ray machine without doing anything; others will reportedly confiscate all of your cosmetics if they are not properly stored in a ziplock bag. Your best bet is to comply with this rule even if you disagree with it.

What if I have a problem with airport security?

It's still a free country. You may express your opinions to the TSA agents you meet at the airport. You may criticize the liquids and gel rule, the scans, the searches, the shoe removal, and anything else you see. However, it isn't unusual for TSA agents to give vocal critics who act suspiciously a secondary screening (I've experienced this myself). My advice? Wait until you're past the checkpoint to speak your mind. Better yet, vote for a candidate who represents your views on this subject.

Should I opt out of the full-body scanner?

If you're unfortunate enough to get into a line with a working full-body scanner, you will be asked to walk through it. The process is pretty straightforward: Empty your pockets, remove your belt, step into the machine, hold your hands above your head, and the machine does the rest. If you refuse, you'll be subjected to a secondary screening, more specifically a pat-down, under the TSA's screening procedures. Even if you agree to use the scanner, you may still be subjected to a pat-down if something suspicious — agents refer to it as an "anomaly" — is detected during the scan.

Passengers object to the scanners for two main reasons: First, the scanners could look through your clothes, allowing the machine to see all of you, although privacy software was said to fix that. Second, some critics worried about being exposed to harmful radiation from the scanners.

As of mid-2013, the scanners that used x-ray technology were decommissioned. They've been replaced by a technology that uses millimeter waves to scan passengers. Some passenger advocates have similar concerns about this technology and are pushing to have all the full-body scanners removed.

The best decision is to avoid having to make a decision in the first place. Find a scannerless line, and you'll

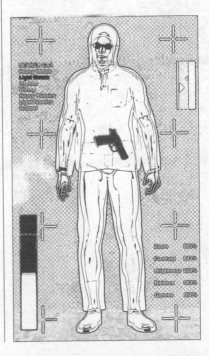

be able to get through the screening area without a secondary screening if your luggage passes the x-ray inspection and if you make it through the magnetometer.

Who should not get scanned?

Whether you allow yourself to be scanned or not is entirely your decision. I've been covering the TSA since its inception and have seen screening technologies come and go. Even though the scanners used today are said to be less harmful than previous versions, I can't personally recommend any of the scanners, and I refuse to use them. Some travelers feel the body scanners haven't been adequately tested. I would emphatically recommend that if you are pregnant or might be pregnant; if you are traveling with young kids; or if you've already been exposed to a lot of radiation or are being medically treated with radiation, you should avoid exposure to scanners. As to privacy concerns, all TSA scanners

have software that claims to make you look like a stick figure on the screen, but some travelers don't believe it. If you don't want a machine to see through your clothes, you'll want to decline a scan.

How do I say "no" to a scan?

Politely tell your screener that you would prefer not to use the scanner. You will then be subjected to a pat-down; you have the right to request that it be conducted by a screener of your gender.

If a screener insists you use the scanner, calmly say, "I would like to opt out, please." You have the right to refuse the scan, and this puts the agent on notice that you are aware of your rights. Try to be as polite and non-confrontational as possible if it gets to this stage.

How do you survive a pat-down with your dignity intact?

Personally, I believe no one should have to choose between being scanned and patted down, and I'm opposed to this method of screening. While a vast majority of pat-downs are conducted without incident, some are not. These strategies can help you get through this unfortunate procedure:

➔ **INTRODUCE YOURSELF.** You want to establish that you are a person, not a suspect. Important: Take a mental note of the agent's name, as you may need it later.

→ ALWAYS ASK TO HAVE THE PAT-DOWN DONE IN A PUBLIC PLACE. In my opinion, the opportunity for misunderstanding or mischief is far higher behind closed doors.

→ MENTION ANY MEDICAL CONDITION YOU MIGHT HAVE, NO MATTER HOW SMALL. If you're just getting over a cold, or you have a sore knee, bring it up. Some pat-downs can be forceful to the point of hurting. Telling the agent you have sensitivities will probably make him or her tread carefully.

→ YOU HAVE THE RIGHT TO ASK THE AGENT TO CHANGE GLOVES. Most will do so as a matter of course.

→ TALK YOUR WAY THROUGH IT. This is not something to be endured in silence. Give the agent constant feedback, and if the pat-down gets too rough, use phrases like "I really have to go to the bathroom," or "Easy there, that's an old baseball injury" to encourage the TSA employee to back off.

→ IF YOU'RE UNCOMFORTABLE, SAY SOMETHING IMMEDIATELY. TSA agents are trained to tell you where they are about to touch you. They should not touch your genital area or conduct a cavity search. If an agent is prodding you in a private area, take a step back, say that you are uncomfortable with the procedure, and politely but firmly ask for a supervisor.

> *Whether you allow yourself to be scanned or not is entirely your decision.*

How to complain to the TSA

If you have a problem with the TSA, what's your next step?

Ideally, the resolution would happen in real time. If you wait until you get home, as with other travel-related grievances, you may never get a fix.

If something goes wrong during your screening and you ask for a supervisor, you should probably know a thing or two about the TSA hierarchy:

 SMART DRESS RIGHT FOR SCREENING.

Avoid short skirts and don't forget to wear underwear when you're flying. Many pat-downs end badly when a passenger isn't fully covered and an agent frisks the wrong place. Gentlemen, I'm talking to you, too. Leave those kilts at home!

→ **TRANSPORTATION SECURITY OFFICER (TSO).** This is the person who is screening you, sometimes also called a "one-striper" because he or she has a single stripe on the shoulder board.

→ **LEAD TRANSPORTATION SECURITY OFFICER (LTSO).** Also called a "two-striper," the LTSO has direct oversight in the screening area and is most likely the first supervisor who will arrive if there's a complaint.

→ **SUPERVISORY TRANSPORTATION SECURITY OFFICER (STSO).** The "three-striper" usually oversees the entire screening area. He or she will be called to the scene if things get serious.

→ **PASSENGER SUPPORT SPECIALIST (PSS).** An officer who is specially trained to screen disabled passengers.

→ **ABOVE THEM, THERE ARE OTHER**

TSA MANAGERS YOU SHOULD BE AWARE OF, including the Transportation Security Manager (TSM), the Assistant Federal Security Director for Screening (AFSD), and the highest-ranking TSA employee at the airport, the Federal Security Director (FSD). They don't wear uniforms and you are unlikely to ever see them.

It helps to know this chain of command if something should go wrong. And remember your manners; being cordial is actually your secret weapon when you're trying to resolve a grievance in real time. No one has ever been arrested for being too polite.

What kinds of grievances should I wait until later to address?

If you're still at the airport and there's a chance a screener can address your problem, you should say something. But if additional paperwork is required to get your problem resolved, you may need to wait until you've arrived at your destination. For example, allegations of serious screener misconduct like assault or theft need to be documented and reported to the TSA *and* airport police, so you'll want to create a paper trail regardless of the outcome of your initial complaint. You'll also need to file a form for lost or damaged property or for a civil rights complaint.

A note about lost, damaged, or stolen property: Some TSA agents have been in the news for pilfering items from checked luggage. Although the agency says it has tried to curb the thefts with a zero tolerance policy, it's better to keep a close eye on your belongings. Don't ever check anything valuable, and take reasonable steps to secure your luggage by closing all latches in your carry-on bag and making it difficult to gain easy access to your valuables. That way, if they decide to go after your bag, they'll have to work for it. (TSA agents can open your checked baggage to inspect it. Don't leave anything of value in there. Ever.)

What do I need to know about the claims process?

Beyond what's explained on the TSA site (*tsa.gov/traveler-information/claim-forms*), there are a few things they won't tell you. The claims process can take two months or more, and I hear from lots of travelers who are unsuccessful at it. One of the problems is that the appeals process seems to be something of a loop. The denials often appear arbitrary and lead to more denials, regardless of whether your case has any merit.

One reason you don't hear more passengers griping about the system isn't because the agency is quickly replacing the items its agents allegedly damaged or stole during screening. It's because passengers simply fail to file a claim when they have one, believing it will never be processed.

Is there an appeal process for damage claims?

Yes. You can send an appeal, along with more information that might persuade the TSA to change its mind, to the following address: Transportation Security Administration, 601 South 12th Street, Arlington, VA 20598-4220. Or you can sue the agency.

Can I shortcut the process on social media?

No. The TSA's two main Twitter accounts, @TSABlogTeam and @TSA, are used for agency messaging and generally don't interact with passengers, but it would be inaccurate to say TSA doesn't pay attention to the online chatter. It does, but mostly for PR reasons. I haven't seen it reverse a claim denial because of something a passenger said via social media.

What about other complaints?

The other major type of grievance is the civil rights complaint. You'll find instructions for how to file one on the TSA site.

BOTTOM LINE

The TSA is an inevitable part of the air travel experience. Whether you agree or disagree with the agency's current practices, you can get through the screening process with your nerves and your dignity intact, as long as you plan ahead and know what to expect.

Resolve Travel Complaints

*Tips, tricks, and strategies for
making sure a travel company addresses
your problem promptly.*

I s your trip not going according to plan? Before you pick up the phone or fire off an angry email, let me share a few insider tricks for fixing a derailed trip. I'll tell you where to write, what to say, and where to go when no one listens.

When to complain:

→ **IF IT'S SOMETHING THAT CAN EASILY BE FIXED IN REAL TIME,** like the wrong food order at a restaurant or a hotel room with a noise problem.

→ **IF YOU LOST A SIGNIFICANT AMOUNT OF TIME OR MONEY** because of something that the travel company directly controls, like a reservation system or a staff decision.

→ **IF THE PROBLEM IS SO SIGNIFICANT** that it could affect future guests or passengers, even if it wasn't a terrible inconvenience to you.

When not to complain:

→ **IF THE PROBLEM IS BEYOND THE CONTROL OF A COMPANY,** such as the weather or a civil disturbance. Those problems, known *as* acts of God or *force majeure* events, can be managed—but not solved.

→ **IF TOO MUCH TIME HAS ELAPSED** between your purchase and your grievance. For example, griping about a bad hotel room six months after your stay makes little

sense. Some airlines require that you fill out a complaint within 24 hours, such as when you're making a lost-luggage claim.

→ **IF YOU CAN'T THINK OF AN APPROPRIATE SOLUTION.** For example, how do you compensate someone for a rude server or a housekeeper who entered your room without knocking? If you don't have any idea, chances are the company doesn't either.

I have a legitimate complaint. Now what?

First of all, let me say, "I'm sorry." Chances are, you haven't heard that yet from anyone—and if you have, it probably wasn't sincere. I'm sorry you had a negative experience. Really.

→ **STAY CALM.** Even though you may feel like ranting, resist the temptation. You're going to need to stay focused to get what you want from the company. If you have to, take a few moments before doing anything.

→ **ACT NOW.** Instead of writing a letter or calling when you get home, mention your problem before you check out,

deplane, or disembark. Frequently, the person behind the counter is empowered to fix the issue on the spot. If you leave without saying something, you'll have to deal with an outsourced call center where operators have 50 ways or more to say "no."

→ **KEEP METICULOUS RECORDS.** When you're having the vacation from hell, record-keeping is critically important. Take snapshots of the bedbug-ridden hotel room or the rental car with a chipped windshield. Keep all emails, brochures, tickets, and receipts. Print screenshots of your reservation.

→ **EXHAUST ALL LEVELS OF APPEAL IN THE HERE AND NOW.** If the front desk employee can't help you, ask for a manager. If a ticket agent can't

fix your itinerary, politely request a supervisor. You're not being difficult: Often, only managers are authorized to make special changes to a reservation, so chances are you're allowing everyone to do their job as opposed to being a jerk.

I missed a real-time opportunity to fix the problem. Should I call or write?

Generally, but not always, a well-written complaint is the most efficient way to resolve a problem.

When to call:
→ **IF YOU NEED A REAL-TIME RESOLUTION AND A PAPER TRAIL IS UNIMPORTANT.** For example, if your flight is delayed and you need to get rebooked, sending an email probably won't work as well as calling.

→ **WHEN YOU DON'T WANT TO LEAVE A PAPER TRAIL.** Let's say you want to complain about a staff member's behavior, but want to keep your correspondence private. A phone call to a supervisor might be the way to do it. Emails can be shared.

→ **WHEN YOU DON'T NEED PROOF OF THE CONVERSATION.** You can call to check on a refund or to verify a reservation, and as long as you don't need to prove you had the conversation, that's fine.

When to write:
→ **WHEN YOU NEED A RECORD OF**

YOUR REQUEST AND THE COMPANY'S RESPONSE. Which is to say, almost always. You don't want the travel company to have the only record of your conversation, which it would if you phoned.

→ **IF YOU THINK THIS MIGHT BE A LEGAL MATTER.** If you think you might have to show proof of your correspondence to an attorney or a judge, you'll want to get everything in writing.

→ **IF YOU CAN'T BRING YOURSELF TO TALK ABOUT IT.** Face it, sometimes you're going to get too emotional to make much sense on the phone. (Been there, believe me.) In that situation, it's better to write.

Write a letter, send an email, or something else?

In the 21st century, you can write and you can *write*. Here are your options and the benefits and drawbacks of each method.

Paper letter
Pros: Can command more attention and respect than anything electronic. Thanks to the U.S. Postal Service's expedited services, FedEx, and other carriers, you can also make it a priority and get it directly into a CEO's office—a useful thing. See my website *(elliott.org/contacts)*

Face it, sometimes you're going to get too emotional to make much sense on the phone.

for details on whom to contact. **Cons:** Letters can be easily lost or "misplaced." They can take several days to deliver and weeks or months to respond to.

Email
Pros: Reaches the intended person virtually instantly and can easily be forwarded to a supervisor, attorney, or (ahem) media outlet if you don't get a desired response.

Cons: Not quite as credible as a real letter. Emails are easy to ignore. Lengthy emails with attachments tend to get filtered to the spam file, which means they may never be seen.

Social media
Pros: The whole world sees your grievance when you post it online with a call-out to the company. Excellent for shaming a company into giving you what you want, but can also backfire when you ask for too much.

Cons: Social media requests generally aren't taken as seriously, and they may be referred to more conventional contacts, such as a company website or phone number.

Online chat
Pros: The immediacy of a phone call, with a record you can keep. Just make sure you remember to save one.

Cons: Agents rely on scripts (prepared answers) and are deliberately vague, so that what they say can't be construed as a promise. I often wonder if there are real people answering the chats, or if they are automated bots programmed to answer your queries, but unable to help.

How do I write a complaint letter that works?

Effective complaint letters are part art, part science. The science part is easy. The art is choosing the right words to convey your disappointment and cajole a company into offering you compensation.

→ **WRITE TIGHT.** The most effective emails and letters are very short— no more than one page, or about 500 words. They include all details necessary to track your reservation, such as confirmation numbers and travel dates.

→ **MIND YOUR MANNERS.** A polite, dispassionate, and grammatically correct letter or email is essential. Remember, there's a real person on the other end of the process reading the email or letter, so something as seemingly insignificant as bad grammar can determine whether your complaint is taken seriously or dispatched to the trash.

→ **CITE THE RULES.** Your complaint has the best chance of getting a fair shake if you can convince the company that it didn't follow its own rules or broke the law. Airlines have contracts of carriage; cruise lines have ticket contracts; car rental companies have rental agreements. Hotels are subject to state lodging laws. Overseas, they may be regulated on a national level.

→ **TELL THEM WHAT YOU WANT, NICELY.** The two most common mistakes that people make with a written grievance are being vague about the compensation they expect and being unpleasant. Also, make sure that you're asking for appropriate compensation. I've never seen an airline offer a first-class, round-trip ticket because flight attendants ran out of chicken entrees.

Why is the company ignoring my letter?

Some travel companies do their best to ignore all complaints, even the legitimate ones. If that's the case, you'll come to that realization fairly soon as you climb through the various layers of appeal. Here are a few reasons your complaint might not be taken seriously.

→ **HAVING A FRIVOLOUS GRIEVANCE.** So the hot water in your hotel room

The most effective emails and letters are very short—no more than one page, or about 500 words.

PROBLEM SOLVED

A NOT-SO-MAGICAL DISNEY VACATION

QUESTION: I need your help with a Disney vacation that turned out to be a disaster. My family of four joined my sister's family and our mother at Walt Disney World recently. Even though we were on the same reservation—called a "Grand Gathering" by Disney—one of our rooms was far away from the rest of us.

Initially, we couldn't get into the Magic Kingdom because our travel agent ordered the wrong tickets. Then, our monorail broke down, making us late for a character breakfast. We had multiple problems with our dining plan, which forced us to spend hours trying to figure out the bill and led to several embarrassing situations. The dining plan was apparently new, and Disney was horribly unprepared to deal with gratuities.

All of this was complicated by problems with our hotel-issued room and park cards, which did not work multiple times at either park entrances or park restaurants.

Then, there were the lines. We arrived at Epcot, hoping to ride on Soarin', only to find a five-hour wait for a FastPass. I expected more and left very disappointed. I wrote a letter to Disney, but haven't received so much as an acknowledgment after eight months. —Troy Pelias, *Dallas, Texas*

ANSWER: Disney should have answered your letter, but I think I know why it didn't. Your initial complaint (the one I published is less than half the length of the one you sent) read like a laundry list. Companies tend to ignore those because they conclude that the customer is just a whiner.

Only, you weren't. You had several legitimate problems, including receiving the wrong tickets and having a dining plan that fizzled. I think the other problems should have been left out of your letter because they probably lessened the effectiveness of your grievance.

The room assignment problems should have been handled while you were at the Wilderness Lodge, not afterward. Similarly, the long wait at Soarin' could have been addressed by showing up at opening time, when the lines are at their shortest. And the monorail breakdown? That happens.

Even so, Disney was a little quick to dismiss your initial letter. A review of its promotional material for "Grand Gatherings" (defined as a group of eight or more) promises a "one-of-a-kind" experience that's "even more magical." Among the special benefits: a dedicated team of Grand Gathering Travel Planners to handle every detail of your itinerary.

I contacted Disney on your behalf. A representative called you to apologize for your less-than-magical experience. Disney refunded the $1,030 you spent on park passes and sent you a $100 gift card that can be used on your next visit.

ran lukewarm? Sorry, but you're not entitled to a free week in a suite. Did a flight attendant get a little short with you on your last trip? Your request for a full refund is unlikely to be granted. Complaints are usually ignored when they're not valid, which means you may not even get the courtesy of a rejection letter. How do you determine if your complaint will fly? I recommend checking out the company's terms and conditions (for example, the airline's contract of carriage, or the cruise line's ticket contract, both of which are available from the company's website). If your problem is addressed there, it's probably the real deal. For the rest, use common sense.

→ **OFFERING A LAUNDRY LIST.** Let's face it, a long list of complaints makes you look like a whiner, and

It can take time to get an acceptable response.

no one takes a whiner seriously. Laundry lists are most common to cruise passengers. The air-conditioning in my berth didn't work right; we didn't get the dinner seating we wanted; our shore excursion left without us—and we want a full refund for the cruise. No can do. Focus on the most important item, and drop the rest.

→ **WRITING TOO LONG.** For some reason, lots of travelers want to compose the great American novel when they complain. Who knows why? The essentials of a long—and likely to be ignored—letter include the following: First, it is incomprehensibly verbose. I've read letters that run more than eight pages, single-spaced. Instead of clear, simple language they are full of big, empty words. Second, it offers a long and detailed timeline. "Saturday morning, 9 a.m., tried to board flight; Saturday late morning, 11:45 a.m., flight delayed; Saturday afternoon, 2 p.m., flight FINALLY boarded." No one needs this information. In fact, these specifics probably are standing between you and the compensation you deserve. Why? Because customer service agents will take a quick look at it and then send—you guessed it—a form response. Save the details for court.

→ **NOT OFFERING A SOLUTION.** Most travelers with a solid case do a fine job of explaining their problems, but not everyone offers a solution. Now customer service agents must guess what it would take to make you happy. Is a letter of apology enough, a voucher, a couple of thousand frequent flier miles . . . or are we talking real money? Here's the problem: The customer service agent will almost always err on the low side, offering a highly restricted certificate instead of a refund, or just sending you a cleverly worded apology, hoping it will be enough. It hardly ever is.

→ **BEING IMPOLITE.** I shouldn't have to tell you that typing in ALL UPPER-CASE is a terrible idea. Your letter will be forwarded to the trash. Remember, the customer service department is staffed with real people. How would you feel if you got an email that said: "This is the WORST HOTEL IN THE WORLD, and you should all be ASHAMED of yourselves." Doesn't make you want to do something nice for that person, does it?

→ **THREATENING.** If you've ever wanted to end a complaint letter— or phone call, for that matter—with the words "I'LL NEVER FLY YOUR AIRLINE AGAIN!" or "I'LL SEE YOU IN COURT!" then let me offer a little advice: don't. Threats won't just guarantee your failure. You could also end up on a company's blacklist (oh yes, they have them), or if your threat is serious enough—say, you threaten the president of the company with bodily harm—you could find yourself

on the wrong side of the law. Interestingly, when I see one of these letters in my inbox, it's often attached to a note sheepishly asking me why the traveler hasn't heard anything from the airline or hotel. Hmm, let's see. Maybe it's because you threatened to boycott the airline?

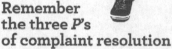

Remember the three *P*'s of complaint resolution

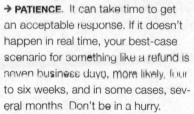

→ **PATIENCE.** It can take time to get an acceptable response. If it doesn't happen in real time, your best-case scenario for something like a refund is seven business days, more likely, four to six weeks, and in some cases, several months. Don't be in a hurry.

→ **POLITENESS.** Kind words can reverse your fortunes and open closed doors. Be unfailingly cordial, and you won't just get a speedier response, but a more favorable one.

→ **PERSISTENCE.** Don't give up. Companies build walls and write form letters that make you want to go away. Don't let it bother you. Stick with it until the problem is resolved. Be the squeaky wheel that is ever-present, but not *too* annoying.

phone. Ask the company to put it into an email or letter. You'll need cold, hard proof that the company gave you a thumbs-down. No worries, you're not out of options yet.

→ **APPEAL TO A HIGHER AUTHORITY.**
Time to send your grievance to a supervisor. I list the names and email addresses on *elliott.org,* my website. Bear in mind that addresses change, so double-check them before writing. Enclose your initial correspondence, along with the rejection and a cordial appeal. You don't have to restate your case, just politely request that the manager review your request one more time.

To whom should I complain?

If you're sending an email, you've got a lot of options. Be sure you don't overlook any of them.

→ **REMEMBER YOUR AGENT OR INTER-MEDIARY.** If you've booked a trip through a third party, then you should start with the agent. Often, that person or agency can act as a go-between and secure a quick resolution.

→ **START AT THE BOTTOM.** If you're already back from your vacation and need to contact a travel company, begin by using its web-based form. If you're filling out a form, be sure you keep a copy of your complaint, since those have a way of disappearing. You're blazing a much-needed paper trail: Companies carefully track each message and assign it a case number. That way, you're in the system.

→ **TURNED DOWN? GET IT IN WRITING.** Don't accept "no" for an answer by

→ **CLIMB ANOTHER RUNG UP THE LAD-DER.** Every travel company has a vice president of customer service, or a manager who is in charge of dealing with passengers or guests. These executives go to great lengths to keep their names and contact information from becoming public, which is why I publish them on my website.

→ **CONSIDER AN EXECUTIVE CARPET BOMB.** By this time in the grievance, you might want to start copying every executive on every correspondence with the company, which is called an executive carpet bomb. Yep, it's annoying, but it also underscores how serious you are about your complaint.

I'm still getting a "no"—now what?

You still have options. They're nuclear options, so use them only as a last resort.

→ **OPTION 1: OVERNIGHT THE CEO.** If the company still says "no," you should consider the "Hail Mary," a respectful but insistent letter overnighted directly to the chief executive officer along with the disappointing string of "nos" you've received.

→ **OPTION 2: DISPUTE THE CHARGE ON YOUR CREDIT CARD.** You can challenge your bill under the Fair Credit Billing Act if you live in the United States. Among other things, the law protects you from any unauthorized charges or incorrect charges and services you didn't accept, or that weren't delivered as agreed. Don't wait too long: You have 60 days after the first bill was mailed to file a dispute. You can find out more about your rights under the FCBA at the Federal Trade Commission site: *consumer.ftc.gov/articles/0219-fair-credit-billing*.

→ **OPTION 3: GO TO COURT.** Most travel-related issues can be handled by a small claims court, which doesn't require that you hire a lawyer. Travel companies like going to court about as much as the average person does, so filing a complaint may be enough

You can challenge your bill under the Fair Credit Billing Act if you live in the United States.

to get the airline, car rental company, or hotel to see things your way. Bear in mind that small claims court limits the amount of your claim (the amount varies based on the state, from $2,500 in Kentucky to $25,000 in Tennessee), and while companies often don't send a representative and lose by default, collecting on a judgment can sometimes be a challenge. Also, you'll have to pay a filing fee, which can cost up to several hundred dollars, depending on where you're suing.

Can't someone help me with my problem?

Yes. If you are reluctant to pull the trigger on a nuclear option—and I don't blame you—then you can reach out to others for help. Remember, your most effective advocate is *you,* but sometimes a neutral third party can be helpful.

→ **THE BETTER BUSINESS BUREAU.** Technically, the BBB won't act as your advocate, but reporting a travel business to the BBB can yield some results. Remember that the BBB is primarily there for its own members, the "better" businesses who fund it, so their decisions tend to be fairly company-friendly. You can get a sense of which way the wind might blow by looking at a company's

PROBLEM SOLVED

AIRLINE WON'T REFUND MY TICKET
AFTER THE DEATH OF MY HUSBAND

QUESTION: I bought a pair of tickets through Expedia for my husband and myself. We planned to visit Germany this fall as part of a retirement trip. Shortly after that, my husband passed away very suddenly.

I contacted Expedia about a refund, but was advised to get in touch with our airline, Lufthansa, directly. Lufthansa told me my husband's ticket was nonrefundable. I asked if they would resell his seat, since he couldn't make the flight, and they admitted they would.

When I said that it appeared that Lufthansa would profit from the death of my husband, they admitted that that was the case. This really offended me. I tried to send an email to Lufthansa's president. What would you advise?
–Ursula Maul, *Wynnewood, Pennsylvania*

ANSWER: My condolences on your loss. Most airlines refund tickets—even nonrefundable ones—when a passenger dies. What's more, it's highly unusual for a representative to admit that the airline will profit from the death of a passenger. Maybe the representative you reached was having a bad day. I certainly hope that explains the response.

I'm concerned about your online travel agency's role in this debacle. Why did Expedia hand you off to Lufthansa in your hour of need? One of the reasons you do business with an online travel agency is that they represent themselves as trusted intermediaries in case something goes wrong with your flight. If they simply sent you to the airline when you needed help, then why not book a ticket directly with Lufthansa the next time, cutting out the middleman?

I might have started the refund process by sending a brief, polite email to Expedia, explaining that you wanted a refund for your husband's ticket. It may have still referred you to the airline, but at least you would have given it a chance to do what it promises it will do, which is to take care of you.

I would have stayed off the phone, too. These days, the odds of you getting put through to an outsourced, overseas call center, where someone is just trying to process your complaint quickly, are too high. Your case required special attention, which neither your agency nor your airline seemed willing to give you.

You had the right idea with the email to Lufthansa's president. I might have started a little lower on the corporate food chain—maybe someone with the word "customer service" in their title. (I list the contact information for Lufthansa and hundreds of other companies on my website at *elliott.org/contacts*.)

If Expedia was unable to help advocate on your behalf with Lufthansa, then a polite email with your husband's death certificate should have worked.

I contacted Lufthansa on your behalf. It apologized for the "inaccurate" response to your request and agreed to refund your husband's ticket.

BBB complaint page, which will show you the number of complaints resolved, compared with the overall number of complaints. Some companies like a spotless BBB record; some don't care. Report your grievance to the BBB chapter in which the travel snafu happened.

Report your grievance to the BBB chapter in which the travel snafu happened.

→ YOUR LOCAL TV STATION OR NEWSPAPER. Some media organizations employ consumer advocates who can mediate your dispute, but as newsroom budgets shrink, their numbers are becoming fewer every year. Even if you happen to live in a city with an "on your side" reporter, getting that person's attention may be difficult. And even if you manage to do so, the advocate may not have the background in travel necessary to understand the case.

→ A TRADE ORGANIZATION. Every industry has its own trade group: Airlines for America (A4A) for airlines, the American Hotel & Lodging Association (AH&LA) for hotels, and the American Society of Travel Agents (ASTA) for travel agencies, among others. These groups often have ethics codes that, if violated, could result in expulsion from the organization. Involving these organizations may result in a speedier resolution of your complaint.

→ THE GOVERNMENT. State and federal agencies may come to your assistance (see Chapters 3 and 4 for details on whom to contact and when to do so). For example, air travel is regulated by the U.S. Department of Transportation, whose Aviation Consumer Protection Division *(dot .gov/airconsumer)* will field and sometimes mediate complaints from passengers with grievances.

When should I give up?

Only you can answer that. Some travelers let it slide after the first rejection; others hang in there until the bitter end. But consider this: Sometimes, the cost of pursuing a complaint, in both time and money, outweighs the benefits. Going after a travel company for nothing more than an apology may not be the most productive thing to do. Pick your battles.

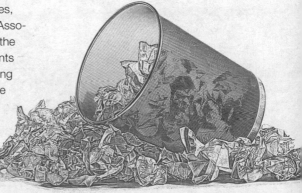

15

Have the Best Hotel Stay Possible

The insider's guide to a successful and problem-free overnight stay.

When it comes to hotel accommodations, most travelers' needs are simple: They want a clean room, a comfortable bed, a reasonable price—and not too many fees. But that's not what they always get. Here's how to make sure you stay happy.

Book a hotel:

→ **IF YOU WANT A RELIABLE LODGING EXPERIENCE** with the convenience of daily linen changes, room service, or an on-property restaurant. Most hotels offer these amenities.

→ **IF YOU NEED TO STAY NEAR AN AIRPORT OR IN THE CENTER OF TOWN.** For many hotels, location and convenience are the biggest selling points.

→ **IF YOU NEED THE PEACE OF MIND** of staying in a secure building.

Don't book a hotel:

→ **IF YOU'RE ON AN EXTENDED STAY**—usually longer than two weeks.

→ **IF YOU NEED THE CONVENIENCE OF A KITCHEN OR EXTRA ROOM** because you're traveling with a larger group. Some extended-stay hotels do offer these amenities, but not always.

→ **IF YOU PREFER THAT OTHER PEOPLE,** like housekeepers and other hotel staff, not have 24/7 access to your living area.

Where should I book my hotel?

You have several options for booking a hotel room, each one with its own set of benefits and challenges.

Direct booking
How it works: You call the hotel or log on to the hotel's website directly, then buy without the help of any intermediary.

Pros: Hotels might offer you a low price guarantee, extra points, or better terms on the room, such as the ability to cancel your reservation without a penalty.

Cons: Since you're dealing directly with the hotel, there's no agency to advocate for you when something gooo wrong. Your first, last, and pretty much only place to go is directly to the hotel.

Go "opaque"
How it works: Sites like Priceline and Hotwire offer aggressive discounts on hotel rooms in exchange for giving up the ability to choose the exact

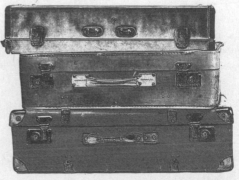

advocate for you if something goes wrong.

Cons: The room may be non-refundable, so pay close attention to the terms before booking.

property and location or collect frequent-stayer points.

Pros: You'll find some of the lowest prices—if not the lowest ones—on opaque sites.

Cons: Your reservation is pretty much nonrefundable. If you want to change your reservation or cancel it, you're usually flat outta luck. You may also get the worst room in the house.

Online agency

How it works: Large websites like Expedia and Orbitz buy rooms at a discount, then resell them to you at a marked-up rate, but one that is still significantly less than if you were booking the sticker price (also called the *rack rate*).

Pros: You'll get a reasonably good discount, but can still have an agent to

Travel agent

How it works: A human agent has access to a wide range of hotel rooms through a reservation system. He or she may even have access to some specially negotiated "unpublished" rates.

Pros: A real agent can take the time to listen to you and find the best possible room, based on your wants and needs.

Cons: You might pay a little more, once you factor in any booking fees or charges above and beyond your hotel rate. Agents also take a commission from hotels—a bonus paid directly to the agent by the hotel—which they do not always reveal to you, the client. Sometimes, even after commissions and other fees

SMART YOU BETTER SHOP AROUND.

No matter how you decide to book a hotel, you'll want to get a good idea of what the going rate is for a hotel room for the dates of your visit. Try Google's Hotel Finder *(google .com/hotelfinder)*, which displays properties on a map and by price. Also, try an aggregator like Kayak *(kayak.com)* to look for the most aggressive deals. Finally, check the hotel company's website to see if it can do better or will offer other incentives to book.

PROBLEM SOLVED

HELP! MY HOTEL IS OVERSOLD

QUESTION: Last fall, I booked a room at the Peabody Hotel in Orlando for a bridge tournament event being held there. A few days before I was supposed to check in, I received an overnight letter informing me that the Peabody was oversold, and that I had been moved to the Renaissance Hotel.

The Peabody offered to pay for my first night's accommodation and offered complimentary trolley passes as compensation. I am 71 years old and recently had hip surgery, so I will not be able to use the trolley.

I called the hotel and got through to a sales manager, hoping to explain my situation. He was rude and unhelpful. My son also called him and the manager was not very pleasant to him, either.

How can I get the Peabody to honor its reservation?

—Virginia Gomprecht, *Jupiter, Florida*

ANSWER: There is no law—at least none that I can find—that would force a hotel in Florida to honor a reservation. I've read all of the relevant statutes, and I am pretty sure that what the Peabody did is legal.

Is it right? Probably not. Yes, overbooking is an industry-wide practice, but there are ways of doing it and keeping your customers happy. I remember arriving at an oversold Ritz-Carlton property a few years ago. I was promptly transferred to a more expensive, smaller inn that ended up being a terrific experience. The Ritz-Carlton even paid my bill. That's how to do it.

Notifying guests at the 11th hour that their accommodations have been changed (and then giving them grief when they try to find an acceptable alternative) is probably not going to make them happy.

What's the hotel's side of the story? It blames a reservation "systems fault" that wasn't discovered until shortly before guests were to arrive. "All of us at The Peabody Orlando deeply regret that this unfortunate situation did not reveal itself [sooner]," a hotel spokeswoman told me.

Although the property is under no obligation to do so, I think it would have been a thoughtful gesture to ask a more able-bodied guest to move to the Renaissance, but the Peabody offered another solution.

In addition to paying for your first night's stay at the new hotel, it also agreed to charge you the rate that you agreed to pay at the Peabody for the duration of your stay at the Renaissance. Because the Renaissance room rate is higher, this accommodation will save you some serious money. The property will also provide you with free door-to-door taxi service from the Renaissance to the Peabody while you are in Orlando.

I think the Peabody's latest offer is a lot better than its first. If you still don't want to stay at the Renaissance, I can think of one other possible fix: Ask one of your bridge tournament colleagues who is staying at the Peabody to switch places with you. I am sure the Peabody would be able to set that up.

are factored in, it can still be a good deal.

How do I pick the right hotel?

Face it: Hotels are basically a bed and a bathroom. Everything else is window dressing. The amenities, the service, the towels, the beach views—they're not essential parts of the product. How do you cut through the clutter to determine what really matters?

There are no credible star ratings for hotels, no single, authoritative guide to help you decide which is the best hotel.

> *Hotels charge a premium for their location, whether there's a quality product on the inside or not.*

→ **REVIEWS MATTER (BUT NOT LIKE YOU THINK).** When deciding on the right hotel, you'll run across user-generated review sites like TripAdvisor, Yelp, and other "star-rating" sites designed to show you the "best" or "favorite" hotel. They can't, and they won't. Why? The ratings are easy to manipulate, and also,

individual tastes and standards vary.

→ **IT'S REALLY ALL ABOUT THE BED.** A few years ago, many hotel marketers woke up and realized that if their beds were uncomfortable, little else mattered. So, they began investing in bedding products, which led to the bed wars, in which hotels tried to outdo one another by offering increasingly extravagant beds. Hotel chains that have their own branded bedding products obviously take the sleep experience—indeed, the guest experience—very seriously. You can find out if they do on their website. Some moderately priced hotels like Holiday Inn have excellent beds, too.

→ **LOCATION MATTERS (AGAIN, NOT LIKE YOU THINK).** Hotels charge a premium for their location, whether there's a quality product on the inside or not. So, unless you absolutely need to wake up and be downtown, or unless you're in the city for a convention, consider staying outside of town. Also check to see if your hotel is close to mass transit; you might even save yourself the expense of a rental car.

→ **PRICE AND SERVICE FIRST, POINTS LAST.** Loyalty programs, which

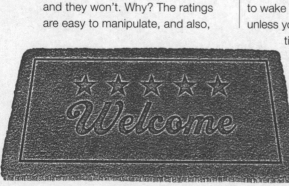

can unduly influence your purchasing decision, should be the *last* thing you factor in to a hotel booking decision. (See Chapter 7 on loyalty programs for more information.) How far down the list? Somewhere around whether they offer mints or chocolates for turndown service. Seriously. To paraphrase Yoda, once you make loyalty programs a central part of your purchase, forever will they control your destiny.

What are the hotel categories and what do they mean, in the United States and abroad?

When you go shopping for hotels, you'll find all kinds of descriptions, from "budget" to "luxury." But these can mean different things to different guests, and no one can seem to agree on the best definition. I like AAA's simple diamond classification system, which can help you quickly find the kind of hotel you're looking for.

One of the most universally accepted rating systems is the one used by Hotels, Restaurants & Café (HOTREC) in Europe *(hotrec.eu),* the umbrella association of national trade associations representing hotels, restaurants, and cafés. It offers a harmonized hotel classification with common criteria. For example, a three-star hotel in Austria will have the same basic amenities and services as one in the Netherlands, Sweden, or

the Baltics. And those would include a reception with a bilingual English and German staff, an in-room telephone, and in-room Internet or online access in a public area. Other countries, notably Britain and France, have similar ratings sanctioned by hotels or tourism organizations. You can find more information at *hotelstars.eu/en.*

What could go wrong with my hotel reservation?

Many hotel reservations aren't worth the paper they're printed on, or the pixels that render them on your computer screen. Here are some of the most common problems you'll encounter.

→ **LOST RESERVATION.** Although your website may generate a reservation number, some guests arrive at check-in only to find that no one has heard of them. The reason? Reservations systems, some of which still are powered by fax machines (yes, *fax* machines), can break down. Fax

sometimes be tricky because your reservation starts on the day you check in and ends the day you leave. That can throw some people off because they think, "I'm planning to be there on Sunday, so I need a room for Sunday," but they are really arriving Saturday night. They actually need a room for *Saturday*. Also, pay extra close attention when booking hotels in Europe and, indeed, most of the world. Date conventions there are Day-Month-Year, not Month-Day-Year as they are in the United States. You could end up with a reservation for the wrong month.

machines run out of paper, you know. The work-around: Always call your hotel to verify your reservation, even if you made a direct booking.

→ **OVERBOOKING.** It's well known that hotels routinely accept more reservations than they have rooms because a certain percentage of their guest are no-shows. That's fine, but the computer algorithm that allows a hotel to do that isn't always accurate. The fix: If your hotel is out of rooms, it will "walk" you to a comparable hotel, which means it will send you to another hotel and pay for the first night's lodging. It's almost impossible to know in advance if a property has overbooked you, but rest assured, if it has, you'll still have a place to stay.

→ **WRONG DATES.** Hotel dates can

What about fees?

By now, you may not be surprised to learn that the hotel room price quoted to you often excludes a number of add-on fees, some mandatory, some not.

→ **BED TAXES AND OTHER GOVERN-MENT FEES.** A bed tax is a levy imposed by local governments on hotel stays. Along with various other fees, it can be used to support tourism promotion efforts and other

---

👍 **SMART** MIND THE FINE PRINT!

When you're self-booking your hotel, pay extra close attention to the terms of your purchase. Many hotels offer a modest discount in exchange for giving up your ability to cancel a room. If you think your plans may change, you'll want to do your due diligence before you click on the "book" button. Otherwise, you might pay for a room you'll never use.

outreach to visitors, or to build new roads and bridges. These taxes are mandatory. A hotel should tell you what the all-in price for your stay is, including these taxes, before you book a room.

→ **MANDATORY RESORT FEES.** Some resorts add a mandatory "resort" fee to your room rate, which includes items that traditionally come with your room, like beach towels or access to the exercise room. What's more, they won't remove the charges even if you promise not to go to the beach or exercise room. To avoid these "gotcha" fees, pay close attention to the room rate when you make a reservation and ask if everything is included.

→ **FEES FOR "AMENITIES" INCLUDED IN YOUR ROOM.** Some hotels add a fee for a room safe (whether you use it or not) or newspaper delivery (whether you want it or not). As soon as you can, tell the hotel that you don't want these "amenities," otherwise they'll be added to your room rate, and they might stick.

→ **FEES TO USE THE PHONE OR WI-FI.** Even hotels that claim to offer "free" local calls or wireless high-speed Internet access for a "low" daily rate may have some surprises in store for you. Making long-distance calls and even dialing 1-800 numbers may subject you to a steep markup, and Wi-Fi connections may end up being billed

per device. Read the fine print before you make a call or log in, and if you have questions, ask first.

→ **MANDATORY TIPPING FEES.** Some hotels add "bellman" or "concierge" fees to their rooms. These surcharges are nothing more than junk fees, meant to pad a property's revenue. If you find yourself staying at a hotel with one of these surcharges, and especially if you prefer to carry your own bags and know where all the good restaurants are, you can and should dispute these fees as soon as you see them on your bill.

What if you don't like your hotel room?

Hey, it happens. Despite your best efforts, you may get stuck with a less than perfect room.

→ **IT'S A SMOKING ROOM.** Yes, some

PROBLEM SOLVED

CHARGED TOO SOON FOR MY HOTEL STAY

QUESTION: I recently had an unpleasant experience with a Holiday Inn in Boca Raton, Florida, that became a Wyndham property. I was hoping you could help me sort things out.

I booked a refundable room for my son at the hotel. I had the choice between prepaying a lower, nonrefundable rate or a higher, refundable rate. I chose the refundable rate because I wanted to be flexible.

I assumed the hotel would charge my credit card at the end of my son's stay, but somewhere between the time I made the reservation and the time my son checked in, the Holiday Inn converted to a Wyndham and my credit card was charged the full $753. From my perspective, the hotel had changed the terms of its reservation by charging the cost of the full visit in advance without informing me.

I disputed the charge with American Express, and they sided with the innkeeper because my son had approved the rate we originally agreed to. I don't think I was treated right. What do you think? —Harvey Kaplan, *Boca Raton, Florida*

ANSWER: I think if you prepaid for your hotel stay, you should have been offered a prepaid rate, which is less expensive than the price you paid for your fully refundable room.

I'm sure the Wyndham would have done this the right way, if it weren't for the reflagging. *Reflagging* is lodging industry-speak for changing the hotel name and affiliation. The property converted from a Holiday Inn to a Wyndham. When that happened, the hotel needed to close out Holiday Inn's records, so it charged your card. If it hadn't, it would have lost all of its credit card information during the conversion, according to Wyndham.

So, why didn't anyone explain this to you? Part of the problem may have been the way you approached the resolution. Although you contacted the hotel in writing, you didn't keep corporate Wyndham in the loop. When the property denied your request for a rate adjustment, you could have appealed your case to Wyndham instead of jumping straight to a charge card dispute. A dispute is your second-to-last option, just before small claims court.

I might have given Wyndham one more chance to make this right, or at least to explain what went wrong. Instead, American Express sided with the merchant, leaving you with only one other choice (besides contacting me): taking this to a judge.

I contacted Wyndham on your behalf. The hotel offered you a refund of $52, the difference between the rate you paid and the prepaid, nonrefundable rate.

states and many countries still allow guests to smoke in their rooms. You may find yourself in a room that's designated nonsmoking (but still smells like smoke), or in a smoking room. You have the right to not breathe secondhand smoke while you and your children are asleep. Ask for a room change, and if none is available, you may want to see if the hotel will walk you to a smoke-free property at no cost to you.

People come to hotels for all kinds of reasons, and not all of them involve sleeping.

→ **UTILITIES NOT AVAILABLE.** A more serious problem is when certain basic utilities are not present. This may include air-conditioning during the middle of the summer, electricity, running water, or hot water; you may find a stopped-up sink or a toilet that doesn't flush. While these basic utilities or amenities aren't specifically promised to you, it's generally understood that your room will come with them and that they'll work. An in-person visit to the front desk is often the best way to fix these problems. Maintenance will be called. The process should be quick. You shouldn't have to spend a night in a hotel room without working air-conditioning, heat, water, or electricity. See page 204 on when to check out of a hotel.

→ **WORST ROOM IN THE HOUSE.** Hotels routinely assign choice rooms to their best guests—the ones who paid the most or who have elite status. The worst rooms often go to the customers who paid discount rates. A number of years ago, one hotelier admitted he had a broom closet that was referred to internally as the "Priceline room." No one should be stuck in that awful room next to the elevator, above the restaurant, and below the disco. Speak up! If the room isn't to your liking, let someone know, and if you're halfway nice about it and there's availability, you'll likely be moved to another room.

→ **LOUD GUESTS.** People come to hotels for all kinds of reasons, and not all of them involve sleeping. If you find yourself next to boisterous guests, remember the chain of complaint. First, if possible, politely ask the loud guests to quiet down. If the guests are belligerent or if you feel you might be in danger, skip to the next step: Call the front desk. If that doesn't work, go to the front desk and ask for a manager. Still nothing? Ask to move, and if that's not an option, and only if that's not an option, call the police.

the hotel placed you in a smoking room with a queen-size bed and a pull-out sofa, with toilets that didn't work, and an air conditioner on the blink—and what's more, failed to remedy the situation—then you should depart ASAP.

→ IF A HOTEL FAILS TO DEAL WITH UNRULY GUESTS. If your complaints about a fellow guest fall on deaf ears, and if you have to call the police and the issues are still unresolved, then you should depart early and find alternate accommodations.

Early checkout protocol: No matter where you made your reservations, a hotel should not charge you for a room you can't or won't use under these circumstances. So, if the hotel insists on charging you even though it asks you to leave early, or delivers the wrong room, or fails to crack down on noisy guests, you should consider disputing the excess charges on your credit card.

When should I check out of a hotel?

Sometimes, you have to say "enough is enough," pack your belongings, and leave.

→ IF YOU'RE ASKED TO LEAVE EARLY. Under most state laws, unfortunately, you don't have a right to stay in a hotel indefinitely. If an innkeeper asks you to go, and you don't, they can call the police to have you forcibly removed. If a hotel believes you've been a bad guest (i.e., it's spring break and you've had a *very* good time), maybe it's time to check out.

→ IF THE HOTEL CAN'T DELIVER WHAT IT PROMISED. If you reserved a nonsmoking room with twin beds, and

Resolving a hotel dispute

Although some of your rights are outlined in the terms contained in your reservation, you have additional legal rights that are detailed in your state's lodging statutes. Each state's laws are slightly different, but these are the major issues you can expect to see addressed in a state's lodging laws:

- Limits of liability for property left in a room.
- Rejection of undesirable guests.
- Telephone surcharges.
- Conduct on the premises.
- Unclaimed property.
- Sanitary regulations.

Not exactly the kind of lodging "bill of rights" you would hope to find— such as a promise that a reservation is a guarantee of a room, for example. But even though hotels appear to have a broad license to play games with their customers, they usually don't. The lodging industry is highly competitive, and hotel managers know that if they treat you like dirt, you won't be back a second time. This contrasts sharply with, say, airlines, which are confident you'll return as long as the fare is low enough.

In most hotels, the staff is trained to address grievances in real time. The staff can offer you anything up to a "comped" room (in other words, zeroing out your bill) if the situation warrants.

When you're dealing with a large hotel chain, you also have a final layer of appeal after you've hit a dead end with the property. You can send your case to the corporate owner. So, for example, if you have a problem with a DoubleTree property and are

Even though hotels appear to have a broad license to play games with their customers, they usually don't.

getting nowhere with the local manager, you can forward your grievance to Hilton at the corporate level. Even the suggestion that you might "take this to corporate" can make a hotel change its tune. Properties are evaluated by their corporate parent based on customer feedback, including how many complaints they generate, and managers will often do everything in their power to make you happy before you go over their head.

BOTTOM LINE

Staying in a hotel can be the best part of your trip, as long as you do a little homework before you make a reservation and keep your expectations in check. You may not have a lot of rights on paper, but in practice, most hotel stays are relatively problem free.

16

Choose Your Ideal Lodging Arrangements

From glamping to yurts, and everything in between—plus, how to handle an Airbnb reservation.

From glamping to yurts, there's a dizzying variety of lodging choices beyond the standard hotel room. One closely related subset of the hotel industry, the all-inclusive resort, comes with meals, activities, and even beverages. There's also a wide range of newer alternative lodging options, from home swapping to couchsurfing, that are no-frills options. Which one is right for you? And what happens if something goes wrong? I'll help you sort it out.

What kind of alternate lodging should I consider?

These lodging options aren't for everyone but, if they fit your comfort level and budget, they can make for great alternatives to standard hotel rooms.

All-inclusive resort

What is it? It's probably best to think of an all-inclusive as the equivalent of a land-based cruise vacation. When you pay for your accommodations, you're getting much more, including activities, meals, and drinks. You can stay on the property the entire time, and that's exactly the point. It's all there. Most all-inclusives are found outside of the United States and often in warmer climates. They operate under names like Sandals, Club Med, Iberostar, Barceló, Riu, Palace Resorts, Secrets, Dreams, and Divi Resorts, among others.

Do it: If you love the cruise experience, but don't like being on the ocean.

Don't do it: If you're more adventurous, like to leave your hotel and tour a destination independently, and like to choose where to eat.

> *There's a dizzying variety of lodging choices beyond the standard hotel room.*

Bed-and-breakfast (B&B)

What is it? Many bed-and-breakfasts, or B&Bs, double as the owner's residence, so the accommodations may be somewhat more homelike than a hotel's. Your room may not have its own bathroom, for example. (Don't forget to ask.) You might also have to deal with the eccentricities of someone else's home. Pets may be present. Also, breakfast may be an event shared with other guests or the owners.

Do it: If you love meeting new people, and like "authentic" accommodations that are priced reasonably.

Don't do it: If you're a private person or are traveling with unruly kids. A B&B is generally not a place for children.

Homeswap

What is it? As the name suggests, home swapping allows you to trade time in your house for time in a comparable house. Most home swaps are handled online through communities like HomeExchange *(home exchange.com)*, but of course they can also be done informally through a relative, friend, or acquaintance. Some online communities charge an annual membership fee—*home forexchange.com* charges $64 annually, for instance. Others are free.

Do it: If you have a house that you don't mind entrusting to strangers, and if you don't mind living in someone else's house.

Don't do it: If you don't like anyone else living in your house.

Online bed, room, or home rentals

What is it? The most explosive growth in alt-accommodations has come from online services that allow you to rent a room or an entire apartment. The most dominant of these sites, Airbnb *(airbnb.com)*, connects homeowners and tenants with spare rooms to offer to travelers who need accommodations. More on Airbnb later in this chapter.

Do it: If you want some assurances that the place will have a minimum level of services and amenities and don't mind a little randomness.

Don't do it: If you need consistent and predictable accommodations.

Glamping, cabins, and yurts

What is it? The mainstreaming of the "adventure" travel movement in the early 2000s has created an entire category of accommodations that our ancestors thought they'd left behind once and for all when they moved to the city: upscale camping—"glamping"—and staying in luxury cabins and yurts. Some amenities, such as individual bathrooms or running water, may be missing. The appeal? It allows you to get much closer to nature without having to make *too* many sacrifices.

> *Staying in a hostel is one of the most affordable options.*

Do it: If you're looking for something different and aren't afraid of a little adventure.

Don't do it: If you require all the amenities you'll find at home, including your own bathroom, a kitchen, and privacy.

Hostel

What is it? For the most budget-conscious traveler, staying in a hostel is one of the most affordable options, aside from staying with friends. It is not necessarily a bad option, either.

Although you'll most likely share a room and a bathroom with other travelers and you may sleep on a bunk bed or a cot, the price can't be beat. At international hostels, private rooms are offered, but in most hostels, it's like being back in college.

Do it: If you don't mind roughing it a little and can handle sleeping with loud noises around you, and possibly large insects, like the ones I fended off when I slept in a New Orleans hostel in my school days.

Don't do it: If you like hotel amenities and privacy. Also, many hostels are coed, so if that bothers you, skip it.

Couchsurfing

What is it? The term *couchsurf,* coined in the 1990s, means moving from one friend's house to another and sleeping on a spare bed, couch, or floor. Couchsurfing also refers to a more organized form of hospitality exchange, which involves sharing space on your sofa with strangers and trading it for space on their sofas. A site called Couchsurfing *(couch surfing.org)* facilitates that exchange.

Its tagline says it best: Couchsurfers: Share your life.

Do it: If you like meeting new people and want to save money on your accommodations. The price is right too—couchsurfing is free.

Don't do it: If you like your privacy and would pay something—anything—for it.

What are the risks of alternative lodging?

Notice any similarities among those alternative lodgings? Often, you sacrifice privacy, convenience, and peace of mind for a better price, or for *no* price. Sometimes the trade-off is worth it, but sometimes it isn't. It's something you should figure out before you hit the road.

→ **ACCOMMODATIONS ARE NOT AS ADVERTISED.** Generally, the less you

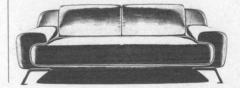

pay for your accommodations, the less sure you can be of the product. "Pay more, get more" certainly applies here, especially when the "more" refers to peace of mind.

→ **THOSE ARE NOT THE TERMS YOU WERE OFFERED.** Some alt-lodgings operate on little more than a hand-shake. That's why it's so important to have every promise in writing, especially the part about refunds and cancellations. Alt-lodging is known to take your money if you change your travel plans, and never return it.

→ **NOTHING WORKS.** Pervasive among alt-lodging complaints—and particularly on the lower end—are complaints that nothing works. There are no towels or sheets. The wireless Internet is down. In extreme cases, the bathroom is unusable.

ALL-INCLUSIVES AND AIRBNB

Let's spend the second half of this chapter diving into two problem areas for travelers: all-inclusives and Airbnb accommodations. Because I receive a regular stream of complaints about these vacation options, they deserve special attention.

What do I need to know about all-inclusive resorts?

Most of the complaints I get about alt-accommodations involve all-inclusive

resorts, which come with their own set of challenges. An all-inclusive looks like a traditional hotel, but in many ways, it isn't.

→ **ALL-INCLUSIVE RESORTS OFTEN HAVE AN UNUSUALLY CLOSE RELA-TIONSHIP WITH TRAVEL AGENTS,** offering generous commissions and incentives. As a result, if an agent recommends an all-inclusive, you should do your due diligence. (See Chapter 2 for details about travel agents.)

→ **ALL-INCLUSIVES ARE OFTEN SOLD AS PACKAGES THAT INCLUDE TRANS-PORTATION TO THE RESORT.** The terms of these vacations can be more restrictive than those of other types of accommodations, so if your plans change, you could lose everything.

→ **YOUR TRAVEL AGENT MAY ENCOUR-AGE YOU TO BUY TRAVEL INSURANCE WITH YOUR PACKAGE,** but again, con-duct your own research before buying. Agents are heavily incentivized to sell the insurance, and you may—or may not—be covered if your plans change. (See Chapter 5 for more on insurance.)

What could possibly go wrong on an all-inclusive vacation?

Although most all-inclusive vacations are problem-free, some are not. Here are a few potential problem areas.

PROBLEM SOLVED

HELP, MY HONEYMOON IN COSTA RICA WENT SOUTH

QUESTION: My wife and I recently booked a honeymoon in Costa Rica through Apple Vacations. On the morning we were supposed to leave, our flights on Delta Air Lines were canceled, and they didn't have any other flights until two days later.

I called Apple, and they refused to help. They simply told me to call the airline. Delta's customer service was only a little more helpful. They ended up getting us to Costa Rica a day later on a different airline.

Because of this, we missed one day at an all-inclusive resort, so we decided to stay an extra day. I again called Apple and asked them to refund our missed day and book an extra day on the end of our honeymoon. They would not refund any money for the missed day, and they charged us for the extra day.

I sent a letter to Apple's customer service office, as they suggested I do. I have not gotten any response from them after two letters. Any advice on this issue?
—Loyd Jobe, *Evansville, Indiana*

ANSWER: It sounds as if Apple could have done more to save your honeymoon. But let's take a closer look at the facts.

Delta canceled your flight, not Apple. So in a sense, Apple was right. You would have to talk with the airline about rescheduling your flight. At the same time, Apple advertises a "beginning-to-end" vacation experience, which includes employees greeting you at your departure airport and meeting you when you arrive.

Perhaps Apple raised the bar a little high when it promised the "ultimate in a quality vacation experience."

I contacted Apple, and a few other details emerged. First, the company says you were offered travel insurance, which would have protected your vacation investment. You declined, according to Apple. So technically, the delay wasn't Apple's fault, and you didn't buy its insurance. It owed you nothing, in a contractual sense.

But who cares about contracts? This is your honeymoon, and you booked a vacation with a company that you believed would take care of you rather than do just what's legally required of it.

I always recommend that for once-in-a-lifetime vacations like yours, travelers consider the services of a travel agent who specializes in honeymoons.

It turns out Apple asked your resort for a date swap, which would have allowed you to stay an extra day at your hotel, but it turned them down. I think you might have started a dialogue with your hotel, letting them know that this was your honeymoon and that you didn't really want to lose the last day of a special vacation.

Next time—and I really hope there isn't a next time—you might want to either send an email to Apple Vacations or ask for a return receipt from the post office. The company had no record of either of your letters.

Apple contacted your resort again on your behalf and secured a $184 refund for the last night of your vacation. It also sent you two $100 travel certificates.

→ **SUBSTANDARD FACILITIES.** One recent guest complained: "The bathroom fixtures were rusted, tiles were cracked and broken in showers, and rooms were in more than a little need of repair but a complete renovation. The whole resort I felt was in need of a renovation." Did I mention it was her honeymoon?

How to avoid it: I document many all-inclusive horror stories on my website *(elliott.org),* but a simple search for "all-inclusive hotel" and "complaints" will yield a treasure trove of useful information.

→ **BAD GUESTS.** You may be able to control where you stay, but you can't always predict who else will be there. I mediated a recent case in which a couple celebrating an anniversary had to share the entire resort with a rowdy group of radio station fans. They were loud. They were obnoxious. They made the couple's vacation an intolerable nightmare. "The daily noise level and filth was unconscionable," says the guest.

How to avoid it: If you're visiting the Caribbean, especially during the off-season, chances are you'll have at least one large convention group at an all-inclusive. Ask about any big groups staying at the property *before* you make your reservations. If you have a problem with the group, or think you might, find another all-inclusive resort for your vacation.

→ **BOTCHED SERVICES OR MEALS.** Since all-inclusives offer so much more than a bed to sleep in, the complaints about service are more common than at other types of lodgings. One recent bride was devastated when a photographer who worked for the hotel inadvertently deleted all of her wedding photos. Seriously, you can't make this stuff up.

How to avoid it: All-inclusives, like other businesses, turn a profit by marking up their services. If those services seem unusually affordable—if not downright cheap—there might be a good reason for it, or maybe I should say, a *bad* reason. Honestly, you get what you pay for. If you go for the cheapest all-inclusive, you might regret your decision.

How do you fix an all-inclusive problem?

Since an all-inclusive resort is so similar to a hotel, you'll want to use many of the problem-solving tactics I outlined in Chapters 14 and 15 on problem solving and hotels. Indeed, the most common problems you'll encounter, from obnoxious guests to bad service, can easily be remedied by saying something immediately. All-inclusives will do almost anything they can to contain a problem, such as a disgruntled guest. In my experience as a consumer advocate, the last thing they want is for someone who is a likely repeat visitor to leave the property unhappy, and potentially complain to a travel agent or, um, an outside party. In other words, a real-time resolution is more important than ever.

If you decide to complain to an all-inclusive after you get home, you may be more successful by asking your travel agent to make the inquiry on your behalf. If that agent is a top producer for the all-inclusive resort, chances are he or she has a personal relationship with a sales manager and can make a refund magically appear in your account. Practically speaking, most all-inclusives try to solve a problem with vouchers that cover lodging nights but not transportation. Beware of these offers: They look good on paper, but they usually expire after a year, and a high percentage of this scrip goes unused. Which may be why resorts give the vouchers away so liberally.

> *You may be able to control where you stay, but you can't always predict who else will be there.*

What about Airbnb?

Ah, Airbnb. This online community, which describes itself as a "trusted community marketplace for people to list, discover, and book unique accommodations around the world," has booked more than ten million nights, in lodgings ranging from apartments to castles, since its launch in 2008. It lists properties in 33,000 cities and 192 countries. The vast majority of those ten million nights are trouble free, but when something goes wrong—and it sometimes does—the failures can be pretty spectacular. Of all the alt-lodging options, Airbnb is one of the most common sources of complaints.

What could go wrong with Airbnb?

Part of the problem with Airbnb is the "trusted" label it generously gives itself. What does "trusted" mean? And is it in any way comparable to the quality standards of, say, a Marriott or Hilton? How about a professionally managed vacation rental? To both of those questions, the answer is "no." While Airbnb's terms and conditions are filled with language that would lead you to believe the company inspects each property, the fact is, the company really has no idea what awaits you. The user-generated reviews may be helpful, but they may also be incomplete. For more on user reviews, please refer to Chapter 1.

So what are the most common Airbnb complaints? Here are the top three:

→ **HOME OR APARTMENT NOT WHAT I EXPECTED.** Owners sometimes embellish a few important facts when they write up their listing on Airbnb. If there's a fine line between hyperbole and lies, Airbnb seems unaware of it. As a result, guests show up at a property and are disappointed with what they find: The home is in a bad neighborhood, the place is a shambles, the amenities aren't there.

How to get around it: Unless you know how to read between the lines, it's difficult to spot the lies, but not impossible. An Internet search can reveal the neighborhood, crime statistics, and even an image of the rental, thanks to the "street view" option on Google Maps (google.com/maps). If, despite your research beforehand, you find yourself stuck with a rental that falls short of your expectations, call Airbnb and ask it to provide you with alternate accommodations.

→ **THE OWNER IS A JERK.** Not everyone gets along, but when your host is being an insufferable idiot, it can make a short stay seem like half an eternity. I dealt with a recent case in which a

guest who complained about an amenity that should have worked—but didn't—was subjected to numerous disparaging comments from the host, who finally threatened to kick him out of his apartment.

How to get around it: It's difficult to see something like this coming. Some reviews can offer clues, but you may find yourself phoning Airbnb for help if you lock horns with a cranky landlord. Airbnb can act as a mediator or help you switch properties.

→ **WHERE'S MY REFUND?** Airbnb offers several refund options, so pay close attention before you give the company your credit card details. Misunderstandings can happen when an owner verbally agrees to a refund—say, after a natural disaster—but the refund policy says otherwise. Again, talk is cheap. It's what's in the refund policy that matters.

How to get around it: Don't waste your breath arguing with a host. If the terms of your rental say you're owed a refund, ask Airbnb for help, and if you don't get it, dispute the charge on your credit card.

How do you fix an Airbnb problem?

In many respects, an Airbnb complaint is a lot like a disagreement with a home rental. The problems, such as they are, can quickly devolve into a personal conflict. Remember, you're staying in someone else's house, sleeping in their bed, eating in their kitchen. How could they *not* take everything you say personally? The difference is that you have a large company, Airbnb, between you.

The trick is to leverage Airbnb to your advantage, if necessary. The company offers numerous assurances that you can invoke, including the following:

→ **A "SECURE" (READ: SUPPOSEDLY FRAUD PROOF) SYSTEM** for handling all the financial transactions between you and the host.

→ **MECHANISMS FOR REQUIRING BOTH HOST AND GUEST** to authenticate their identity via social media.

→ **A MESSAGING SYSTEM THAT ALLOWS YOU TO COMMUNICATE DIRECTLY WITH THE HOST** when you have questions about your upcoming stay.

You can also refer to Airbnb's terms and conditions, which is a dense and sometimes difficult-to-read document that describes your rights and obligations when you rent through the company. It's possible that Airbnb's security guarantees and terms won't address a specific problem you have, but they suggest the company is trying

> *Airbnb can act as a mediator or help you switch properties.*

to offer you the kind of peace of mind you'd get with a hotel reservation. So even if your grievance isn't directly addressed, it's implied that your Airbnb stay will be problem free—and that's often enough to get a desired resolution.

Airbnb is the neutral third party that stands between you and the owner and tries to keep things humming along smoothly. As with most other types of travel disputes, the best results come from someone who quickly and politely addresses any problem with a rental, as opposed to waiting to get home before saying something. Airbnb responds fairly quickly to complaints and is hypersensitive to any criticism it gets online, via social media. But I would do everything you can to resolve this through direct channels before launching a shame campaign. Don't forget, you always can dispute a charge on your credit card if you need to, but use this as a final option instead of trying it first.

BOTTOM LINE

The galaxy of alternative lodging is constantly expanding. Whether you like to rough it in a hostel or tent, or prefer to "glamp," remember: At the end of the day, it's still just a bed to sleep in. Everything around it is window dressing.

17

Find the Right Vacation Rentals

A few secrets for zeroing in on the ideal rental and getting what you paid for.

Why stay in a hotel when you can rent a house or condo? That's a question many travelers are asking themselves, particularly at a time when some hotels are adding new fees, surcharges, and restrictions to their rooms. Renting a home or condo can be a great lodging alternative, as long as you know what awaits you.

Consider renting:

→ **IF YOU'RE TRAVELING WITH A LARGE GROUP** or a family and need extra room. You can also find a smaller vacation rental for one or two people.

→ **IF YOU DON'T LIKE BEING BOTHERED BY HOUSEKEEPERS,** room service, or close proximity to other guests, as you might well be in a hotel. At many rentals, housekeeping, where available, is optional and often incurs an additional fee.

→ **IF YOU REQUIRE THE FACILITIES FOUND IN A HOME,** like a full kitchen or a living room.

→ **IF YOU VALUE THE COST SAVINGS AND CONVENIENCE THAT VACATION RENTALS ALLOW,** such as preparing meals, enjoying in-home entertainment, or splitting multiple bedrooms with your friends and family.

→ **IF YOU ENJOY GETTING TOGETHER WITH FAMILY AND FRIENDS IN A HOME-LIKE ENVIRONMENT,** with the benefit of your own space and privacy.

Don't rent:

→ **IF YOU LIKE HAVING A CONSISTENT, PREDICTABLE LODGING EXPERIENCE,** including full room service and daily towel and linen service when you're traveling.

→ **IF YOU DON'T NEED LOTS OF SPACE,** but want to be somewhere centrally located, such as a city center or near a popular attraction.

→ **IF YOU LIKE TO EAT MOST OF YOUR MEALS IN A RESTAURANT** and don't mind paying extra for things like laundry service.

What do I need to know about vacation rentals?

Vacation rentals are a vast, unregulated market that can be divided into professionally managed properties—those offered by a vacation rental professional and those for rent by owner, which are offered directly through

is a fake, you could lose everything. Always look for a secure Internet reservation site or the option to book by phone, along with the ability to accept major credit cards.

→ **NOT RESEARCHING THE PROPERTY.** The property description on a rental site is often filled with hyperbole.

Don't rely on just one source when you're shopping around for vacation rentals. Consult independent reviews and pick up the phone and speak with the owner or manager before you sign any contract. Make sure you ask for references from previous renters.

→ **FAILING TO READ THE CONTRACT BEFORE SIGNING.** Again, a home rental isn't a hotel, and certain terms and conditions may apply that you won't find at any hotel. For example, the rental may insert a "nondisparagement" clause that prohibits you from posting an unauthorized review. If you do, your credit card could be charged extra. Fortunately, this is not a common practice.

homeowners. Generally speaking, professionally managed rentals may be more expensive, but will have higher quality standards and more guest services, while "by owner" rentals may be less expensive and vary qualitatively.

What are the biggest mistakes renters make?

A vacation rental is not a hotel. Perhaps the biggest mistake travelers make is thinking their rental will be just like a bed-and-breakfast, minus the breakfast. It isn't. It is, in some respects, better than a hotel, and in some respects it can be worse.

→ **WIRING MONEY.** I've said it before many times in my role as a travel adviser, but it merits repeating. Never, never, *ever* wire money to a homeowner or rental manager. The rental may be legit and the owner might sound like a perfectly nice person, but you're giving up many of your rights when you wire money. If the "owner"

How do I find a vacation rental?

Most vacation rental apartments and homes are found online, but that's not the only way.

→ **ONLINE.** Explore a listing website like VRBO *(vrbo.com)*, or FlipKey

(flipkey.com). VRBO lists mostly "by owners" properties, while Flip-Key deals mainly with professionally managed properties, although there's some overlap.

→ **THROUGH A TRAVEL AGENCY.** Agents can offer vacation rental homes through their reservation systems or through a third party like the Travel Rental Network *(travelrentalnetwork.com)*, which pays agents a commission.

→ **THROUGH THE CLASSIFIEDS SEC-TION.** Newspapers and magazines sometimes list short-term rentals, and there are always the online classifieds, such as Craigslist *(craigslist.org)*, but be warned — online classifieds can sometimes be scams.

→ **IN PERSON.** If you're staying at a destination and planning to return, and see a "for rent" sign, it's worth asking if there's some availability next year. By reserving a property a year in advance, you might be able to lock in a more favorable rate. Plus, you'll meet the owner or manager, which is always helpful.

What are some more differences between professionally managed

and "by owner" vacation rentals?

A vacation home is a vacation home, right? Well, not necessarily. At some level, you're getting essentially the same or a similar product, no matter whom you're renting from, but behind the scenes, there are some noteworthy differences.

> *Above all, a professionally managed rental will come with a baseline level of services.*

→ **PROFESSIONALLY MANAGED.** A management company will probably charge a rate that's competitive with a nearby hotel and offer several payment options, including a credit card. Professional managers also use a more standard contract, so you're less likely to find a surprise, but you should still read your agreement *thoroughly*. You will also find a 24 hour customer service contact, in case something happens while you're renting. Some higher-end rentals also offer a concierge service for restaurant reservations and events.

Above all, a professionally managed rental will come with a baseline level of services, such as professionally cleaned properties, towels, linens, and a guarantee that everything will be in working order when you check in. In some areas, towels and linens are never included, no matter how you rent. In North Carolina's Outer Banks, for example, linens are almost always extra. Keep an eye out for "junk" fees like a "reservation fee" or a "damage waiver fee" that might pop up without warning.

→ **"BY OWNER" RENTALS.** An independent homeowner may or may not offer you a competitive rate for your vacation home. You'll have to research comparable properties to find out if it's right on the money, overpriced, or too good to be true. Since the owner is responsible for maintenance, upkeep, and any customer service aspects of your rental, the service and amenities might vary. Pay close attention to any online reviews and references provided by the owner. Don't expect any 24-hour hotline or concierge service, although I've found that owners are typically very responsive to their customers.

How professional is my professional rental?

Membership in the Vacation Rental Managers Association indicates that a management company is dedicated

> *You'll have to research comparable properties to find out if it's right on the money, overpriced, or too good to be true.*

to elevating the vacation rental industry as a whole, and therefore your stay as well. Its members hold themselves to a high standard, including following best practices to stay abreast of industry trends and the example set by the VRMA's Code of Ethics and Standards of Practice.

You can expect these companies to have a variety of properties to choose from, with reservation agents that can help you pick the property that will fit your needs. VRMA companies also offer 24/7 service, so if something happens during your stay, you have access to a real person on standby who can be there quickly to help.

Should I avoid renting a "by owner" property?

No. While you'll get some peace of mind from a managed property, you can find many quality "by owner" properties on the market, too. In fact, if you're a hands-on property owner,

COTTAGE FOR RENT

it may not make much sense to hand your property over to a real estate agency. Consider a few of these numbers from my colleague Christine Hrib Karpinski, who publishes the website *How ToRentByOwner.com*. Once you factor in a 30 percent commission paid to the manager and up to 3 percent to use a credit card, she says it's often more profitable to handle the rental yourself, as a vacation rental owner. What those numbers tell me is that by ruling out "by owner" properties, you're ignoring a huge segment of the market—and possibly the perfect vacation rental.

Is that listing for real?

A vacation rental listing may be legit in the sense that the place exists, but how can you tell if it is what it says it is? Online reviews and testimonials can help, but remember—those can be doctored and manipulated. Sometimes you can ferret out a fake by reading the property description carefully.

➔ DO THE PHOTOS LOOK LIKE THEY'RE RIGHT OUTTA *ARCHITECTURAL DIGEST?* Do they use wide-angle lenses or angles that make the home appear as if it's the only house on the beach? Are the interior shots over-staged? These could be signs that the property owner is trying to make the home look better than it actually is. Then again, the property could live up to its billing. If possible, cross-check it on Google Maps *(google .com/maps)* and use the "street view" option, which may give you a better idea of what the rental looks like.

What do they really mean?

Property descriptions can predict the actual experience. But mind the buzzwords! The vacation rental industry sometimes uses the same tired phrases to describe its product, and just seeing these words in a property description makes me suspicious, because they're so cliched. Here's how I interpret them:

• Classic—Like staying at Grandma's, only you pay for it.
• Clean—But the rest of the neighborhood is chaos.
• Cozy—It's a closet.
• Inviting—Takes a good picture, but nothing works.
• Private—You'll never find it.
• Romantic—Kids not welcome.
• Rustic—No sign of civilization.
• Secure—It's in a bad neighborhood, so lock your doors.
• Warm—The AC doesn't always work.

What kind of vacation rental traps should I know about?

➔ RENTAL DOES NOT EXIST. Here's a problem with some "by owner" rentals

PROBLEM SOLVED

NO REFUND FOR MY COLORADO CONDO?

QUESTION: I need your help getting a refund for an advance resort rental paid to Winter Park Lodging Company in Winter Park, Colorado. I made a reservation to stay in a two-bedroom condo during the New Year's holiday.

I had to cancel my reservation almost a month before I was supposed to arrive. The company refunded the sales taxes and linen charges of $69 out of the prepaid $965. But it kept $896 for the rental.

Winter Park Lodging's cancellation policy says, "If you must cancel, let us know as soon as possible and we will try to rebook your property for your reservation dates, and will reimburse you for any nights we are able to rebook for you." I asked the company if it rented my unit. It says no, but I question its honesty. If you look at the property availability on its site, you'll see that all of the weekends from January to April were fully booked. What can be done? —May Tong, *Houston, Texas*

ANSWER: You have to take Winter Park Lodging Company at its word. Which is something you're unwilling to do, and for good reason. Its site appears to contradict what it's telling you.

The company's cancellation policy, which it emailed to you, has one other disclaimer: "We strongly encourage that you purchase vacation insurance for your reservation. Without vacation insurance, there is no guarantee that you will receive any money back for your lodging reservation."

That's excellent advice, but the overall policy leaves something to be desired. How do you verify whether a unit was rented? Wouldn't it just be easier to say "no refunds," and not even leave open the possibility of getting your money back, as many other properties do?

As a matter of fact, travel insurance might have covered you. Or not. Some policies do allow a cancellation for any reason, but others only offer refunds for specific reasons, and there's no telling if your reasons would have been good enough for your insurer.

I wouldn't have booked a condo in Colorado with an iffy refund policy unless you were absolutely certain you'd be able to stay there, or unless you had reliable insurance. Once you sign on the dotted line, you might not be able to get a refund.

I thought it might be worth asking Winter Park Lodging Company if it could verify that the unit you rented was actually empty during the peak of high season, so I contacted it on your behalf.

"I spoke with the owners of this property and convinced them to give the guest all of her money back minus the $100 cancellation fee," a spokeswoman told me. "Normally we don't do this, but she seems to be after our reputation despite her signing a legal contract that explains the cancellation policy."

listed online or through a classified section: They insist that you wire money, and when you arrive to check in, the home doesn't exist. The best way to avoid it is to refuse to wire money. If in doubt, check with the state and/or local municipality to confirm whether the manager or owner has a business license and is paying lodging taxes.

→ YOU PUT *WHAT* IN THE CONTRACT?

Since there's no "standard" home rental contract, you can find all kinds of surprises in the fine print. The most unpleasant ones allow the homeowner or manager to pocket your deposit for virtually any reason. Others permit the owner to add cleaning fees and other surcharges to your final bill. These can be negotiated, but *before* you sign.

→ OWNER DOES NOT EXIST.

In the last few years, phishing scams have proliferated that target the owners of vacation rentals. (See "How does the vacation rental phishing scam work?" below.) The only way to be certain that you're dealing with a real owner is to call the number of a listing on a site like VRBO or FlipKey. Phone numbers are harder to fake.

→ I CAN'T DO THAT IN MY RENTAL?

Since you're renting a home, you may face some unusual restrictions on how you use the property. To comply with local ordinances, the contract may specifically forbid you to have more than a certain number of guests join you in the rental. You may not be able to park your car in front of the building. Bear in mind, there are no standards when it comes to vacation rentals, so pay attention to *every* page of your contract.

How does the vacation rental phishing scam work?

Scammers sometimes steal vacation rental owners' email passwords to assume their identity, a crime called *phishing*. These crimes have affected rentals sold online, mostly through large sites like *VRBO.com* and *HomeAway.com*.

One victim thought she'd found the ideal rental home in Playa del Carmen, Mexico, for her Christmas vacation: a two-bedroom penthouse condominium with a hot tub and an impossibly perfect view of the Caribbean. She was getting it for the impossibly low peak-season rate of $160 a night through *HomeAway.com*.

"Impossible" being the operative word. Shortly after she wired the money to Mexico, the guest discovered that she'd paid the wrong person. Her vacation dollars didn't go to the property owner, but to someone who was pretending to be the owner.

These vacation rental phishing criminals aren't dummies. They use clever techniques to harvest the email password of a vacation rental owner and then assume that person's identity. They have real-looking contracts. They mimic their messages with uncanny accuracy. They'll even negotiate with you, pretending to offer you a better rate.

You can avoid this scam by taking the following simple precaution: Never. Wire. Money.

What are some essential questions to ask before signing?

→ WHAT'S THE DEPOSIT FOR THE RENTAL? When is it owed, and when is it refunded? Are there any special circumstances under which it can be kept?

→ IS THERE A DAMAGE WAIVER? More travelers today will find damage waivers as an alternative to the traditional security deposit. The damage waiver is often a lower cost, nonrefundable fee that protects you against any accidental damage to the property up to a certain dollar limit. Each of these options will be detailed in the rental agreement.

→ WHAT'S THE CLEANING FEE? Cleaning fees can vary as widely as vacation rental properties do, so there's not an average fee travelers can come to expect. Location matters, and since property sizes can range from studio suites to homes with upward of 20 bedrooms, the cost will also, obviously, be relative to the size of the rental or the number of rooms.

SMART HOW TO PROTECT YOURSELF FROM SHAM RENTALS.

Some large websites that deal with vacation rentals offer insurance that will cover your rental. For example, VRBO will sell you what it calls a Carefree Rental Guarantee that covers losses related to phishing. You should also speak directly to the owner before you sign your paperwork. By calling the number on an official listing, you can be reasonably sure you're dealing with the actual owner.

→ **ARE THERE ANY TAXES?** If taxes are not required for your rental, it could be a red flag that the rental is not licensed or approved for short-term rental. Lodging taxes are typically collected in line with local regulations, and they vary from state to state. Some states allow for tax-inclusive rates, so be sure to ask what the total tax rate will be for your stay and whether it's included in the price you've been quoted. Travelers should plan to pay standard sales and bed taxes, which are dictated by the county in which the property is located.

Cleaning fees can vary as widely as vacation rental properties do.

→ **HOW ABOUT PETS?** If you're thinking of bringing Rover on vacation, check the fine print in your contract first. You may not be able to, or you may have to pay a hefty cleaning fee for the privilege, even if your furry friend stays outside.

→ **AM I OLD ENOUGH?** Some vacation rental managers and owners refuse to do business with anyone younger than 25—even if they're responsible 25-year-olds with jobs and mortgages. Spring Break ruined it for everyone! Unfortunately, in the United States, federal law doesn't explicitly prohibit landlords or managers from turning you down based on your age.

→ **IS THERE A MINIMUM LENGTH OF STAY?** During peak season or holidays, some rentals require that you stay at least a week. You can find particularly attractive two- or three-night stays during the off-season, when booking at the last minute, or even in specific rental properties. Some areas have ordinances banning short-term rentals. If you're not planning to stay more than a couple of days, you may need to look for a hotel.

What's a vacation rental survival kit?

Did I already mention that a vacation rental isn't a hotel? A time or two, maybe. You need a vacation rental survival kit.

→ **TOILET PAPER.** Every vacation rental should have full rolls of toilet paper in every bathroom. Extras? Don't count on it.

→ **TIN FOIL, PLASTIC WRAP, AND GARBAGE BAGS.** If you're planning to cook, you'll need a few basic items. Some vacation rentals are stocked with these, but you can't depend on it.

→ **OILS AND SPICES.** Again, some homes may have these basic cooking ingredients, but they might not. By the way, unless the items are unopened, they may violate safety regulations and standards.

→ **LAUNDRY AND DISH DETERGENT.** Some rentals come with more than you can use; others don't even have a bar of soap. You're better off asking before you arrive, and if the kitchens and bathrooms aren't properly stocked, visit a grocery store for the essentials before you check in.

→ **WI-FI HOTSPOT.** Many vacation rentals claim to have wireless Internet, but it's sometimes slow or unreliable. If you positively need to stay in touch with the outside world, bring your own hotspot or connect your cell phone to your laptop or tablet to access the Internet. See Chapter 18 on phones for details.

→ **LINEN SUPPLIES.** Some rentals do not come with sheets or towels. Don't assume; always ask if linens will be included in the rental. Many properties will add a surcharge for linens, and others don't offer them at all. The last thing you want is to be stuck at a property at 11 p.m. without any sheets for your bed. I've been there.

How do I resolve a dispute with a vacation rental owner or property manager?

I outline many strategies for avoiding a protracted fight in my chapter on dispute resolution. With a vacation rental, there are a few other items to consider, as well.

→ **REAL TIME IS BETTER THAN LATER.** Minor problems, such as a TV that doesn't work or a refrigerator that isn't making crushed ice, can and should be addressed then and there, not after you return from your vacation. The property owner or manager has more options, including fixing the problem (obviously) or knocking a few dollars off your bill. If you've rented from a professional, you have some added assurance—they are typically on-site or nearby to handle any issues or to cover repair costs. If you need to move, a company may have dozens if not hundreds of other properties available.

→ **YOUR RENTAL CONTRACT IS YOUR FRIEND.** Just like the airline contract of carriage or the cruise ticket contract, you'll want to refer to the actual agreement when you have a major complaint. If you've read it before you rented (you *did* read it, didn't you?) then you know what your rights are and can make an informed argument.

→ **STATE AND LOCAL ORDINANCES APPLY.** You don't have to be a lawyer to look up state or local laws that apply to your rental. Generally, state lodging laws, which often apply to rentals, favor the innkeeper. However, citing a law that may apply underscores your seriousness, and it may eliminate a trip back to your destination to visit small claims court.

Generally, state lodging laws, which often apply to rentals, favor the innkeeper.

→ **BE NICE.** Whether you're dealing with a vacation rental professional or an owner, it matters not. Remember, this is someone's home. They're bound to take your displeasure personally. Politeness has never been more important—or more helpful.

BOTTOM LINE

Whether you're renting from a professional or an owner, a vacation rental can be the perfect lodging option for your next vacation. Remember to research the property carefully, pay close attention to the contract—and never, *ever* wire money.

18

Keep Connected

Avoiding the connection "gotchas" that could make your vacation more expensive.

In the days before cell phones staying in touch while you were on the road was pretty straight-forward. You found a landline, made a call, and paid your bill. But in the Information Age, it's anything but easy. Now, your cell phone may or may not make or take a call when you're away (is it a GSM phone or CDMA?). It may work if you can connect to a wireless hotspot. Then again, it may not. And then there are all those roaming charges! Communicating while you're traveling, it turns out, isn't that simple. I'll help you make a connection.

Don't bring your cell phone:

→ **IF YOUR PHONE IS INCOMPATIBLE** with the system used in the country you're visiting.

→ **IF YOU'RE PLANNING TO LEAVE THE COUNTRY FOR AN EXTENDED PERIOD OF TIME.** Most international calling plans aren't worth keeping for longer than a month.

→ **IF YOU ARE NOT ENTIRELY SURE HOW TO CHANGE THE PHONE'S SETTINGS,** but plan to "just use Wi-Fi" to communicate. You may hit the wrong button, and then get hit with a big roaming bill.

Bring your cell phone:

→ **IF YOU'RE TRAVELING SOMEWHERE YOUR CALLING PLAN COVERS.**

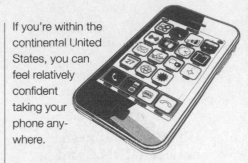

If you're within the continental United States, you can feel relatively confident taking your phone anywhere.

→ **IF YOU'RE TRAVELING INTERNATIONALLY,** and you've negotiated a reasonable calling plan.

→ **IF YOU'RE A POWER USER,** know how to turn the roaming options on and off, know how to use a Wi-Fi hotspot, and consider yourself comfortable around a cell phone. *If you have any doubts, don't chance it; leave the phone turned off or don't take it with you.*

How do I know if my phone will work when I'm away?

The fastest way to determine whether your wireless device will work is by calling your cellular phone provider. As a general rule, if you live in the United States, your phone should work in North and South America. Depending on the handset, it may work in Europe and Asia. Remember: Even if it's compatible with a foreign carrier, that doesn't necessarily mean it will make a call. You may need to activate a calling plan before you leave. Not surprisingly, the system favors the cell phone carrier when the tables are turned. If, by chance, your phone *does* work overseas and someone calls it, you may be charged for the cost of the call (as high as $5 a minute) *even if you don't answer the call.*

What's the difference between CDMA and GSM—and does it really matter?

There are two major cell phone systems in current use: CDMA (Code Division Multiple Access) and GSM (Global System for Mobiles). CDMA phones are dominant in North America, and GSM phones are used in much of the rest of the world. For travelers, here's how that translates: First, the systems aren't compatible with each other. But some phones have the technology embedded so you may use either CDMA or GSM. The benefit of a GSM phone is that you can remove your personal information, which is stored on a tiny card called a SIM card. That allows you to swap accounts without having to change your phone. Theoretically, that allows you to take your phone with you when you travel. The gap between GSM and CDMA may be

partially bridged by new 4G technology, but don't hold your breath— some incompatibilities will remain, probably for years to come.

So what's the best way to communicate when I'm overseas?

Unfortunately, there's no "one size fits all" solution. If you're traveling internationally on business and need to be in touch with the office at all times, your employer will probably cover the high cost of a calling plan or a SIM card. If you're on vacation, it's up to your budget and communication needs. Each wireless company and manufacturer has slightly different rules and technical specifications for its handsets. Check their websites or visit one of their stores if you have specific questions. For most leisure travelers, the following options are worth considering:

→ **STAY OFFLINE.** It's your vacation, after all. Obviously, you'll want to have *some* way of communicating with friends and family back home, but isn't that what we have landlines for? Between a public phone (get a calling card; see page 233,) and the occasional Internet cafe, you'll have plenty of choices when you're away. Why keep your devices on while you're off the clock? Seriously, consider powering down your cell phone for the duration of your trip. You can do it!

→ **CONSIDER A SUBSCRIPTION-BASED WI-FI SERVICE.** Companies such as Boingo, a subscription-based service that lets you connect to a network of hotspots at airports and other public areas, may offer the most bang for your buck. For a monthly subscription fee, you can connect to a relatively fast wireless network. Boingo connects to more than 700,000 hotspots, and its iPhone app also helps you detect any wireless hotspot, free or otherwise. You can use the high-speed connection to access a service like Skype or Google Voice to make free or reduced-rate phone calls.

→ **TRY PAY-AS-YOU-GO WI-FI.** Another popular option is the pay-as-you-go wireless option. You can connect to a wireless network in your hotel, which allows your smartphone to make Internet-based calls and get online. In most full-service hotels, the wireless connection in the lobby is free, but you pay a daily fee to use it in your room. At budget hotels, the price of an unlimited Wi-Fi connection is usually included with the cost of your room.

Free Wi-Fi
Hot coffee, hotspot

→ **SPRING FOR THE PRICEY CALLING PLAN.** Your wireless company would be happy to add a calling plan to your phone, but pay close attention to the pricing. Not only will you pay extra for the plan, but you'll probably also prepay for a certain number of minutes, and you'll only get a discount on calls made and received internationally—a discount from the cellular phone company's steep markup. If you're on vacation, you may use it only a few times.

→ **SIM CARD.** The SIM card, a small electronic memory card that identifies and configures your phone, can be swapped out on some phones, depending on the type of handset and whether the manufacturer allows it. The most sophisticated phone users buy inexpensive SIM cards and use them for local phone calls and to receive international calls (see "Buy a calling card," page 233, for details on how to make cheaper long-distance phone calls). You can buy an inexpensive SIM card when you arrive, or you can buy one online. You will get a new local phone number when you switch

> *Your wireless company would be happy to add a calling plan to your phone, but pay close attention to the pricing.*

231

PROBLEM SOLVED

A COSTLY CALL FROM COSTA RICA

QUESTION: During a recent trip to Costa Rica, I decided to call my housemate on her birthday. I knew I should have used a calling card, but decided just to make a quick call with my credit card, instead. I used one of those "international long distance" phones that are in hotel lobbies.

So, I made phone call number one. No answer, so I tried to track her down on her cell phone. Call two—no answer. Call number three—oops, wrong number.

Okay, here we go. Call number four. Finally, an answer. I sing "Happy Birthday" in Spanish, we have our conversation, and all is well. Or is it?

I fully expected that the actual conversation was going to cost a fair bit. What I didn't expect was to come back and see that I got charged $43.31 for each of the three calls where I didn't even make a connection.

My credit card statement has a company called NCIC listed on it. I'm a bit apprehensive about contacting them directly for fear that I could get dinged with even more outrageous long-distance charges or hidden charges.

In the end, it cost me $190.49—that's three times $43.31 for no connections and $60.56 for the one actual call. Can you help me get rid of the extra charges?
—Ian Rosenfeldt, *Toronto, Canada*

ANSWER: It's no secret that calls made from your hotel are more costly. But $43.31 for a call that didn't even go through? Come on.

I've experienced the same thing in Europe, particularly Eastern Europe (my phone bill for two nights in a Warsaw hotel set me back $500 once). It turned out that every call—even the attempted calls—were subject to a ridiculous markup.

Thanks to Poland, I came up with a rule that's served me well on my travels: Don't even *look* at the phone in your hotel room. Pretend it doesn't exist. (I wouldn't be surprised if some of the more entrepreneurial hotels one day begin charging for incoming calls, too.)

Your situation is slightly different, because the hotel had nothing to do with the pricey calls. You were dealing with Network Communications International Corp. of Longview, Texas, which bills itself as the largest privately owned operator service company in the United States. A look at its rates suggests that your credit card charges were far too high.

I asked a company representative to look at your record. She determined that, indeed, a mistake was made when you placed the calls. NCIC credited your account for $129.93, leaving you with only a charge for the call you actually made.

So what went wrong? "The technicians are researching that," the representative told me. "They are really not sure."

Well, I am sure of this: When you need to make a call, either use a card or get a cell phone. There's only one reason I can think of to pick up an "international long distance" phone, and that's in a life-or-death emergency.

Next time, try writing a postcard.

👎 NOT SMART
MAKING A LONG DISTANCE PHONE CALL FROM A HOTEL PHONE.

Hotels are waiting for you to pick up that phone and call home, and at no time is that more true than when you're abroad. A hotel may charge you several dollars a minute for the convenience of making a call from the landline in your room.

It's almost never worth it. (See "What are hotel phones good for, anyway?" page 235 for details.) A phone card can help you shortcut those charges, but be warned: Some properties are known to charge even for those calls. Ask before dialing.

cards. If you're planning to receive long-distance calls or need to conduct conference calls while you're on vacation—and I sincerely hope you don't—then a SIM card in most countries allows free incoming calls. You only pay when you call out. In the United States, both ends pay for a wireless call. Go figure.

→ **RENT A PHONE.** Companies such as PlanetFone and TravelCell will rent a phone on a weekly or monthly basis, which will allow you to make local calls. The rates are pretty reasonable—less than $100 a month—but there's a catch: You're not getting a state-of-the-art smartphone that lets you conduct all of your social media business, take photos, and shoot videos. It's a basic phone that makes calls. Plus, the per-minute call rates may be significantly higher than on your regular cell phone.

→ **BUY A CALLING CARD.** A prepaid phone card is a card that allows you to make long-distance phone calls for a flat fee. To use a card, you call an access number—either a toll-free number or a local number—then follow the voice prompts to enter your personal identification number. The cards can save a significant amount of money if you need to make a lot of phone calls to home base, whether you're traveling domestically or internationally, but there's a downside: They may also have a few surprise fees waiting for you. (See "Help, I've been scammed by a phone card!" below.)

ANY QUESTIONS?
If everything went smoothly all the time, I'd be out of a job. Here are some questions and concerns I hear from time to time.

Help, I've been scammed by a phone card!
Phone cards can save you a lot of money if you need to make frequent phone calls back home when you're overseas. They can also cost you more

money than you expect.

One pitfall is your hotel, which may offer "free" and unlimited local calls, but charge a per-minute fee for calling certain numbers, including 1-800 numbers. The best way to avoid this communication trap is to use a public phone or to use a cell phone to make the call.

The other potential problem is the calling card. Your card may advertise that you can make thousands of minutes of calls for one low fee, but it often fails to also disclose that you'll be assessed multiple surcharges that could make the phone card worth a lot less. Be careful to read the terms and conditions associated with the card.

The Federal Communications Commission, which regulates phone cards in the United States, has issued millions of dollars of fines against phone card providers for trying to deceive consumers. It recommends that, in addition to reading the instructions, users pay close attention to all of the fine print included on the back of the card or the packaging, and that they make sure they understand the rates, conditions, and limitations that apply. Look for additional fees, including terms like *post-call, disconnect, hang-up,* and *maintenance,* all of which refer to additional charges you pay when you make calls. (For more, check *fcc.gov/guides/prepaid-phone-cards-what-consumers-should-know*.)

If you think you've been scammed by a phone card, you can file a complaint with the FCC's Consumer Center by calling 1-888-CALL-FCC (1-888-225-5322). That is, if you still have minutes left on your card.

My cell phone is locked.

What should I do?

Many cell phones in the United States are "locked," which means you can't just swap out a SIM card. The only way to be sure if this is the case is to call your provider. Your phone can be unlocked independently, but you may run afoul of your mobile contract, the law, or both. While it's possible to unlock a phone via a repair specialist, a better way is to buy an unlocked phone. You'll be able to use it on any compatible network. Unlocked phones can be purchased directly through a wireless company, but you can also find them on Craigslist or eBay. Your carrier will also unlock your phone at the end of your contract. All you have to do is ask.

Many cell phones in the United States are "locked," which means you can't just swap out a SIM card.

What are hotel phones good for, anyway?

If you need to call another guest in the hotel or get in touch with the front desk, then by all means, use the phone in your hotel. Otherwise, don't touch it. For years, hotels made obscene profits from their phones. Since wireless devices have cut into those profits, hotels in some countries have looked for clever ways of keeping the money coming. Look out for the phone trap in the following places:

→ HOTELS IN REMOTE AREAS WITH LITTLE OR NO CELL PHONE RECEPTION. When the landline is the only game in town, then you'll pay more. *Lots* more, probably. Years ago, I was hot on the trail of one hotel that installed cell phone blocking devices in-house, ostensibly to boost its landline profits. Very clever!

→ HOTELS OFFERING "FREE" LOCAL CALLS. Some hotels offer "free" local calls as an enticement to use their phones. Only, they don't really define "local," and may not mention that they charge a fee to call a toll-free number. Read the fine print in your guest directory for the unfortunate details.

→ HOTELS IN COUNTRIES WHERE CELL PHONES HAVEN'T BEEN WIDELY ADOPTED. In developing countries where cell phones aren't widely used, you're much more likely to find a predatory hotel. But remember, these unscrupulous hotels can be anywhere.

BOTTOM LINE

If you need the convenience of a cell phone while you're abroad, be prepared to spend money on a calling plan or a SIM card. If you don't require 24/7 access, you can still get all the conveniences of wireless communication by using a Wi-Fi signal from your hotel or at the airport. Or, you can unplug.

19

Troubleshoot Your Travel Tour

Package tours, escorted tours, and fixing things that could go wrong.

A tour gathers various components of a trip into a single package. It comes in two basic varieties. An *independent tour* will include transportation, lodging, and sometimes meals and activities, which you can assemble on your own to fit your itinerary; an *organized tour* has some or all of the components of an independent tour but follows an itinerary set by a tour company and is escorted by an experienced guide. Both options have advantages and disadvantages. I'll help you determine which one is best for you.

An independent package tour might be for you:

→ **IF YOU VALUE FLEXIBILITY** and don't want to be limited to a seven- or ten-day "experience."

→ **IF YOU LIKE TO EXPLORE NEW PLACES** and would prefer to determine where you eat and how you spend your time while you are on vacation.

→ **IF YOU LIKE TO KEEP TABS ON HOW MUCH EACH COMPONENT OF YOUR VACATION COSTS** and who is directly responsible for it.

Consider an escorted package tour:

→ **IF YOU'D LIKE TO HAVE EVERYTHING PLANNED FOR YOU** where you stay, what you see, how you get there. Some meals are included in an escorted tour. A few newer tours also

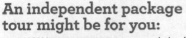

SMART CAST A WIDE NET WHEN YOU'RE SHOPPING FOR TOURS.

You can buy a package tour through your travel agency or online travel agency, or you can purchase it directly from a tour operator. The tours you'll find all basically work the same: They're a vacation in a tidy package that eliminates some of the hassle of planning and can save you money. But there are important differences. Online travel agencies may offer deeper discounts, but their terms tend to be more restrictive than those of tours found through a travel agent. When you book a tour directly through a tour operator, you may also get a price break, but you won't have an agent who can advocate for you if something goes wrong with your vacation.

have more "flex" time built into them, so they aren't as rigid as a traditional escorted package would be.

→ **IF YOU DON'T REALLY LIKE EXPLORING A PLACE ON YOUR OWN,** and enjoy traveling with other people.

→ **IF YOU'RE CONCERNED ABOUT DEALING WITH A FOREIGN LANGUAGE** and unfamiliar customs.

What's so great about a package?

The appeal of a tour is obvious once you understand how it works. But since tours can be a little complicated, even to someone who has written about them for most of his career, the benefits aren't necessarily self-evident. Why should you consider entrusting your entire vacation to a tour operator?

→ **IT'S AFFORDABLE.** Tour operators buy hotel rooms, flights, and activities and pass the savings along to you (see "A tour by the numbers," below, for details).

→ **IT'S ORGANIZED BY A PRO.** Knowing that a vacation was planned by an industry professional can be reassuring, especially when

you're traveling overseas.

→ **YOU PAY UP FRONT.** You'll know exactly how much your vacation will cost, minus tips and incidentals. But there's a downside to this, too. I'll have more on tour operator bankruptcies later in this chapter.

→ **BETTER ACCESS.** It's true that tour groups almost never have to wait in lines for the museums and the choice attractions. Also, they often get into places other travelers can't and are frequently given VIP treatment on the ground.

A tour by the numbers

A tour is almost always less expensive than buying all of the components individually, as I just mentioned. The economics of a package can make a lot of sense. Let's take a look at this typical Las Vegas vacation package:

À LA CARTE

Airfare: $299
Car rental: $149
Show tickets: $100

Total: $548

PACKAGE

Cost to tour operator:
Airfare: $229
Car rental: $99
Show tickets: $89

Company pays: $417

You pay: $509

Tour operator profit: $92
Your savings: $39

PROBLEM SOLVED

CAN MY TOUR OPERATOR POCKET MY AIRLINE REFUND?

QUESTION: My wife and I have traveled together for more than 45 years. Our destinations have included many developing countries and remote places. We have had no real problems with tour agencies and travel companies—until now.

We were returning to the United States after a tour of India and, because of bad weather in London, our flight back to the States was canceled by British Airways. We were able to make alternate arrangements with Air India for a direct flight to the United States, for which we paid separately, since British Airways did not resume flights for three days. British Airways refunded the cost of our flight to the tour operator, Overseas Adventure Travel (OAT). But the tour operator claims it is their policy not to pass along the refund to us because it is part of a land-plus-air package.

Our travel insurance company paid us for all the expenses we incurred but not for the cost of the flight, since they said we should be reimbursed by OAT.

I have talked several times to a representative from OAT, but they say this is their policy. Before I consult an attorney, I would like your comment.
—Donald Kne, *Chagrin Falls, Ohio*

ANSWER: Here's my comment: It's your money. OAT should return it. Immediately.

If British Airways refunded the unused portion of its flight to your tour operator, the operator shouldn't pocket the money. But here's the problem: Airlines typically don't offer refunds on nonrefundable tickets when there's a weather-related delay. But in this particular instance, British Airways bent its own rules and offered a refund.

The OAT representative with whom you spoke didn't believe British Airways would do that. She thought you'd made alternate arrangements with Air India to come home and were asking for a refund to which you weren't entitled.

A company representative told me they were unaware of the refund in their system, and that the phone agent was simply repeating the company's policy that it can't refund a nonrefundable airline ticket.

Putting your grievance in writing might have changed the answer, forcing OAT to either consult with British Airways or to check with its own accounts receivable department, both of which would have readily confirmed the refund.

For what it's worth, I don't think OAT would have kept your money. If you'd asked an attorney to send a letter to the company, it would have coughed up a refund quickly.

How to avoid a situation like this? You could have either asked British Airways to refund your ticket directly to you at the time of the cancellation, and if it couldn't, to verify in writing that it had sent the money to your tour operator. Sending OAT that documentation might have persuaded it to do the right thing.

None of that should have been necessary. The company should have sent you a check for the refund as soon as it had the money. "Clearly, we didn't communicate well internally on this one," a spokeswoman told me.

OAT refunded you $882 for the unused airline tickets.

Looks like a win-win, right? How does the tour operator get to pay such low rates for its products? It's based on economies of scale. The operator buys thousands of rooms, show tickets, and airline tickets at a time. In fact, when travelers happen to see the "bulk" rates travel companies pay, they often demand to pay the same rate. Answer: No problem. Just buy a thousand hotel rooms, and you'll get the same price the tour operator does!

You probably will never know exactly how much the tour company paid for the various components of your trip—only that you're saving 20 percent or more off the cost of your vacation.

But the savings can be even more dramatic. I've found tour packages through which, even if you were to remove one component, you would *still* save more money than you would by pricing the vacation *à la* carte. Under those scenarios, you could book a package, simply throw away certain components, and still save money. Quite a deal, isn't it?

What are the risks of buying a package?

Booking a package may save you money, but it isn't without risks.

You probably will never know exactly how much the tour company paid for the various components of your trip.

→ **BANKRUPTCY.** One of the biggest potential downsides of doing business with a tour operator is that you're handing all of your money to one company. If that company were to go out of business, you would lose everything. Even if you had purchased insurance, some tour operators self-insure, which means your coverage is essentially worthless. (See Chapter 5 on insurance for details.) I recommend you buy a reliable travel insurance policy from a third party—*not* from the tour operator.

→ **REFUNDS OF INDIVIDUAL COMPONENTS.** When all goes smoothly with your trip, a package or guided tour can be a real pleasure, but when one part doesn't live up to your expectations, then you can have a problem on your hands. Why? Well, remember that you don't know how much that one component cost. So how does your tour operator or travel agency calculate a refund? Based on its price? A percentage of your price? Do you just get a voucher? I've had many complaints from unhappy customers who believe they deserved more of a refund. Your right to a refund is discussed in your tour operator's terms and conditions. Make sure you know what's in the fine print before asking for, or accepting, any refund.

→ **LOYALTY POINTS.** If you're a point collector, you may be unhappy with the terms of your tour. Since airfare and hotels are bought in bulk by your operator, there's a chance you won't earn as many frequent flier miles as you thought you should. You may not earn any at all. If loyalty is important, I strongly recommend you book a package that doesn't include airfare, so that you can maximize the miles

you earn. This is especially important when you're flying long distances and the miles flown are enough to bump you to the next elite level.

Isn't there a "Good Housekeeping" seal for tour operators?

Kind of. The United States Tour Operators Association (ustoa.com) is a professional, voluntary trade association for tour operators. Interestingly, USTOA was founded in 1972 by a group of California tour operators

 SMART MIND YOUR AIRFARE!

Airfare might be included in the cost of your package tour. Or not. Airline tickets can usually be added to both types of tours, or you can make your own airline reservations. Bear in mind that the prices for most escorted tours are not guaranteed until just before the final payment. If you're mulling airfare arrangements for an escorted tour, you might consider booking the escorted tour's air, which could cost a little more than if you booked it yourself—but if the tour is canceled and refunded, you'd also get your airfare back.

concerned about tour operator bankruptcies. USTOA has high standards, which include the following:

→ REQUIRING EACH MEMBER COMPANY TO SET ASIDE $1 MILLION of its own funds specifically to protect consumers' deposits and payments.

→ COMMITMENT TO TRUTH, accuracy, and clarity in advertising.

→ ADHERENCE TO A CODE OF ETHICS, which includes a pledge to encourage and maintain the highest standards of professionalism, integrity, and service.

Membership in USTOA can mean you're protected, but because only businesses that have been in operation for at least three years are eligible, it can also mean that a smaller or newer tour operator—one perfectly deserving of your business—is left out. So, while the USTOA symbol is a good sign, you shouldn't necessarily assume that the absence of the sign is bad news.

What's a tour participation agreement, and why should I care about it?

A tour participation agreement, sometimes simply referred to as the terms and conditions, is the contract between you and your tour operator. It's usually used for organized, escorted tours, but it is sometimes also used for specialized tours, such as river cruises. As with anything else in travel, it can be littered with "gotchas."

→ DON'T HOLD US TO OUR BROCHURE PRICES. The terms may say that a price you see in a catalog can change. No price is final until your purchase is completed. If you read about a tour that interests you, contact an agent or the tour company and get the most up-to-date specifics, including the price.

→ MIND THE FEES, PLEASE. Tour operators should disclose their fees—some routine, some not. For example, some operators will charge a fee of up to $300 if you make any change to your itinerary within a month of your departure. That *doesn't* include the airline or hotel fees.

→ DID WE MENTION THE "SINGLE" SUPPLEMENTS? Prices are usually based on double occupancy. If you're traveling solo, you may pay anywhere from 10 to 100 percent more for your accommodations. To cater to the single travel market, some tour operators offer reduced or waived single supplements, while others have "share" programs that team up like-minded travelers.

→ PASSPORT PROBLEMS? NOT OUR PROBLEM. If your passport gets lost or expires and you're unable to travel, your tour operator isn't liable for your cancellation and won't issue a refund. So, make sure your paperwork is in order if you're traveling internationally. I've mediated numerous cases with tours that had to be canceled because of a paperwork misunderstanding (see Chapter 3 on travel documents for more).

→ WE CAN CANCEL, BUT YOU CAN'T.

One of the most vexing portions of the tour agreement involves cancellations. If enough people don't sign up for a tour or a portion of the tour, then the operator sometimes reserves the right to cancel the entire tour. But if *you* decide not to go on the tour, you are still governed by its strict cancellation rules.

→ THIS ISN'T THE ONLY CONTRACT. Since it's a package with multiple components, other contracts may apply to your purchase. Also, you only have a limited amount of time—usually a year—to sue the tour operator, if it comes to that, and it can only be done in certain jurisdictions, as outlined in the contract.

→ OTHER GOODIES. It's worth reading the entire contract from beginning to end. You'll find some gems you wouldn't expect. For example, one company's contract says that your participation grants the company the right to photograph you and to use the image in an ad—without explicitly asking permission. You're welcome!

👎 NOT SMART BUYING A PACKAGE WHEN YOU SHOULDN'T.

Since most components of your vacation are bundled together in package tours, it would follow that one of the most common questions I get is this: Can I *unbundle* them? What if you want to skip a city or extend your vacation? Some tours offer optional extensions. But if you find yourself saying, "This tour looks perfect, but . . ." enough times, then an escorted tour might not be for you and you should consider an independent tour. If you still feel too restricted, you're better off skipping the tour altogether and flying solo.

PROBLEM SOLVED

NO REFUND FOR THE WRONG CHICHÉN ITZÁ TOUR

QUESTION: I'm trying to get a refund for a tour, and I'm getting the runaround. Last year, my husband, my niece, and I traveled to Cancún for two weeks. Before our departure, I told my travel agent I wanted to book a tour to Chichén Itzá, a popular pre-Columbian archaeological site. She recommended Gray Line.

I went online and booked an overnight tour that included a light show and a room at the Mayaland Hotel. This cost me $99 per person.

When we got to Cancún, I asked the concierge at my hotel to confirm the arrangements. She phoned and I thought it was all set.

When we arrived, we were told that we were booked on the day trip. This did not include the light show. When I explained that I had paid for the overnight trip, the woman at the counter told me there were no hotel rooms available at all. There was nothing she could do. She also told me that she couldn't issue a refund since I had booked on the Internet. She told me to get my refund through the website.

I have contacted Gray Line Cancun several times in the past year. Each and every time, I am promised a refund. Each time, they fail to deliver it. Can you help?
—Nancy Giese, Swan Hills, *Alberta, Canada*

ANSWER: Gray Line should have refunded the difference between the day tour and your overnight tour as quickly as it took the company to withdraw the money from your credit card. Which is to say, instantly.

So why are you still waiting?

That's a question a lot of travelers—from airline passengers to hotel guests—struggle to answer every day. Travel companies are quick to take your money and slow to return it, even when you have every right to a prompt refund. The best explanation is that they want to keep your money, and they figure that dragging their feet increases the chances you'll give up.

But not you. You copied me on several email requests to Gray Line Cancun, in which you politely and persistently asked for your money. Gray Line's terms and conditions are clear about giving its customers refunds: It doesn't. "All tickets purchased on *grayline.com* are nonrefundable," it says.

Curiously, while the Gray Line terms address your own behavior down to an interesting level of detail ("You will only provide truthful and accurate information. You will not harass, threaten or abuse other people when using this site in any manner."), it doesn't really talk about the company's obligations to you. Too bad. Obviously, the company should adjust the rate you paid for your Chichén Itzá tour immediately.

While you dealt directly with the Cancún location, you had three other options. You could have appealed to Gray Line at the corporate level. You could have disputed the charges on your credit card. And you could have sued Gray Line in a Canadian small claims court.

Fortunately, you didn't need to do any of those things. I contacted Gray Line on your behalf, and it sent you a full refund.

Common tour problems from my readers

Oh, the trouble my readers get themselves in to! Here are a few common tour-related queries I've handled:

→ I DON'T LIKE MY TOUR GUIDE OR FELLOW TRAVELERS. Perhaps the biggest unknown is your professional tour guide and the other members of your tour. If you have a personality conflict with one, it can make your vacation miserable. The only way to avoid this is to plan your tour very carefully, preferably with the help of a competent travel agent. An agent will know what types of travelers are likely to take a particular escorted tour and will probably know if you're a good match. If you're part of a larger group offering concurrent tours—for example, if there are two buses, each with its own guide—it may be possible to switch buses. But don't count on that as an option.

→ I HAVE A SPECIAL NEED. Attractions, hotels, and restaurants overseas may not be accessible to all guests, although some tour operators have a great reputation for accommodating visitors with special needs. Contact the Society for Accessible Travel and Hospitality *(sath.org)* for a recommendation or ask your travel agent.

→ THE FOOD, ACCOMMODATIONS, OR TOURS ARE NOT WHAT I EXPECTED. Sometimes, tour operators cut corners, paying a restaurant just a few dollars for a meal they buy at a volume discount, but advertising it as a "five star" experience. These tour operators don't deserve your business; in fact, they don't deserve to be *in* business at all. If one part of your tour isn't up to standards, say something *then*— don't wait until you get home (see Chapter 14 on complaint resolution for more). Again, a knowledgeable agent or a recommendation from a trusted friend can help you avoid such tours in the first place.

Canceled tour? Don't expect a full refund.

The advantage of a package is that you get a price break. The

disadvantage? Refunds.

When an airline cancels a flight, you can get your money back. When a hotel turns you away, you're entitled to a refund. Same thing when your cruise is canceled, or your car rental company doesn't have the vehicle for which you prepaid.

Put it all together into a package, however, and curiously, the rules change. Your tour may not be refundable at all. Don't believe me? Check your participation agreement and see for yourself.

I heard from one reader whose Egypt tour and Nile cruise was canceled during a recent period of civil unrest in that country. She'd paid $6,032 for the tour, but when the tour operator canceled, it offered her only two choices: Either rebook the same tour later in the year, or transfer all of her credit to a different tour within a year.

Unfortunately, her travel insurance didn't cover civil unrest. So, that left her to try to deal with her tour operator, which stipulated that "a full refund will be made to all participants only if the cancellation does not result in a loss of monies" to the company. Unlikely, since its tour guides were busy with a revolution.

Why no refund? When there's a cancellation, a tour operator has already incurred expenses for advance reservations and arrangements, and they may be liable for paying hotel and other services contracted on your behalf. Besides, a tour operator doesn't want to refund your money (it's in the company's DNA), but would happily welcome you on another tour. Even when you deserve to get all of your money back.

Resolving a tour dispute

If you've booked an independent tour, there's a looser connection between you and the supplier (the airline, hotel, or cruise line). If you booked through a travel agent or an online travel agency, that would be the first point of contact for addressing the cancellation and any refunds.

As I mentioned before, a leading problem travelers encounter with any tour is having part of their tour canceled and then asking for a refund. The agency or tour operator will always use *its* math, which is to say, whichever formula is more advantageous to it. I've seen well-deserved refunds shrink and virtually disappear under this funny accounting.

Applying *à*-la-carte logic to a refund problem won't work. Remember, your tour operator probably didn't pay full price for the airfare and accommodations, so it doesn't make sense to request the sticker price as a refund. The most effective strategy is to ask the operator or agency to explain its decision in writing. If the reasons don't make sense, appeal the decision—to both the tour operator and the supplier. You may be entitled to more, and you may get more.

Next to cruises, escorted tours are the most frequent subject of laundry-list complaints. In other words, it's not one big thing that goes wrong, but a lot of little ones. It's a late pick-up, missing luggage, a bad meal—things you can't necessarily put a price on. But cumulatively,

Whether you're buying an independent package or taking an escorted tour, the package can be a terrific way to save money.

they have the capacity to ruin a vacation.

The good news is that tour operators who don't maintain high quality standards throughout their entire product don't last long. There's just too much competition, and in the Information Age, it only takes one angry customer to destroy a business. My best advice for resolving an escorted tour-related complaint is to hammer on this one issue—overall quality—particularly if you've got a compelling list of complaints.

Many tour operators will respond to a complaint by sending you a form letter, which is totally insincere, apologizing for "the way you feel." If you can make a polite and persuasive case that the overall experience was below the standards of quality that the tour operator advertised, then you have a reasonable chance of getting the boilerplate mea culpa upgraded to a voucher or even a refund.

BOTTOM LINE

Whether you're buying an independent package or taking an escorted tour, the package can be a terrific way to save money. But it can also go sideways if you don't do your research. Review your contract carefully and buy a tour from a trusted source.

20

Manage Your Vacation Cash

Sidestepping currency traps and
payment problems when you travel.

Travelers tend to spend a lot of time before a trip obsessing about money—specifically, not spending too much of it on airfare, hotel, and meals—but once they're on the ground, it becomes an afterthought. It shouldn't be. Have you thought about whether you'll withdraw cash or use a credit card, for example? What about exchanging your money—do you know how much you'll pay for the privilege? You need to know before you go. I can help.

When to carry cash

→ **WHEN YOU'RE VISITING A COUNTRY WHERE MOST TRANSACTIONS ARE STILL HANDLED IN CASH.** Many countries still favor cash transactions, for a variety of reasons. The only way to know is to ask. On the other hand, some African countries, such as Nigeria and South Africa, for example, are virtually cashless, using cell phones to handle their transactions electronically. As I write this, Sweden is on the verge of becoming a "cashless" country. A good travel agent can offer guidance.

→ **IF YOU'RE MAKING PURCHASES THAT ARE TRADITIONALLY CASH ONLY.** Some businesses remain stubbornly cash only. Many popular restaurants in urban areas and small vendors at markets, for example, only accept cash, preferring not to shoulder the extra cost and infrastructure required to accept plastic.

→ **IF YOU WANT TO AVOID CREDIT CARD FEES.** Many credit card companies impose fees on transactions that take place in foreign countries. In order to steer clear of them, you'll have to use cash. Bear in mind that withdrawing cash from an automated teller machine (ATM) could cost you a pretty penny, too. (A 2 to 3 percent foreign transaction fee and a 3 percent cash withdrawal fee—that's 7 percent just to access your money. Ouch!)

When to carry a credit card

→ **IF YOU WANT TO RENT A CAR OR CHECK INTO A HOTEL.** In these cases, you'll usually need a credit card, not a debit card. A merchant may refuse to do business with you if you don't

SMART PAYING WITH PLASTIC?
MEMBERSHIP *DOES* HAVE ITS PRIVILEGES.

One of the benefits of paying with a credit card is that if something goes wrong, you may have the option of disputing the purchase. Your rights to dispute a purchase are outlined in the Fair Credit Billing Act (see "How to dispute a charge," pages 255–256).

A word of advice if you have a dispute: The sooner you say something, the better.

have a credit card. If you don't carry plastic, you'll need to make special arrangements in advance and pay a deposit.

→ IF YOU NEED THE PROTECTION OFFERED BY A CARD. Some credit cards offer additional protection, such as secondary car rental insurance coverage (see Chapter 8 on car rentals for more). They may also extend your warranty on purchases. Also, if a credit card is lost or stolen, it can quickly and easily be replaced, while limiting your liability. Some credit card companies will even overnight a replacement card to your hotel.

How do I get money while I'm overseas?

→ YOUR CREDIT CARD. If credit cards are accepted, you can use yours without having to extract cash from an ATM.

Pros: Credit cards offer some protection against fraudulent purchases. They can give you a more favorable inter-bank exchange rate and

save you from having to carry large amounts of cash.

Cons: Many credit cards add a 2 to 3 percent "foreign exchange fee" to any transaction that happens in another country, even if it's in dollars.

→ ATM. The automated teller machine is a great option if you have to make a cash purchase, but would prefer to not carry around too much cash.

Pros: You can withdraw just enough to make the purchase, and the rest of your money stays in your account in your native currency. As your bank will charge per withdrawal, though, you may want to make a more sizable withdrawal at once.

Cons: Fees! Your bank will charge a transaction fee, which will probably be significantly higher overseas. You may not get the best exchange rate. Your receipt may not show you the exchange rate—just the amount you are taking out in local currency.

→ BUYING CURRENCY FROM A BANK. You may be able to buy a commonly used foreign currency (such as Euros) from your bank before you leave for your destination.

Pros: You'll have the money before you leave.

Cons: The exchange rate may not be favorable; fees may apply to the transaction; and you might be in for some extra paperwork, such as forms to fill out, to get the currency.

→ **DOLLAR BILLING.** Some businesses, notably hotels, will offer to bill you in your home currency.

Pros: You'll get your bill in dollars, so you'll have a good idea of how much you're being charged and there's no need to do any mental math.

Cons: Your credit card may still charge a currency exchange fee or foreign transaction fee. Your exchange rate might not be competitive, either. (See section on "dynamic" currency conversions, pages 256–257, for more information.)

→ **AN EXCHANGE KIOSK.** These booths, conveniently set up at airports and train stations, give you access to foreign currency quickly.

Pros: If you need money fast and don't care about the exchange rate, go for it.

> *Fees! Your bank will charge a transaction fee, which will probably be significantly higher overseas.*

Cons: Pay close attention to the terms, which may be onerous. In addition to various junk surcharges and fees for the "convenience" of using the booth, the "buy" and "sell" exchange rate may be far apart (the so-called *spread*). That difference is profit to the business. Also, they don't always do coins. Use this as a last option.

Should I use a debit card?

A debit card is your ATM card, although some also can work as credit cards, offering some protections for purchases made. Remember, many hotels won't accept an imprint from a debit card when you check in, so don't try to travel with only a debit card. A debit card withdraws money directly from your bank account and it may have a daily limit. Banks normally charge a flat fee for each transaction. But some now also add a conversion surcharge when you access an ATM overseas, up to $5 per transaction and 3 percent for the conversion. Thank you, may I have another?

👎 NOT SMART USING TRAVELER'S CHECKS.

Traveler's checks used to be a terrific way to keep money while you were on the road. Not so much anymore. Even if you can find a bank that issues traveler's checks, you may have some trouble locating a business that accepts them; however, foreign banks that exchange currency still take them. My advice: You probably *do* want to leave home without them.

NOT SMART ACCUMULATING COINS.

If you're making a day trip into another country and need a small amount of native currency, don't try to exchange coins when you leave. Currency exchange facilities at the airport or train station may not accept coins, and you'll have to wait until the next time you're in that country to use them.

What about wiring money to a business?

You may be asked to conduct something called a retail money transfer using a service like Western Union or MoneyGram. Wiring money is often used to pay for a vacation rental either in the United States or overseas, but it can also be used to settle the bill on a high-end vacation or package tour offered by a smaller, independent tour operator.

While it may be tempting to wire money in advance, and while the company may offer a deep discount for paying cash up-front, I would strongly advise you not to do it. Once the money has been sent, there's no way to get it back. I receive regular complaints from readers who have lost thousands, and often tens of thousands of dollars, to scammers who insisted on having money wired.

How do I keep my money safe while I'm traveling?

Many travelers swear by a money belt, a fabric strap for holding your passport and cash. Some travel experts even peddle their own branded belt for security-conscious

travelers. There are variations on this solution, including socks and neckwear with pouches for storing valuables, but they're not the most elegant solution. Retrieving something from them means partially disrobing, and thieves know to look for hidden pouches on tourists. However, a belt is better than nothing.

Another option, one favored by security experts, is the dummy wallet or pocketbook—a decoy containing a small amount of cash and IDs. I've mentioned this strategy already, but it merits repeating. If you're ever asked to hand over your valuables, give the robber the bogus wallet. It's better than taking off your clothes and handing over your money belt.

CREDIT CARDS

In today's day and age, you may be able to cover most of your travel expenses with credit cards. But which cards, and what should you look for?

How do I choose the right credit card for my trip?

Credit cards come with all kinds of bells and whistles for

travelers—everything from airport lounge access to a concierge service. But what do you actually need? The time to make a decision about what card to carry is weeks, and preferably months, before you go anywhere. It takes time to sift through the contracts and decide which card is best for you.

What to look for in a credit card:

→ **CAR RENTAL COVERAGE.** This allows you to skip the optional car rental insurance when you rent a car—but note that often the coverage will be secondary, meaning that it kicks in after your primary insurance coverage, such as your personal auto insurance. (See Chapter 8 on car rental for more information on credit card coverage.) Don't forget, you have to use the card to pay for your rental in order to benefit from the coverage.

→ **TRIP CANCELLATION OR INTERRUP-TION COVERAGE.** If your vacation is interrupted or canceled, you might be covered. Significant restrictions, including a clause for preexisting medical conditions, normally apply, so you may still need to get an insurance policy. Some cards also insure you against accidental loss of life, limb, sight, speech, or hearing.

→ **BAGGAGE DELAY INSURANCE.** If your luggage goes astray while you're away, you can get reimbursed for emergency purchases, even when

your airline, cruise line, or motor coach operator won't help. Typically, the coverage will pay for one or two people to buy a change of clothes and toiletries.

The things your card definitely shouldn't have:

→ **AN ANNUAL FEE.** You shouldn't have to pay an annual fee for your credit card. Banks have other ways of making money from you. If the card you're considering costs something, make sure it does something pretty amazing that no other card can do. And if the benefits outweigh the costs, you have my blessing. (I have yet to find such a card, but there may be one out there. I'm open to it.)

→ **A CURRENCY EXCHANGE FEE.** If you're traveling overseas, get a card that exchanges your money without a fee. Some cards charge as much as 3 percent and impose the fee on any foreign currency transaction.

→ **A HIGH APR.** Your annual percentage rate (APR) should be between 8 and 10 percent. Anything higher than

PROBLEM SOLVED

CURRENCY CONFUSION AND THE CAR

QUESTION: Avis overcharged me for a one-month car rental in England, and I've had absolutely no luck in getting the error removed. I'm hoping you can help.

I booked the car rental through the British Airways website. When I arrived at the rental counter, I gave the employee my U.S. driver's license and my U.K. credit card.

Avis's computers were down when I returned the car, so the agent couldn't give me a receipt. You can imagine my surprise when I checked my Visa statement and found that Avis had converted my U.K. pounds into dollars because I had used my U.S. license. As a result, I paid an extra $124 for my car.

I called Avis's customer service number, which was a complete waste of time. I also sent them an email, but I have heard nothing back from them.
—Laura Cattell, *Houston, Texas*

ANSWER: The Avis contract should have offered a choice of currencies—yours or theirs—but if you didn't make a selection and there is no record that you did, its reservations system would have defaulted to the currency of your country of residence. So, if you live in America, you would be charged in American dollars even if you are a British citizen renting a car in Britain with a credit card issued in the United Kingdom, which pays the bill in pounds.

That would mean your pounds would be converted into dollars, and then back into pounds, incurring a processing fee of up to 3 percent each time. That doesn't make any sense, and I don't think any reasonable person would expect you to pay that.

Determining the Avis policy on currency conversions is maddeningly difficult. The terms on its website contain separate contracts for different parts of the world, and it is utterly confusing when it comes to currency conversion.

According to the European contract, the rate of exchange used for any currency conversion will be "conclusively determined by Avis." I take that to mean the company can basically do whatever it wants, but I've been assured that it doesn't. In fact, Avis's policy in Britain is to give renters a choice of paying in the currency of their native country or in pounds. An agent should have reviewed those options with you when you picked up your car.

Currency conversions are a tricky business in the best of circumstances. Credit cards charge a fee and travel companies often do, too. If you don't pay attention, you could rack up a lot of surcharges without realizing it. Any time you plan to cross a border, check with your credit card and travel company to make sure you're using the payment option that allows you to avoid unnecessary surcharges.

I checked with Avis to get its side of the story. According to a spokeswoman, an agent explained the charges to you, but you then "hung up the phone on one of our representatives." Hanging up on a phone agent doesn't help your case. Travel companies can attach notes to your reservation that follow you around like a rap sheet. A little politeness sometimes dramatically improves your chances of resolving a dispute. Avis refunded the $124 in fees as a gesture of goodwill.

15 percent, and you're throwing away your money. Note that your APR may change if you make a late payment. Some cards offer a low—in some cases a ridiculously low—introductory APR. Pay attention to the rate *after* your introduction.

Things you should consider *not* getting with your credit card:

→ **THE ABILITY TO EARN MILEAGE.** Earning miles is always good for the travel company or credit card, but not necessarily for you. Personally, I recommend staying away from mileage-earning cards, not just because they encourage extra spending, but also because they may come with higher fees. (See Chapter 7 on managing your loyalty program for more.)

→ **CONCIERGE SERVICES.** Cards for big-spending customers sometimes come with "concierge" services that help you book everything from event tickets to restaurant reservations. You may find these services useful, but in my experience, they are often redundant. Typically, you can get the same attentive service from a hotel concierge.

→ **DISCOUNTS THAT HAVE NOTHING TO DO WITH TRAVEL.** Credit card companies try to distinguish their products by adding special offers, such as discounts from wineries. It's a nice perk, but does little to help you when you're on the road.

How do I handle a credit card dispute?

Your credit card purchases are regulated by the Fair Credit Billing Act, which limits your responsibility for unauthorized charges to $50 and protects you against billing errors, including charges for goods and services you didn't accept, that weren't delivered as agreed, math errors, and incorrect charges. You can find out more about the FCBA at the Federal Trade Commission site *(consumer .ftc.gov)*.

The best way to avoid a dispute is to review your credit card statements as soon as you can, and to contact the merchant directly if you see something incorrect.

How to dispute a charge:

→ **FIND OUT IF YOU'RE COVERED.** Review the FCBA if you're planning to challenge a purchase. Even though the law has provisions that say the purchase price must exceed $50 and the transaction needs to occur within the same state as the cardholder's address, or within 100 miles of the cardholder's address, banks will often accept disputes for smaller amounts or if the distance exceeds 100 miles.

→ **CONTACT YOUR BANK.** You can initiate a dispute on your credit card company's website. If you prefer to phone, you can call your bank's credit card dispute department, and they'll walk you through the process.

> ## 👍 SMART
> CARRY AT LEAST TWO CARDS AND
> LET YOUR BANK KNOW YOU'RE TRAVELING.
>
> If you're traveling anywhere—not just outside the country—take at least two credit cards, if you can. That way, if one is frozen, the other one will still work. Your bank's fraud detection algorithms can be triggered by anything from buying a latte across a state line to shopping for souvenirs while you're on vacation. The only way to be sure your cards will still work is to call your bank at least one business day before you travel. A representative should make a notation on your account and your card won't shut down when you have to settle the tab at that Michelin two-star restaurant in Paris.

→ **KEEP ALL YOUR RECEIPTS, AND TAKE PICTURES.** Paperwork is extremely important during the dispute process. Any receipts, emails, or invoices you receive that may support your case are critical. That's not all: Photos or video recordings can also help the dispute department determine if the product you purchased was the one you did—or didn't—receive.

→ **BUILD AN AIRTIGHT CASE.** If a company has violated federal or state laws or breached its own contract, then you stand an excellent chance of prevailing in a dispute. For example, say your airline charges you a fee for your luggage, but then loses your suitcase. If the fee was not refunded, it failed to deliver on its promise, and you should dispute the purchase. So-called nuisance disputes—say, a customer felt slighted by a server and wants to dispute the charge for an entire restaurant meal—will go nowhere.

→ **IF YOUR CREDIT CARD SIDES WITH**
THE MERCHANT, APPEAL. You can appeal a decision made by your bank. I have never dealt with a traveler who has successfully appealed a denial, but it's worth noting that there are provisions for an appeal in the FCBA.

→ **IF YOU LOSE, COMPLAIN TO THE FTC OR SUE.** As a last-ditch effort, you can complain to the Federal Trade Commission, and you can sue if the dispute is not resolved properly, but know that taking your case to court may be more trouble than it's worth.

Scam alert: Watch for "dynamic" currency conversions

Beware of dynamic currency conversion (DCC), a practice that can allow an unscrupulous merchant to skim a little off the top of your purchase, at your expense. Here's how it works: If you're paying by credit card overseas, a merchant will sometimes ask if you want to make the purchase in dollars, "for your convenience." If you agree, your money is converted from the local currency into greenbacks and sent to your credit card, but at an awful exchange rate. Bizarrely, you may still have to pay your credit card company a fee for a foreign transaction—so you basically convert the money twice.

The exchange rate is terrible because a third party is helping the merchant make the dollar conversion, taking what amounts to a commission, and splitting it with the business. And you are none the wiser. Except, now you are.

Although the benefit of DCC is that you get to see exactly how much you paid in dollars, it is more than offset by the disadvantageous exchange rate. Moral of the story: Always insist on being billed in the local currency when you're paying by credit card.

How do you prevent card skimming?

Travelers are easy prey for "carders" who take illegal credit card impressions through a crime called cloning or skimming. It can happen almost anywhere. I had my card skimmed at a deli in Whistler, Canada. One reader believes her credit card was cloned when she made an in-flight purchase. The most common skimming site is an ATM, where magnetic strips and PIN numbers are harvested from unsuspecting customers.

> *Moral of the story: Always insist on being billed in the local currency when you're paying by credit card.*

→ **GET A CHIP-AND-PIN CARD.**
These new credit cards use secure computer chips and personal identification numbers to make the card more secure. They're commonly used in Europe and are available from some banks in the United States. They're much more difficult to skim.

→ **PAY ATTENTION.** ATMs with skimmers are fairly easy to spot; they sometimes have a bulky extra layer of electronics where the skimmer is hidden. Also, a sign will sometimes advise you to input your PIN number slowly. If you see a teller machine like that, report it to the authorities and don't use it.

→ **USE CASH PURCHASED FROM YOUR BANK BEFORE YOU LEAVE.** It's a foolproof way to pay for items when you're traveling. As long as you have the right currency you can avoid the ATM completely.

BOTTOM LINE

If you're traveling abroad, you'll want to carry at least one credit card (preferably two) and some local currency. Both payment forms have their risks and rewards but for now, at least, both will serve you well. Mind the fine print and the fees, as always, and you'll avoid most trouble.

(21)

Find the Best Places to Eat on the Road

The lowdown on restaurants, tipping, and why picnics are still cool.

Where to eat is one of the first questions—if not *the* first question—travelers ask. Yet surprisingly, they spend relatively little time planning meals, and, as a result, food can easily become one of the most disappointing parts of a vacation, with travelers falling back on "first available" choices wherever they go. You can do better.

The hospitality industry wants you to believe that when you travel, you *should* eat at a restaurant three times a day. Perhaps the most pervasive myth of all about travel, this self-serving conventional wisdom will, if followed, lighten your wallet while expanding your waistline.

When to dine in:
→ **WHEN PREPARING A MEAL YOUR-SELF** is more convenient, economical, and healthy for you and your traveling companions.

→ **WHEN NONE OF THE RESTAURANT OPTIONS ARE APPEALING.**

→ **IF YOU'RE ON A SPECIAL DIET,** like low-carb, vegetarian, or gluten-free.

When to eat out:
→ **IF YOU DON'T HAVE THE TIME** to prepare a meal.

→ **IF YOU LACK THE FACILITIES TO COOK,** such as a kitchen or microwave.

→ **IF YOU WANT TO EXPERIENCE LOCAL CUISINE** that isn't available where you live.

What's "road food"?
I define "road food" as any dining option along your route, which in the United States typically involves automobile travel. Road food is comfort food or fast food and its location justifies its existence. Anecdotal evidence suggests it's the road food—not the restaurant meals at your destination—that accounts for the bulk of the unwanted calories devoured by travelers.

Is there an equivalent of "road food" for air travelers?
Airport food, a close cousin to road food, is often worse for travelers. Why? The options are limited, because you're behind the security checkpoint, which means you're a captive audience. Often, it's even less healthy

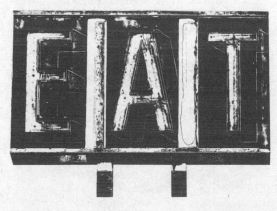

than what you'd find just off a highway exit. What's more, the prices are significantly higher because there's no meaningful competition. As an added bonus, security restrictions mean air travelers can't bring soup, yogurt, or any liquids through the checkpoint (see Chapter 11 for details).

How do I battle the bulge when I'm on the road?

Experiencing new foods is one of the joys of travel. I still remember the pot of crawfish I ordered along a two-lane road in Louisiana back in 1986. My mouth burned all the way to the Texas border.

→ **PLAN YOUR MEALS.** Just as you plot the day's drive on a map, you should also plan for meal breaks near a place where there are either abundant restaurant options or a grocery store. Don't get caught at 8:30 p.m., starving, with a greasy spoon the only option for miles around.

→ **INVESTIGATE YOUR FOOD CHOICES.** If you're resigned to fast food, you don't have to order a burger and fries.

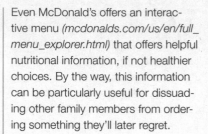

Even McDonald's offers an interactive menu (mcdonalds.com/us/en/full_menu_explorer.html) that offers helpful nutritional information, if not healthier choices. By the way, this information can be particularly useful for dissuading other family members from ordering something they'll later regret.

→ **SNACK OFTEN INSTEAD OF STARVING YOURSELF.** Some of the worst decisions are made at the end of a long road, when dining options are few. Human instinct kicks in; you order the all-you-can-eat ribs and gorge yourself, as your cave-dwelling ancestors did after the hunt. If you hadn't allowed yourself to go hungry, you might have made a better choice. I recommend packing a generous supply of trail mix, just in case.

→ **EXERCISE.** If possible, take frequent walks, swim, surf, or ski—whatever gets your heart rate up. You'll burn those extra calories in no time.

Should I pack my lunch when I'm traveling?

Yes, there's something decidedly unglamorous about buying your food from a grocery store when you're traveling. Don't worry about that. I would strongly suggest that you plan one or two special meals in a well-researched restaurant and buy the rest of your meals like everyone else: in a grocery store or at a local market. Here's why:

→ **YOU'LL SAVE MONEY.** A lot. My family's food bills are roughly 60 percent lower when we leave restaurants off the menu when we're traveling.

→ **PICNICS ROCK.** If you think the view of the lake from the expensive restaurant is amazing, you should see it from the picnic tables across the street. It's like you're *right there.* Even some highway rest areas can offer an amazing setting. Interstate 90 in the South Dakota Badlands is one of my favorite places to stop for lunch.

→ **YOU'LL GET TO KNOW THE LOCALS.** If you want a truly authentic experience, skip the restaurant where all the tourists cluster and visit the grocery store. You'll meet real people and you'll find out what they *really* eat. Wherever you are, remember two words: farmers market. If you don't get out, you'll miss what is arguably the best part of any trip—a walk to the local bazaar or marketplace. Their culinary offerings may not be available anywhere else.

→ **YOU'LL STAY HEALTHY.** I probably don't have to tell you that a diet of fresh fruits and vegetables and low-fat meats or fish will keep you trim while you're traveling. On the road, where the standard fare is carb-heavy, dripping in heavy, delicious sauces, how easy it is to forget what keeps you healthy.

Some of the worst decisions are made at the end of a long road, when dining options are few.

Where should I eat?

In Chapter 1, I mentioned that there are more—and less—credible sources for reliable recommendations. Many of those principles hold true for restaurants, but there are a few exceptions.

→ **USER-GENERATED REVIEWS ARE HELPFUL FOR SOME INFORMATION.** For example, information about pricing (how many "$" signs are displayed next to the rating) can offer a general idea of how much your meal will cost. But as I've warned earlier in this book, I'd recommend a healthy dose of skepticism when it comes to the actual star ratings.

→ **SEEING IS BELIEVING.** A long line out the door is a sign that the food is pretty decent. In fact, I've never been disappointed by a restaurant with a lengthy wait. Pay attention to what you see, and less to what they say. By the way, if you see guests walking out the door and shaking their heads in disgust, it might be a sign you've picked the wrong place.

→ **"FIRST AVAILABLE" MAY BE WORST AVAILABLE.** There's an old saying that in New Orleans, a favorite conversation around the lunch table is what to have for dinner. That's great advice for travelers. By planning your restaurant visit well in advance, you can avoid defaulting to the "first available" place, which may end up being a terrible choice.

Should I tip?

In the United States, tips are used to subsidize the poverty-level hourly wages paid to restaurant staff, who are exempt in most jurisdictions (California is one notable exception) from minimum wage laws. In a perfect world, you would pay the total on your check, and, if you liked the service, you could add a few dollars if you wanted to. It's not a perfect world. Servers may follow you out onto the street if you forget to tip or don't tip enough. It's happened to me. Tipping rules are different outside the United States. Ask before tipping in other countries (see below).

How about tipping while I'm abroad?

In most other countries, servers are paid a living wage and don't need

> *Hotels add a room service surcharge and a mandatory tip to most room service bills.*

gratuities in order to survive. It may even be considered offensive to tip, or to tip too much. In most of Europe, for example, a 15 percent tip is almost always too much, and in some countries a service charge is included in your meal. (Five to ten percent is more like it.) In Costa Rica, tips are also included in your meal. And in China, tipping is not allowed. Aren't you glad you asked?

Tipping scams you should watch for when you're traveling

→ **"MANDATORY" TIPS.** Some restaurants add a compulsory tip to large parties, usually of ten or more patrons, but sometimes fewer. The tip is usually 18 percent and it's automatically added to your bill. To avoid it, you can break large groups into two, or even ask for separate checks. They may agree to split the bill, but you could still see a fee, so watch for it.

NOT SMART DON'T FALL FOR THE MENU TRAP.

Many restaurants offer at least two menus: one for lunch, the other for dinner. If you're just driving through, that might not be immediately apparent. But if you compare the entrées on each menu, they're often identical. What's different? The price, usually. Just as with movie theater tickets, you're paying more because of the time of day. To be fair, some restaurants *do* offer larger portions for dinner, but do you really want to eat that much? To avoid this late p.m. premium, plan your "out" meal for lunch, and have a more modest dinner that you prepare in your room or buy in a grocery store.

→ **"PRE-CALCULATED" TIPS.** New handheld, point-of-sale machines that handle your credit card transaction at the table can be convenient, but for whom? If you said the restaurant, you're right. I've heard from patrons who claim the on-screen prompts offer pre-calculated tips that are based on post-tax totals, not pre-tax totals, as they should be. In other words, they're adding a few cents to each bill unless you calculate the tip instead of letting them do it, for their convenience.

→ **ROOM SERVICE TIPS.** Hotels add a room service surcharge and a mandatory tip to most room service bills. They then allow you to add a discretionary amount on top of it, vastly inflating your food bill. One guest complained to me after paying 60 percent over the menu's prices once the hotel added delivery surcharges and he'd tipped. It's tricky. The hotel doesn't always itemize the bill, so you think you're tipping the employee. In fact, you're probably overtipping.

What should I do if I have a problem with my meal?

Of course, the best time to resolve any kind of problem with a business is at the moment the problem occurs. Nowhere is that truer than at a restaurant. Is there a hair in your entrée? Call a server over and ask him or her to address the problem. Once you pay your bill and leave the establishment, the business assumes you're a happy customer. Maybe they shouldn't.

Here are a few strategies for avoiding/resolving a restaurant dispute:

→ **BE CLEAR WHEN YOU ORDER YOUR MEAL.** Regional dialects and language issues may lead to confusion. When in doubt, point to the entrée you're ordering. If you aren't sure your server has understood the order, ask him or her to repeat it.

→ **IF SOMETHING IS MISSING, SPEAK UP.** Don't assume your server will return with a missing item. Mention if a side order or drink has been omitted.

→ **DON'T FORGET YOUR (TABLE) MANNERS.** Being rude to a server can have direct and unwanted consequences in a restaurant. You want to be as polite as possible, particularly when you have a grievance. In other words, be dispassionate, unfailingly cordial, and friendly—even if the meal is a total disaster.

→ **LET THE PUNISHMENT FIT THE CRIME.** Too many restaurant patrons demand that the bill be torn up if something goes wrong ("Waiter, there's a fly in my soup"), but that's hardly an appropriate response. A sincere apology, a replaced bowl of soup, and maybe a complimentary dessert is far more fitting. Let the server be the one to say, "The meal is on us."

→ **ESCALATE TO A MANAGER, AND THEN TO A CORPORATE OWNER.** If a server doesn't do the right thing, ask to speak with a supervisor, manager, or owner. If that doesn't work, try sending a brief, polite email to the owner or to the corporation that runs the restaurant chain.

How do I get a restaurant to see things my way?

You may be faced with an intransigent server, manager, or owner who either belittles your complaint or dismisses it. Travelers are often subjected to that kind of treatment because they're unlikely to return—why go

the extra mile to make them happy? But you can easily get the upper hand.

→ **USE YOUR POLITENESS AS A WEAPON.** When you point out a flaw in the meal, a restaurant's reaction may be defensive, if not hostile. The business may expect you to lose your temper. Also, tourists sometimes have a well-deserved reputation for being rude. When you defy the stereotype, it dampens the blow and can boost your chances of getting what you want.

→ **TAKE PHOTOS.** Nothing is as persuasive as a picture of that soufflé that caved in before its time. You can upload the image to the Internet in the time it takes for a manager to come to your table. Whether or not you actually share it with your social media friends is really up to the restaurant, isn't it?

→ **END YOUR MEAL EARLY.** If things take a turn for the worse, you don't have to stay and order a dessert. You can note your displeasure by cutting your meal short. Don't forget to pay.

→ **WITHHOLD YOUR TIP.** If the service was truly awful, don't tip. Remember: In the United States, that's more or less the same thing as not paying your server, so be sure it's actually deserved. Write "sorry, no tip for this meal" on the subtotal, and wait. Chances are a manager will be called over to see if something's fixable. If it is, please consider restoring your tip.

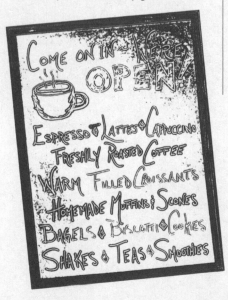

When should I walk away from a restaurant meal?

The best time to abandon a restaurant meal is *before* ordering. When the billing outside the restaurant didn't live up to the offerings inside (fewer menu choices, bad ambiance, noisy guests) politely take your leave. As a traveler, you have a great excuse. Don't you have a plane to catch?

If you've already ordered your food, it'll get a little complicated. Walk out and the restaurateur could call the police. Better tell your server that you're done with your meal—even if it's clear you're not done eating—and ask to settle up. If your server is halfway perceptive, he or she will know there's a problem and call a manager. That will at least guarantee you'll leave a tip of some kind. If not, then pay up and leave, and if you believe the server is culpable for the less-than-desirable restaurant experience, omit the tip. I would not abandon a restaurant meal and leave the premises without paying unless you felt as if you were in imminent physical danger.

What about other surcharges on my bill?

Normally, the price on the menu should be reflected on your bill when you are in the United States, not including any applicable sales tax. In recent years, restaurateurs have added surcharges of anywhere from 2 to 5 percent to cover other items such as healthcare costs. Restaurants in San Francisco are known for adding these fees, and at Oakland Airport your meal comes with a side order of an employee healthcare surcharge. How convenient—for *them*. These extras may make your total bill more difficult to estimate.

→ **IF A RESTAURANT INSISTS ON TACKING A SURCHARGE TO YOUR BILL, YOU CAN DEDUCT THE FEE FROM YOUR TIP.** This will, of course, incur the wrath of a server. But adding a surcharge is not a sound business practice and shouldn't be rewarded.

→ **IF YOU SEE A SURCHARGE YOU DON'T LIKE, SOUND A WARNING.** User-generated reviews may lack credibility, but that doesn't mean you can't leverage them to warn others about a fee that was added without notification. In this case, Yelp and TripAdvisor are your allies.

BOTTOM LINE

When it comes to food on the road, think outside the lunch box. Choose your restaurants carefully, not by default. Try a picnic even if you can afford to eat every meal out. And visit a grocery store to find out how the locals *really* cook. You'll probably have a more culturally enriching trip and maintain a healthy weight if you do.

22

Survive a Timeshare and Travel Club Presentation

The truth about vacation ownership and a travel club you should never join.

Why pay for a hotel when you can own your own vacation home or condo? That's the promise the timeshare industry offers. The pitch typically comes when you're on vacation and your guard is down. An equally compelling come-on happens when you're back at home and are lured into a sales presentation for a travel "club" that could save you tens of thousands of dollars—as long as you're a member. Let's take a closer look at both.

TIMESHARES

A timeshare is a resort property— usually condominium units—in which multiple parties hold rights to use the property. Each owner is allotted a period of time, usually one week a year, to use the property. The weeks can be traded with other timeshare owners through an exchange company. Timeshares are often also referred to as fractional ownerships, but they both are essentially the same thing.

When should you consider a timeshare?

→ **IF YOU SPEND A LOT OF TIME VACATIONING IN A POPULAR VACATION DESTINATION** where there are timeshare units or places where you can exchange your timeshare unit for accommodations, including hotel rooms.

→ **IF YOU REQUIRE THE EXTRA SPACE** and amenities that a timeshare unit can offer.

When should you not consider a timeshare?

→ **IF YOU TAKE ERRATIC VACATIONS** and can go many months or even years without staying at a popular vacation destination, or if you normally stay in a hotel and you like it.

→ **IF YOU PREFER TO EVALUATE YOUR LONG-TERM VACATION LODGING OPTIONS** on your own without the pressure inherent in a direct sales approach.

What kind of timeshares can I buy?

Although this book isn't a buyer's guide for timeshares, it's helpful to know some of the main differences among timeshares.

→ **DEEDED.** A deeded vacation ownership is the traditional real estate timeshare. You buy a week-long increment and it's yours to rent, trade, or give away. You can resell a deeded vacation ownership or give it to your heirs.

→ **RIGHT TO USE.** A right-to-use property, as the name suggests, gives you the right to use the property for a specific period of time through a legal contract, but you do not receive an interest in real estate. Why limit it? Because in some countries, outright ownership by foreigners is restricted. At the end of the specified period, the property reverts to the original owner.

→ **POINTS.** Points should be thought of as a representation of an owner's reservation power: either a deeded or right-to-use interest. As part of your purchase, the developer may assign a number of points to your timeshare interest (your deed, leasehold, or right-to-use interest), which will depend on many factors such as unit type and season in which you own. In turn, those points are then used to make a reservation in a timeshare unit.

If you haven't already noticed, timeshares can be extraordinarily complicated.

If you did it for the tickets, be honest. Tell them.

What are the biggest timeshare pitfalls?

As a consumer advocate, I don't get many questions about whether, for example, a fixed week or a floating week is a better buy. Those queries are best left to a timeshare consultant who is not paid on commission and who can offer objective recommendations. Rather, the complaints I receive fall into three broad categories:

→ **THE INITIAL PITCH.** The come-ons and promises with which timeshare resort representatives try to lure you into a tour and sales presentation.

→ **THE SALES PROCESS.** The presentation, which is often highly persuasive, can leave you signing away your life savings. Literally.

→ **BUYER'S REMORSE.** The morning after your timeshare purchase,

---

SMART KNOW THE DIFFERENCE BETWEEN A SALES PITCH AND A CONTRACT.

Talk may be cheap, but it could end up costing you a lot if you're buying a timeshare and you rely on a salesman's verbal promises. Even timeshare insiders will warn you that understanding the difference between a sales pitch and a contract, which spells out exactly what is being provided, is the key to a satisfying timeshare experience. If a sales representative says you can exchange your unit within the resort group, look for the precise wording in the contract to see which terms apply. The paperwork trumps everything.

you wake up and realize that you didn't get what you paid for—and you want out. Fortunately, the vast majority of states in America require a rescission period or a mandatory exit clause of three to ten days, by law.

What's an OPC and how do I avoid one?

Off-property consultants, or OPCs, are some of the most aggressive salespeople in the world, and they happen to sell timeshares—or more specifically, they sell the *opportunity* to sell a timeshare.

→ **STAY AWAY FROM OPC TERRITORY.** Timeshare OPCs lurk in touristy areas. If you want to avoid being pitched, steer clear of places like the Vegas Strip or a popular beach.

→ **HAVE A READY ANSWER.** A comeback like "I'm leaving tomorrow," or "I've already been to a timeshare presentation" might work. "We have a timeshare we're trying to sell" can do the trick, too.

→ **JUST SAY "NO."** I've counseled many heartbroken vacationers who were enjoying margaritas on the beach one minute, and writing a check for $25,000 the next, thanks to an aggressive sales pitch. A simple "no" could have saved them a world of hurt.

How do I survive a timeshare tour and sales presentation?

If you take the bait by accepting the "free" theme park tickets or dinner vouchers, then you've just agreed to take a 90-minute tour and presentation of a property.

Remember what I mentioned before? A vacation is hardly the time to buy real estate or make long-term decisions on vacation options. You are either doing this to look at the property up close, or, more likely, for the "free" gifts. Either way, you want to get through the process without buying a timeshare. If you want to buy a timeshare, you can always do it later.

→ **REPEAT AFTER ME: "I'M HERE FOR THE FREE TICKETS."** If you did it for the tickets, be honest. Tell them. Actually, you'll want to use this line often, without being rude. If someone asks how you're doing, tell them you're just here for the tickets. If they want to know how many kids you

PROBLEM SOLVED

A BROKEN DISNEY VACATION CLUB PROMISE

QUESTION: We recently purchased 350 points in Disney Vacation Club, Disney's timeshare program. New members of Disney Vacation Club are given help with their first reservation, and salespeople can go into Disney's cash inventory, if necessary, to get a better selection.

About six weeks ago our salesperson promised to help us with our second reservation as soon as we had our dates decided, because we had booked our first reservation on our own.

When we called, we found out he is on indefinite medical leave and were directed to speak with another salesperson about the reservation. The second salesperson said she couldn't help because Disney only offers to help on the first reservation.

We tried to appeal to a supervisor, but she also refused to help. And her tone on the phone was not what one expects of a Disney representative—very negative and condescending.

It is not our fault that our salesperson is on medical leave and we feel Disney should honor what he told us. Can you help us get that magic that we expected from Disney? —David Willard, *Newtown, Pennsylvania*

ANSWER: Disney's policy may be to give priority to first-time reservations, but it is not something that is openly promoted, as far as I can tell. Nonetheless, if your timeshare salesman promised you could use your first-reservation credit on your second reservation, it's something Disney should make good on.

I've attended the Disney Vacation Club presentation in Orlando, and it's a pretty impressive program. Disney offers a lot of properties, and the rates were reasonable enough that I even considered buying in. Why didn't I? Like a lot of Americans, I don't have nearly enough vacation time to use it.

The problem with the agreement you had with your first salesman is that it was verbal. Of course, you had no way of knowing that he'd go on medical leave, but what happened underscores the importance of getting absolutely everything in writing.

Even a brief email from Disney, agreeing to help you with the second reservation, would have prevented this from taking away the magic of your vacation. If you didn't have something in writing, you could have started a paper trail—or in your case, an email trail—with your request. Disney would have been compelled to respond to you by email, and it may have answered differently (and almost certainly without the attitude you got from the supervisor).

I think the Vacation Club staff you dealt with could have done better, from finding a new salesman who had been properly briefed on your needs, to ensuring that all of the promises he made to you were being kept, even if the promises weren't necessarily in line with stated company policy. Of course, there's no excuse for being unpleasant with a customer—ever.

I contacted Disney Vacation Club on your behalf. A representative called you and helped you make a reservation at the timeshare you wanted.

have, you're just here for the tickets. If possible, secure the tickets, prizes, or dinner vouchers before the presentation begins.

> *Questions will make your sales associate think you're interested in buying today, which you are not.*

→ **LEAVE YOUR WALLET AT HOME.**
One surefire way to avoid making a purchase is to leave the tools necessary to buy a timeshare at home. Your credit card, debit card, and, of course, your checkbook. Don't bring 'em. You may be asked for a credit card and ID when you pick up your "free" tickets. I recommend a debit card with a low spending limit.

→ **DON'T ASK TOO MANY QUESTIONS.** They'll needlessly prolong the presentation. Also, questions will make your sales associate think you're interested in buying today, which you are not.

→ **BRACE YOURSELF FOR THE SALES TEAM.** Most timeshare sales teams consist of at least three levels: A sales associate who makes a presentation, which always ends with an offer to buy a timeshare. Many prospects say "no" or, if they've been paying attention, "I'm just here for the tickets." You may be referred to a manager, who will offer to dramatically cut your rate if you buy *now*. If all else fails, you'll be referred to a closer, who can make more promises and reduce the rate for your timeshare further.

→ **JUST SAY "NO."** These salespeople are used to rejection, and if they're professionals, they'll appreciate your polite firmness.

Help, I'm tempted to say "yes"

If you're sitting in a presentation with a sudden urge to buy, do this: Pull out your smartphone and run a search on the timeshare along with the keyword "complaints" or "scam" and see what pops up. That's usually enough to give you second thoughts. Check out the Timeshare User's Group (*tug2.com/timesharemarketplace*) or

---

👍 SMART IF YOU CAN'T HELP YOURSELF, DON'T GO.

You know the old Greek saying "Know thyself"? There's no travel purchase for which that is more appropriate than timeshares. If you can't exercise self-control, it's best to not attend presentations where you'll feel tempted by the gifts, dinners, and weekends away.

IntervalMLS at *intervalmls.com* and see if there are any resales on the same unit you're being pitched. It's not unusual to find units that cost $1 (maintenance fees not included, of course). If that doesn't convince you to walk away, chances are, nothing will.

Membership in the American Resort Development Association (ARDA), the trade group for timeshares, can be a positive sign. You can find the membership directory online at *arda.org/membership/memberdirectories/corporate.aspx*.

How do I get out of a timeshare I shouldn't have bought?

A legitimate timeshare has a rescission period—anywhere from 24 hours to more than a week—during which time you can escape from your contract. Rescission periods may also be set by state law. Consult your state's applicable timeshare laws for details. You can find them on the state legislature website. Bottom line: Once you sign your name, the clock is ticking. You may have days—or hours—before you are stuck with your purchase. Ask the deeding or verification officer to show you the rescission portion of the paperwork, and make sure you understand exactly what needs to be done for you to officially rescind.

TRAVEL CLUBS

A travel club is a timeshare's distant cousin because it is marketed and sold in a similar way, but make no mistake: Whereas timeshares are legitimate, regulated travel products, clubs are usually not. In order to skirt the long arm of the law, many travel clubs move from state to state, changing their names to avoid prosecution.

Should I buy a travel club membership?

No. With the exception of AAA, which is a not-for-profit member service organization, travel clubs are either really bad deals or outright scams. If someone asks if you want to attend a presentation for a travel club, don't walk away—run!

What does a travel club offer?

A typical club will try to sell you an annual membership and may also charge an initiation fee to join the club. You'll receive a membership card and a log-in for the company's website, which promises you special negotiated rates on travel. "Benefits" may include:

• A 50 percent or higher discount on travel.
• Buy one/get one free airfare, or a companion certificate.
• A "free" cruise.
• A "free" two-day vacation.
• A discount access card that offers special deals on non-travel items, such as restaurants and attractions.

These "deals" look terrific, but a closer look reveals they aren't. The discounts may be comparable to the discounted prices you'll find on Expedia, Orbitz, or Travelocity. The companion certificate? It requires you to buy a full-fare economy class ticket, which costs twice what you'd pay for a normal coach seat. The discount access? Your AAA or AARP card can often do better. The one area that's consistently the biggest source of frustration among victims is the "free" vacation or cruise. Let's dive right into that one.

Read the fine print on the travel club application really carefully. The offers are highly restrictive, if not fraudulent.

Is that "free" cruise for real?

Many vacation clubs try to hook you into a presentation with the promise of a "free" cruise—but it's not a free cruise. Trust me, it's not. I've fielded numerous complaints from travelers who believed they had received a legitimate offer, by mail, of either a free cruise or vacation, in exchange for attending a presentation for a travel club.

Read the fine print on the travel club application *really* carefully. The offers are highly restrictive, if not fraudulent.

You'll have to pay your own way to the port and cover fees that, once paid, may total more than the cost of a cruise you'd buy from a regular travel agent. Also, blackout dates apply to the offer. Once you've jumped through all the hoops to collect the "free" vacation, chances are you will have spent more money than you would have by simply booking a cruise the old-fashioned way—plus, you might be stuck with a membership in a useless travel club.

How do I survive a travel club pitch?

Most travel clubs use direct mailings (or bombard you with emails or faxes) that offer a free vacation as bait. The goal is to attract you to one of their sales events, which normally take place either in a rented space in a strip mall or in a hotel conference center.

These high-pressure presentations put the timeshare industry to shame, both in terms of the huge amount of pressure they apply and the enormous promises they make. At the same time, because travel clubs are so mobile—they're not tied to a particular product, or to real estate in the same way timeshare salespeople are—they can get away with almost anything. And they often do.

If you go, gather a little intel on the club first. A simple Internet search for the club, under its name, along with keywords like "scam," "fraud," or "rip-off" can reveal a mother lode of useful information. Remember, fraudulent travel clubs change their names and locations often, and they use sophisticated search engine manipulation techniques (sometimes called *reputation management*) to guarantee nothing bad shows up when you search for them. Here's a tip: Don't search for the name of the club, but the owners. I've seen travel clubs that looked squeaky-clean online, but their owners . . . not so much.

Here are a few tips for getting through a travel club presentation:

→ **SECURE YOUR PRIZE BEFORE THE PITCH.** If you can claim your "free" cruise or vacation before the action starts, so much the better. No prize, no presentation.

→ **REPEAT AFTER ME: "I'M NOT READY TO BUY."** Never, ever buy a travel club in a presentation. If you must, give yourself a cooling-off period to reflect on the offer. To that end, you should leave your credit card and checkbook at home.

→ **BEWARE OF AUDIENCE "PLANTS."** A favorite tactic of fraudulent travel clubs is having operatives planted in the audience. They applaud, and ask enthusiastic questions to which, inevitably, there's a canned response. ("How do I know if I'm getting the best deal?") Ignore those around you. For all you know, you may be the only prospect in the room.

$ $ $

→ **IF YOU THINK YOU'RE INTERESTED IN THE CLUB, ASK TO REVIEW THE CONTRACT.** Like timeshares, travel clubs have ridiculously convoluted and restrictive agreements. Ask your sales associate if you can take the contract home to review it, which is a perfectly reasonable request. Better yet, say you want to show it to your attorney. Odds are, your associate will balk and tell you that's not allowed. That's your sign to head for the exit—*now!*

→ PREPARE FOR A CLOSER WHO WON'T TAKE "NO" FOR AN ANSWER. During travel club presentations, the closer does not take "no" for an answer. You must be prepared to walk out the door anyway. Closers will keep cutting the price of the club, or offer to waive the initiation fee. It's a sign of desperation. Be prepared to be guilted about accepting the "free" cruise without also considering the club. Walk away.

Can I get out of a travel club?

Your options to escape the clutches of a travel club are limited. You may have an "out" in your contract, but as before, you should pay attention to what's written in your contract—not what a salesperson tells you. If you've paid with a credit card, you can dispute the charge, but you'll have to show that you didn't get what you paid for, and that may be difficult once the travel club has shown your super-restrictive contract to your bank dispute department.

Small claims court or your state attorney general's office is another option, but by the time the law catches up to a travel club, it's usually long gone, and for you, it's an expensive lesson learned.

BOTTOM LINE

Timeshares are not for everyone. If you're prepared to accept theme park tickets or restaurant vouchers in exchange for attending a presentation, you're playing with fire. You could end up owning a timeshare you wish you hadn't bought. You wouldn't buy a house on a whim, and a timeshare is a type of real estate purchase. Don't be taken in by a high-pressure sale. Take your time, and think about what you're doing.

Travel clubs, which are marketed in a similar way, are practically worthless. Responding to the direct mailer that offers you a free cruise or vacation is like walking into a trap. You're better off throwing the offer into the garbage and never looking back.

👍 **SMART** HERE'S A LITTLE INDUSTRY INTEL TO HELP YOU SAY "NO."

It helps to understand how products are priced in the travel industry. It's true that airlines, cruise lines, and hotels discount their products, and often aggressively. But they also have contracts with online travel agencies and computer reservations systems that prevent their rates from being reduced by too much from their sticker prices. This prevents them from being undercut on their own websites. In other words, the promised savings a travel club offers either violates a contract or, more likely, doesn't exist at all. Either way—run!

Afterword

Congratulations! You are now the world's smartest traveler. But this isn't the end of the book. Keep reading for an appendix with the contact information for many major travel companies. And if you need to take your problem up the ladder, don't forget to check out my website, *elliott .org/contacts,* which lists names and contact information for specific corporate executives. This completely unsanctioned resource is a guaranteed shortcut to solving your next travel problem.

Think of this book as the beginning of an important conversation. When you're done here, please join the debate on my website, *elliott .org,* or follow me on social media. I'm at @elliottdotorg on Twitter and on Facebook at *facebook.com/ ChristopherJamesElliott.*

If you need help, I'm here for you. You can also turn to Travelers United (formerly the Consumer Travel Alliance), an organization I helped create. Travelers United also advocates for the big issues affecting many people, whether they cruise, drive, or fly. You can learn more at its website, *travelersunited.org.*

How to Be the World's Smartest Traveler is the result of years of consumer advocacy, but it is also a direct result of the many friendships with real travelers I've developed along the journey.

If you're one of them, I thank you for being there for me, so that I could be there for travelers like you.

Safe travels.

Acknowledgments

This book wouldn't have happened unless Norie Quintos, my editor at *National Geographic Traveler,* had noticed my work back in 1998. She was looking for a consumer reporter who wasn't afraid to tell the truth about an industry that has a reputation for buying positive coverage. I was younger and fearless—maybe a little *too* fearless. We've been working together ever since. Thank you, Norie.

Keith Bellows, *Traveler*'s editor in chief, made a brave decision when he hired me as the magazine's first reader advocate in 2002. He's defended my stories, and me, against angry advertisers and unhappy readers on so many occasions that I've lost count. Along the way he also lent me his incredible literary agent, Cynthia Cannell. I can honestly say I wouldn't be here without you, Keith. Thanks.

I'm also grateful to my friends and colleagues at Tribune Content Agency who saw some potential in this blogger turned magazine writer and offered me a syndicated column in 2006. *Mahalo* to TMS editor Mary Elson; to my immediate editor, Tracy Clark; and to the phenomenal sales team at TMS, led by J. Scott Cameron. I'm so pleased that they agreed to let me republish some of my syndicated columns in this book.

As I mentioned in the introduction, I am not the world's smartest traveler. I sent an early draft of this book to the people I *do* consider to be the world's smartest travelers. I am eternally grateful to them for making this a great book. Instead of listing them individually here—there are more than 100 "smartest" travelers—I decided to create a series for my website called "The World's Smartest Traveler" in which I thank them and ask them to share their favorite travel strategies.

Also, I wanted to give a big shout-out to my friends and readers on the social networks, who have shown me, through comments, emails, and tweets, that there *is* a smarter way to travel. I have listened. I travel better because of you.

Finally, I owe a debt of gratitude to my family: to my better half, Kari, who generously allowed me to take a leave of absence from many of my duties to write this book; and to my kids, Aren, Iden, and Erysse, for understanding that even though Daddy is in his office, it doesn't necessarily mean he's available. I hope one day, when you look back on the months I spent on this project, you'll think it was worthwhile. And I hope you'll grow up to be smarter travelers.

Appendix

Specific instructions for initiating an inquiry, complaint, or dispute vary from company to company and can be found by checking the individual corporate websites listed below or by calling the company. For regularly updated contact information for specific customer relations managers and other corporate executives—including names and phone numbers—check out *elliott.org/contacts*.

Consumer Advocacy

Better Business Bureau
Council of Better Business Bureaus
3033 Wilson Boulevard, Suite 600
Arlington, VA 22201
703-276-0100
bbb.org/us/Contact-BBB
• The Council of Better Business Bureaus, which includes your regional Better Business Bureau, describes itself as one of the nation's "recognized leaders in developing and administering self-regulation programs for the business community." This is the bottom line for you, the consumer: While your local BBB is a useful tool for finding a reputable business, you should rely on it to advocate on your behalf as forcefully as any other self-regulating group.

Call For Action
11820 Parklawn Drive, Suite 340
Rockville, MD 20852
240-747-0229
cfadatabase.org/cfa/submit-a-complaint.aspx

• A nonprofit network of consumer hotlines founded in 1963 to empower consumers by giving them a voice larger than their own. Volunteer professionals in offices around the world are trained to assist consumers through mediation and education to resolve problems with businesses, government agencies, and other organizations. Call For Action's services are free and confidential.

The National Association of Consumer Advocates
1730 Rhode Island Avenue NW,
  Suite 710
Washington, DC 20036
202-452-1989
Fax 202-452-0099
naca.net/contact-us
• A nationwide organization of more than 1,500 attorneys who represent consumers. If you are going to take the legal route, NACA might be able to help with a referral.

Hotels

Hilton
7930 Jones Branch Drive, Suite 1100
McLean, VA 22102
703-883-1000
1-800-445-8667
1-800-445-8667 (Puerto Rico and the
  U.S. Virgin Islands)
901-374-6476 (Guest Relations)
hilton.com
• Hilton operates several hotel brands, including Conrad, DoubleTree,

Embassy Suites, Hampton, Hilton, Homewood Suites, and Waldorf Astoria. Some of the brands experienced a brief spike in complaints after a recent ownership change. But overall, Hilton's properties aren't known for their preponderance of customer grievances.

InterContinental

InterContinental Hotels Group
  (Americas office)
3 Ravinia Drive, NE, Suite 100
Atlanta, GA 30346-2149
770-604-2000
Fax 770-604-8442
1-800-621-0555 (Customer Service
  for the Americas)
Fax 801-975-1846 (Customer Service for the Americas)
ihg.com
• InterContinental's brands include Candlewood Suites, Crowne Plaza, Holiday Inn, InterContinental, and Staybridge Suites. Its brands usually handle customer service complaints quickly.

Marriott

10400 Fernwood Road
Bethesda, MD 20817
301-380-3000
1-800-228-9290
Fax 301-380-3967
801-468-4000 (Guest Services)
1-800-450-4442 (Guest Services)
Fax 801-468-4033 (Guest Services)
marriott.com
• Marriott is the corporate parent of several well-known hotel chains, including Courtyard, Fairfield, Marriott,

Renaissance Hotels, and Ritz-Carlton. Overall, it is one of the least complained-about lodging companies.

Information, Reviews, and Trip Planning

AAA Travel

1000 AAA Drive
Heathrow, FL 32746
1-800-529-3222 (Travel Inquiries)
407-444-7000 (AAA Headquarters
  in Heathrow, Florida)
407-444-8402 (National Office,
  Member Relations)
travel.aaa.com
• AAA Travel Services offers travel products and services for air, car, hotel, tour, and cruise bookings to worldwide destinations via its network of local and regional offices. Each regional club is an affiliate of AAA National, which serves some 53 million AAA members in the United States and Canada.

TripAdvisor

141 Needham Street
Newton, MA 02464
617-670-6300
tripadvisor.com
• TripAdvisor claims to be the world's largest travel site. It promises to help travelers "plan and have the perfect trip." TripAdvisor says it offers trusted advice from real travelers and a wide variety of travel choices and planning features. As a practical matter, TripAdvisor accepts reviews from anonymous readers and does not have a uniform or transparent way to deal with fake ratings.

Yelp

706 Mission Street, 7th Floor
San Francisco, CA 94105
415-908-3801
yelp.com

• Yelp describes itself as an online urban city guide that helps people find "cool" places to eat, shop, drink, relax, and play, based on the informed opinions of a vibrant and active community of locals in the know. Like TripAdvisor, it accepts anonymous reviews, which has created some credibility problems.

Travel Booking

American Express Travel

200 Vesey Street
New York, NY 10080
1-800-297-2977
312-980-7807
travel.americanexpress.com

• American Express Travel is a full-service travel agency that can assist you with travel plans for hotels, flights, cruises, or vacation packages. It operates in more than 140 countries.

Expedia

333 108th Avenue NE
Bellevue, WA 98004
1-877-787-7186
404-728-8787
expedia.com

• Expedia is the largest online travel agency in the world. Complaint volume has decreased in recent years as the company has worked to improve customer support.

Hotwire

655 Montgomery Street, #600
San Francisco, CA 94111
1-866-HOTWIRE or 1-866-468-9473
415-343-8400
Fax 415-343-8401
hotwire.com

• Hotwire is a discount travel site that offers a lower price in exchange for concealing certain details about the airline, car rental company, or hotel. The most common Hotwire problems include amenities or services promised but allegedly not delivered, and confusion over its star-rating system.

Orbitz

500 W. Madison Street, Suite 1000
Chicago, IL 60661
312-416-0018
1-888-656-4546
orbitz.com

• Orbitz is one of the big three online travel agencies. It has a reputation for using technology creatively to help travelers and receiving relatively few service complaints.

Priceline

800 Connecticut Avenue
Norwalk, CT 06854
1-800-774-2354
203-299-8000
Fax 203-299-8901
priceline.com

• Priceline is a travel agency that provides users with plane tickets, hotel reservations, car rentals, vacation packages, and a number of weekend or last-minute deals. They specialize in discount pricing and a "Name Your

Own Price" feature that allows customers to negotiate their own rates.

Travel Leaders
3033 Campus Drive, Suite W320
Plymouth, MN 55441
763-744-3700
1-800-335-TRIP (8747) for leisure travel inquiries (to be connected with travel agency franchisees in your area)
travelleaders.com
• Travel Leaders is a system of full-service travel agencies operating throughout the United States. The brand includes 1,250 systemwide franchised locations. Travel Leaders' support services desk mediates disputes between its franchisees and their customers.

Travelocity
11603 Crosswinds Way, Suite 125
San Antonio, TX 78233
682-605-3000
1-888-709-5983
1-888-872-8356 (Customer Support)
travelocity.com
• Travelocity is a subsidiary brand of Sabre Holdings. After adopting a service guarantee several years ago, the agency has made significant strides toward improving its customer service experience.

Transportation and Cruise Lines
American Airlines
P.O. Box 619616
DFW Airport, TX 75261-9616
817-963-1234
1-800-433-7300
817-967-2000 (Customer Service, pre-recorded)
Fax 817-967-4162 (Customer Service)
aa.com
• American's recent bankruptcy hurt its customer-service reputation. As this book goes to press, it is trying to merge with US Airways, which could take a further toll on service.

Amtrak
60 Massachusetts Ave N.E.
Washington, DC 20002-4285
1-800-872-7245
amtrak.com
• The National Railroad Passenger Corporation, Amtrak, is America's national passenger rail carrier. Most service complaints involve Amtrak's aging equipment and infrastructure, which is chronically underfunded by Congress.

Avis
6 Sylvan Way
Parsippany, NJ 07054
973-496-3500
1-800-352-7900
avis.com
• Avis owns the Avis and Budget brands. It generally offers a quality car rental product, although I've heard occasional complaints about overly vigilant damage claims.

Carnival Corporation
3655 N.W. 87th Avenue
Miami, FL 33178-2428
305-599-2600
1-888-227 6482

Fax 305-471-4700
1-800-929-6400 (Guest Care)
carnival.com
• Carnival Corporation is the parent company of several cruise lines, including Carnival Cruise Lines, Holland America Line, Princess Cruises, Seabourn, AIDA Cruises, Costa Cruises, Cunard, P&O Cruises, P&O Cruises Australia, and Iberocruceros. Some have excellent reputations for customer service. Others, not so excellent. All appeals should go to Carnival.

Delta Air Lines

Hartsfield-Jackson Atlanta
  International Airport
1030 Delta Boulevard
Atlanta, GA 30354-1989
404-715-2600
1-800-221-1212
delta.com
• Delta Air Lines has a reputation for lightning-fast response times via social media. After merging with Northwest Airlines, it has steadily improved in the customer service department.

Enterprise Holdings

600 Corporate Park Drive
St. Louis, MO 63105
1-800-261-7331
Fax 314-512-4706
enterprise.com
• Enterprise, through its regional subsidiaries, operates Enterprise Rent-A-Car, National Car Rental, and Alamo Rent-A-Car. It generally offers a quality car rental product, but watch for damage claims.

Greyhound

PO Box 660362
Dallas, TX 75266
214-849-8000
1-800-231-2222 (Fare and Schedule Information)
1-877-463-6446 (Customer Service Resources)
greyhound.com
• Greyhound Lines, a subsidiary of the British transportation company FirstGroup plc, is the largest provider of intercity bus transportation across North America, serving more than 3,800 destinations with 13,000 daily departures. Complaints about bus service problems are rare.

Hertz Car Rental

225 Brae Boulevard
Park Ridge, NJ 07656
201-307-2000
1-800-654-3131
1-800-654-4173 (Customer Relations)
hertz.com
• Hertz has a better-than-average reputation for customer service, although recent efforts to collect new fees from its drivers have made a dent in it. Still, the company generally rates far higher than many other car rental companies.

Norwegian Cruise Line

NCL Corporation Ltd.
7665 Corporate Center Drive
Miami, Florida 33126
305-436-4000
1-866-625-1164 (Customer Relations, post-trip)
ncl.com

• Norwegian Cruise Line operates a fleet of 12 ships, specializing in an upscale "freestyle" cruising experience. Complaints about NCL service are relatively rare.

Royal Caribbean Cruises Ltd
1050 Caribbean Way
Miami, FL 33132
305-539-6000
1 800 390-9019 (Customer Service)
1-800-256-6649 (Corporate
    Guest Relations)
royalcaribbean.com
• Royal Caribbean Cruises Ltd operates the Royal Caribbean International, Celebrity Cruises, Azamara Club Cruises, Pullmantur, and Croiseres de France. Although they are distinct brands, many of the customer service functions of these companies are integrated. Any complaints should go to the individual cruise line and appealed to Royal Caribbean, if necessary.

Southwest Airlines
2702 Love Field Drive
Dallas, TX 75235
1-800-435-9792
214-932-0333
southwest.com
• Southwest is consistently among the least complained about carriers in the United States. If something goes wrong, the airline's employees usually fix it before you have a chance to pick up the phone or write a letter.

United Airlines
77 West Wacker Drive
Chicago, IL 60601

1-800-864-8331
312-997-8000
united.com
• The merger with Continental Airlines has left its mark on United's customer service reputation. It's too soon to tell if the new company will more closely resemble the old United—which had a so-so reputation for service—or the old Continental, which was well regarded among passengers. We'll see.

Travel Insurance
Allianz Global Assistance from Access America
PO Box 72031
Richmond VA 23255-2031
1-800-284-8300
804-281-5700 (International Collect Calls)
Fax 1-800-346-9265 (Customer Service Inquiries)
Fax 804-673-1469 (Claim Inquiries)
allianztravelinsurance.com
• Allianz Travel Insurance (formerly Access America) is the travel insurance brand of Allianz Global Assistance USA, a unit of Allianz, one of the world's largest insurance and financial services conglomerates.

CSA Travel Protection
PO Box 939057
San Diego, CA 92193-9057
858-810-2000
Fax 1-877-300-8670
csatravelprotection.com
• CSA Travel Protection is a travel insurance company serving United States residents.

Index

Illustrations Credits

All artwork created based on the following:

Published by the National Geographic Society
1145 17th Street N.W., Washington, D.C. 20036

Library of Congress Cataloging-in-Publication Data

Elliott, Christopher, 1968-.
How to be the world's smartest traveler (and save time, money, and hassle) /
Christopher Elliott.
p. cm.
ISBN 978-1-4262-1273-4 (pbk.)
1. Tourism--Social aspects. 2. Tourism--Psychological aspects. 3. Tourism--
Economic aspects. I. Title.
G155.A1E426 2014
910.2'02--dc23

2013039842

The National Geographic Society is one of the world's largest nonprofit scientific and educational organizations. Its mission is to inspire people to care about the planet. Founded in 1888, the Society is member supported and offers a community for members to get closer to explorers, connect with other members, and help make a difference. The Society reaches more than 450 million people worldwide each month through *National Geographic* and other magazines; National Geographic Channel; television documentaries; music; radio; films; books; DVDs; maps; exhibitions; live events; school publishing programs; interactive media; and merchandise. National Geographic has funded more than 10,000 scientific research, conservation, and exploration projects and supports an education program promoting geographic literacy. For more information, visit www.nationalgeographic.com.

National Geographic Society
1145 17th Street N.W.
Washington, D.C. 20036-4688 U.S.A.

For information about special discounts for bulk purchases, please contact
National Geographic Books Special Sales: ngspecsales@ngs.org

For rights or permissions inquiries, please contact National Geographic Books
Subsidiary Rights: ngbookrights@ngs.org

Interior design: Elisa Gibson

Printed in the United States of America

13/QGT-CML/1